T0383827

Healthcare and Economic Restructuring

Philip C. Aka • Joseph Abiodun Balogun

Healthcare and Economic Restructuring

Nigeria in Comparative Perspective

Philip C. Aka
Robert H. McKinney School of Law
Indiana University
Indianapolis, IN, USA

Joseph Abiodun Balogun
College of Health Sciences
Chicago State University
Chicago, IL, USA

ISBN 978-981-16-9542-1   ISBN 978-981-16-9543-8   (eBook)
https://doi.org/10.1007/978-981-16-9543-8

© The Author(s), under exclusive license to Springer Nature Singapore Pte Ltd. 2022
This work is subject to copyright. All rights are solely and exclusively licensed by the Publisher, whether the whole or part of the material is concerned, specifically the rights of translation, reprinting, reuse of illustrations, recitation, broadcasting, reproduction on microfilms or in any other physical way, and transmission or information storage and retrieval, electronic adaptation, computer software, or by similar or dissimilar methodology now known or hereafter developed.
The use of general descriptive names, registered names, trademarks, service marks, etc. in this publication does not imply, even in the absence of a specific statement, that such names are exempt from the relevant protective laws and regulations and therefore free for general use.
The publisher, the authors and the editors are safe to assume that the advice and information in this book are believed to be true and accurate at the date of publication. Neither the publisher nor the authors or the editors give a warranty, expressed or implied, with respect to the material contained herein or for any errors or omissions that may have been made. The publisher remains neutral with regard to jurisdictional claims in published maps and institutional affiliations.

Cover pattern © Melisa Hasan

This Palgrave Macmillan imprint is published by the registered company Springer Nature Singapore Pte Ltd.
The registered company address is: 152 Beach Road, #21-01/04 Gateway East, Singapore 189721, Singapore

For our families; To Obadaiah Mailafa (1956–2021) and countless other victims of Nigeria's broken healthcare system, including fatalities from COVID-19

Preface

Funding for healthcare is severely inadequate to meet the needs of the teeming population of Nigeria in the first quarter of the twenty-first century. With this proposition as starting point, this book makes a proposal for restructuring Nigeria's oil-based economy to generate more—and dependable—funding for health services. The proposal is based modestly on the incremental concept of a postindustrial economy anchored on diversification. Because each country is different, in applying this concept to Nigeria, we do *not* suggest that a restructured Nigerian economy will necessarily achieve the status or near-status of a postindustrial economy in the manner of advanced countries like the United States and Japan. The thrust of the book is confined to economic restructuring. Political restructure of the country, a major issue of debate as this book goes to press, is outside the scope of this study.

To support our argument and proposal, this book comprises five parts, plus an introduction. Chapter 2 is a historical account revolved around the perception of Nigeria as a giant of Africa, testament to its vast material and human resources. The main takeaway from the discussion is a distillation of four features, along with their ramifications for healthcare funding: demography, colonial history, federalism, and largest economy. Chapter 3 presents the features of the Nigerian healthcare system. Six such features, more illustrative than exhaustive, are: a high burden of disease relative to resource allocations, predominant influence of private facilities relative to public initiatives, continuing influence of traditional medicine, privileging of curative healthcare over preventive medicine, low public trust indicated by the practice of medical tourism, and the deleterious legacy of long military rule on the healthcare system.

Chapter 4 elaborates the theme of economic restructure for better healthcare funding that drives this book. Key highlights in the discussion include the impact of the imminent shift to electric vehicles on Nigeria's oil-based economy, diversification as tool for economic restructure, and the creative use of health services as diversification technique. Chapter 5 builds on the theme of healthcare reform through economic restructure from a more tailored angle with its analysis on the influence of politics on healthcare in Nigeria. The focus is on the record of the Fourth Republic since 1999 with tailored suggestions on the possible role of the legislative branch using its power of oversight over the executive branch. Takeaways from the discussion include nine recommendations on what the Nigerian National Assembly could do, using its oversight powers, to generate dependable funding for safe and affordable healthcare in Nigeria. Chapter 6, the conclusion, includes introspection on the comparative values of this book, including its contributions to comparative healthcare studies, and comparative human rights.

Major features that set this book apart from comparable or similar works include its innovative perspective to healthcare reforms in Nigeria built on economic restructuring, and its contributions to the fields of comparative healthcare studies, and comparative human rights studies—using Nigeria as case study. Numerous studies and policy statements, including materials we use in building our argument in this book, have commented on the need to diversify Nigeria's economy away from oil and gas. What sets this book apart is that, in addition to sounding that urgency, it also concretely points the way on means for achieving that diversification to the benefit of healthcare funding. Instructively, publication of this book coincides with back-and-forth debates on healthcare reforms in Nigeria, climaxed most recently, in September 2021 with the formation of a Health Sector Reform Committee by the Nigerian national government. The Committee, chaired by Vice President Yemi Osinbajo and whose membership includes state governors and members of the National Assembly, was charged with the responsibility of reviewing all healthcare reforms adopted in the past 20 years, under the Fourth Republic, including teachable lessons from those reforms. This book is our packaged contribution to that larger debate.

Every book is a work of collaboration and tribute to the solidarity of numerous parties whose antecedent energies made the work possible. This book is no different. Among the parties who deserve acknowledgment in this preface are the authors of the numerous sources in the references whose ideas we drew upon to support our argument in this work. We thank them immensely. We are also indebted to the team of anonymous reviewers whose conscientious evaluations of our proposal immensely improved the overall book. We hope that they like this final product. We equally extend our appreciation to Josh Pitts, erstwhile senior commissioning editor at Palgrave Macmillan in charge of the Pivot program under which this book is published. Consistent with canons of academic practice, we alone take the blame for any errors of analysis and interpretation in this work. We gratefully acknowledge the permission of the United Nations Publications Board to reproduce the map of Nigeria on p. viii.

Indianapolis, IN   Philip C. Aka
Chicago, IL   Joseph Abiodun Balogun
October 2021

Table of Nigerian National and International Laws

African Charter on the Rights and Welfare of the Child. OAU Doc. CAB/LEG/24.9/49, 1999

Child's Rights Act, Act No. 26 (2003). refworld.org/pdfid/5568201 f.4.pdf

Constitution of the Federal Republic of Nigeria (1999)

Disease Control and Prevention (Establishment) Act, 2018, Act No. 18. Federal Republic of Nigeria Official Gazette, 145(105). November 12, 2018

International Covenant on Economic, Social, and Cultural Rights. UN General Assembly Resolution No. 2200A (XXI) (December 19, 1966), 993 U.N.T.S. 3 (1976)

National Health Act, Act No. 8. Federal Republic of Nigeria Official Gazette, 145 (101). October 27, 2014

National Health Insurance Scheme, Decree No. 35 (1999)

National Health Insurance Scheme: Operational Guidelines (revised October 2012)

Universal Declaration of Human Rights. G.A. Res. 217A. December 10, 1948

Map of Nigeria

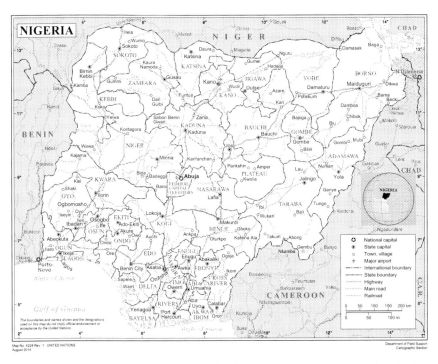

Map No. 4228, Rev. 1 (August 2014), set forth above, is gratefully reproduced with permission from the United Nations Publications Board

Contents

Abbreviations

ACA	Affordable Care Act
ACRWC	African Charter on the Rights and Welfare of the Child
AU	African Union
COVID-19	The novel coronavirus, a respiratory disease that can result in serious illness or death. The disease is caused by a new strain of coronavirus not previously identified in humans and easily spread from person to person. The World Health Organization declared it as a pandemic.
CMS	Church Missionary Society
CRA	Child's Right Act
HHMI	Hillebrand-Herman-Moyer Index Scale
ICESCR	International Covenant on Economic, Social, and Cultural Rights
LNUHC	Legislative Network for Universal Health Coverage
MDGs	UN Millennium Development Goals. Replaced after 2015 by Sustainable Development Goals (SDGs)
MRI	Magnetic Resonance Imaging
NASC	National Assembly Service Commission
NEAC	National Economic Advisory Council
NEEDS	National Economic Empowerment and Development Strategy
NHA	National Health Act
NHIS	National Health Insurance Scheme

NMA	Nigerian Medical Association
NMI	Magnetic Resonance Imaging
NNPC	Nigerian National Petroleum Corporation
OAU	Organization of African Unity
ODA	Official Development Assistance
OECD	Organization for Economic Cooperation and Development
OPEC	Organization of the Petroleum Exporting Countries
R & D	Research and Development
RMAFC	Revenue Mobilization, Allocation, and Fiscal Commission
UDHR	Universal Declaration of Human Rights
UK	[The] United Kingdom [of Great Britain and Northern Ireland]
UNICEF	United Nations International Children's Emergency Fund
US	The United States of America
WHO	World Health Organization
WHO-AIMS	World Health Organization Assessment Instrument for Mental Health Systems

List of Tables

1

Introduction

Abstract This chapter embodies a concise statement of the problem that animates the book. It comprises four interrelated conversations: the book's argument, debate outside its scope, two recent developments within the context of the healthcare debate in Africa that inspired and lent impetus to the research, and the organization of the book.

Keywords Economic restructuring • Abuja Declaration • Imminence of electric cars • Healthcare debate • Health Sector Reform Committee

This book is a study on the influence of economic restructuring on healthcare reforms featuring Nigeria as case study and geopolitical window into the world that also applies helpful insights from accumulated knowledge about other countries in analyzing the country. This chapter is an introduction to the study and comprises four main elements characteristic of any introductory material: the argument of the book and debate outside its scope, recent developments within the context of the healthcare debate in Africa which inspired the research, and the organization of the book.

© The Author(s), under exclusive license to Springer Nature Singapore Pte Ltd. 2022
P. C. Aka, J. A. Balogun, *Healthcare and Economic Restructuring*,
https://doi.org/10.1007/978-981-16-9543-8_1

Argument

This book explores the intersection between healthcare delivery and national economic health, using Nigeria as case study and analytical window into the world. Specifically, the issue this book tackles revolves around how to repair Nigeria's dysfunctional healthcare system through the medium of a healthier economy that provides sufficient revenue to meet the healthcare needs of citizens. Its argument is that the key to healthcare reform in Nigeria is economic prosperity realizable through a restructure of the Nigerian economy to provide more revenue for healthcare delivery to the masses of the Nigerian people. Insufficient funding of healthcare runs against the grain of the Abuja Declaration and it is antithetical to Nigeria's international obligations related to healthcare. In 2014, the Nigerian national government adopted the National Health Act.[1] The law "provides a framework for the regulation, development[,] and management of a national health system" as well as "set[s] standards" for rendition of health services in the country and related matters.[2] However, only one of the law's 65 sections, Section 11 on the "Establishment of Basic Health Care Provision Fund,"[3] dealt with funding.

The story is similar with respect to the Disease Control and Prevention (Establishment) Act four years later.[4] The legislation created a Center for Disease Control and Prevention charged with responsibility for promoting, coordinating, and facilitating "the prevention, detection[,] and control of communicable diseases in Nigeria and other events of public health importance."[5] However, just like the National Health Act, only

---

[1] See National Health Act, 2014, Act No. 8, Federal Republic of Nigeria Official Gazette, 145(101) (October 27, 2014), https://www.ilo.org/dyn/natlex/docs/ELECTRONIC/104157/126947/F-693610255/NGA104157.pdf.
[2] Ibid. (citation).
[3] See ibid., §11 ("Establishment of Basic Health Care Provision Fund").
[4] See Disease Control and Prevention (Establishment) Act, 2018, Act No. 18, Federal Republic of Nigeria Official Gazette, 145(105) (November 12, 2018), http://extwprlegs1.fao.org/docs/pdf/nig195227.pdf.
[5] Ibid. ("Explanatory Memorandum"). Just like the National Health Act of 2014, elaborated in Chap. 5 on the influence of legislative politics in Nigeria, this law has seven parts. Part I deals with the objectives and administration of the Center. Part II deals with the establishment and function

one out of its 28 sections dealt with healthcare spending. That provision was Section 14 mandating the Center "to establish and maintain a fund."[6] Because we perceive no silver bullet solution to the economic problems Nigeria confronts in the first quarter of the twenty-first century,[7] our argument is a proverbially incremental one, hinged modestly on the concept of a postindustrial economy, comprising three sectors: agriculture, industrialization, and services.[8] The trick is how to increase the contributions of the industrialization and service sectors of Nigeria's economy without undermining agriculture on which sector, Nigeria, like many other nations, depends upon for its self-sufficiency in food production. Herein lies the main contribution of this book.

The Abuja Declaration and Its Aftermath

During a meeting in Abuja in spring 2001, Nigeria and other African countries pledged to earmark 15 percent of their annual budgets toward healthcare services for citizens of their respective countries.[9] The pledge is famed as "the Abuja Declaration."[10] However, by April 2011, ten years later, few of these countries met this self-imposed, nonobligatory, revenue target necessitated by the dire state of healthcare delivery in their countries and Africa in the lead up to the Declaration. Two notable exceptions were Tanzania and Liberia which, respectively, devoted 18.4 percent and 16.6 percent of their budgets to healthcare.[11] Many European countries

---

of the Center. Part III deals with the establishment and functions of Center's governing board. Part IV deals with the management and staff of the Center. Part V focuses on financial provisions. Part VI deals with a National Advisory Council and its functions. Part VII deals with miscellaneous issues, including the power of the Minister of Health to give directives. Ibid.

[6] Ibid. ("Fund of the Center").

[7] See Chap. 4 (expounding the outcome of various development programs and projects designed to achieve economic prosperity in Nigeria since the country's independence from the United Kingdom in October 1960).

[8] See Chap. 2, notes 75–6.

[9] See "The Abuja Declaration: Ten Years On," World Health Organization (2011), 4, https://www.who.int/healthsystems/publications/abuja_declaration/en/.

[10] Ibid.

[11] Ibid., p. 3. See also *The World Health Report: Health System Financing: The Path to Universal Coverage.* Geneva, Switzerland: World Health Organization, 2010), xii [hereinafter *World Health Report 2010*]

devote an average of 10 percent of their GDP to healthcare,[12] and the World Health Organization (WHO), a global health czar, recommends about 6 percent as ideal.[13] Therefore, the figure of 15 percent in the Abuja Declaration ranges beyond these numbers by 5–9 percentage points.

However, the number is a reflection of the depth of underinvestment in healthcare in many African countries that dates back a long time in the period since independence in these countries. Historically, "government spending on healthcare in many African countries [is] inadequate to scratch the surface of healthcare delivery, a situation then compounded by corruption which leaves even less money available for health services."[14] In 2015, per capita, Africa spent one-tenth on healthcare than the rest of the world.[15] More elaborately, although the region comprised 16 percent of the world's population and carried 23 percent of global disease burden, in 2015, it accounted for just 1 percent of total global spending on healthcare.[16]

A brief history on the lead up to the Abuja Declaration sheds much-needed light on its 15-percent-of-the-GDP commitment. In September 2000, 189 heads of state, including those from Africa, met and adopted the United Nations Millennium Development Goals (MDGs), eight targets UN member states committed themselves to achieve by 2015.[17]

---

[12] See Philip C. Aka, *Genetic Counseling and Preventive Medicine in Post-War Bosnia* (Gateway East, Singapore: Palgrave Macmillan, 2020), 52.

[13] *World Health Report 2010*, note 11, p. xv. According to this report, this level of spending on health will limit out-of-pocket payments to an amount that makes the incidence of financial catastrophe negligible.

[14] Philip C. Aka et al., "Ghana's National Health Insurance Scheme (NHIS) and the Evolution of a Human Right to Healthcare in Africa," *Chicago-Kent Journal of International & Comparative Law*, 17(2) (2017), 47.

[15] Osondi Ogbuoji et al., "Closing Africa's Health Financing Gap," *Brookings* (March 1, 2019), https://www.brookings.edu/blog/future-development/2019/03/01/closing-africas-health-financing-gap/.

[16] Ibid.

[17] See United Nations Millennium Declaration, Doc. A/RES/55/2, UN General Assembly (September 18, 2000), https://www.un.org/en/development/desa/population/migration/general-assembly/docs/globalcompact/A_RES_55_2.pdf. The eight goals were to: (i) eradicate extreme poverty and hunger; (ii) achieve universal primary education; (iii) promote gender equality and empower women; (iv) reduce child mortality; (v) improve maternal health; (vi) combat HIV/AIDS, malaria, and other diseases; (vii) ensure environmental sustainability; and (viii) develop a global partnership for development. Ibid. Following its expiration in 2015, a new program, the

Three of the eight goals—reducing child mortality rates, improving maternal health, as well as combating HIV/AIDS, malaria, and other diseases—relate to healthcare. To make progress on the MDGs, African leaders met in April 2001 in Nigeria's capital city Abuja. Such was the setting in which the Declaration took place. In the aftermath of the Abuja declaration, subsequent declarations took place in various African countries, all of which, to some extent, dwelt on increased healthcare funding: one in Ouagadougou, Burkina Faso, in 2009; another in Tunis, Tunisia, in 2012; and a third in Luanda, Angola, in 2014.[18] But the fact that Tanzania and Liberia met this standard means that, with discipline, the budgetary target is reachable.

A vibrant healthcare system is predicated on a sound economy. User fees as a condition for accessing healthcare services is the bane of a good healthcare system.[19] Nor are foreign aids of much help as funding method.[20] Because they are often dependent on the vagaries of economic fortunes, political goodwill, and related idiosyncrasies of donor countries, rather than on altruism or philanthropy as such, receipt of foreign assistance is unpredictable.[21] Instead, as the African Charter on the Rights

---

Sustainable Development Goals (SDGs) succeeded the MDGs. See "From MDGs to SDGs," SDGF: Sustainable Development Goals Fund, https://www.sdgfund.org/mdgs-sdgs.

[18] Marie-Paule Kerry, and Matshidiso Moeti, "Foreword," *in Public Financing for Heath in Africa: From Abuja to the SDGs* (Geneva, Switzerland: World Health Organization, 2016), 5. Kerry was WHO Assistant Director-General for Health Systems and Innovation. Moeti was WHO's regional director for Africa.

[19] This is irrespective of what innocuous name government officials in a country use to sugarcoat these out-of-pocket expenses." In Bosnia and Herzegovina in southeastern Europe, these fees go by the name "contributory fees." See Aka, *Genetic Counseling and Preventive Medicine in Post-War Bosnia*, note 12, p. 35. However, the nomenclature does not take away from the reality that putative contributions are user fees with negative ramifications for access to healthcare. Ibid., pp. 45–70 (assessing the Bosnian healthcare system based on its ability to meet the requirement of health as a human right).

[20] In the lingo of international development, these measures of foreign assistance go by the name "overseas development assistance" (ODA). The Organization for Economic Cooperation and Development (OECD) defines ODA as government assistance that targets and promotes the economic development and welfare of developing countries. *Official Development Assistance (ODA)* (Paris, France: OECD), https://www.oecd.org/dac/financing-sustainable-development/development-finance-standards/official-development-assistance.htm. In 1969, the Development Assistance Committee of the OECD adopted ODA as the "gold standard" of foreign aid and till date ODA remains the main source of financing for development aid. Ibid.

[21] See Philip C. Aka, "Bridging the Gap Between Theory and Practice in Humanitarian Action: Eight Steps to Humanitarian Wellness in Nigeria," *Willamette Journal of International Law &*

and Welfare of the Child (ACRWC), elaborated upon shortly, advised, African countries should mobilize "local community resources" to develop healthcare for African children.[22] Echoing this position, Ogbuoji and his colleagues stated that "[i]ncreased donor funds will not be enough to close" health financing gap in Africa, given that "[e]xternal support for health is a tiny share of global health spending," and also because in the wake of the global financial crisis in 2008, "[d]evelopment assistance for health has been more or less stagnant."[23]

There is no attempt made to discredit external donors, as they can play an important complementary role in healthcare delivery, under certain clearly specified conditions.[24] In the final analysis though, as one African adage goes, no serious traveler depends wholly or even largely on the legs of another person for his or her own journey.[25] Depending on the legs of another person for one's own journey engenders vulnerabilities inconsistent with a good travel.

The adage obviously applies in healthcare funding. Ruling out user fees and foreign aids as reliable sources of healthcare funding leaves out revenue generated from a strong economy as the only viable option. Adequate financing is "the mother's milk of any healthcare system, and key to both access in healthcare and health outcomes."[26] A robust health system is not built on a shoestring budget. Instead, as the WHO pointed out, "[n]o country has made significant progress toward universal health coverage

---

Dispute Resolution, 24(1) (2016), 1, 48–9 ("External Support or Assistance") (statement within the context of humanitarian assistance that ranked external assistance as secondary); and Thierry Kangoye, "Does Aid Unpredictability Weaken Governance?: Evidence from Developing Countries," *Developing Economies*, 51(2) (June 2013), 121–44 (answering the question in the affirmative).

[22] See note 58 and accompanying text.

[23] Ogbuoji et al., note 15.

[24] See, for example, Chap. 5, notes 10–17 (commenting on the commendable activities of the Legislative Network for Universal Health Coverage, LNUHC, in Nigeria). As one health analyst aptly observed, to be effective, donor funding must be predictable, rather than erratic, and offered over extended periods for, say, 20–30 years. Otherwise, she said, "many African countries will not be able to handle the recurrent fiscal contingencies generated by" donor funding. Ola Brown, *Fixing Healthcare in Nigeria: A Guide to Some of the Key Policy Decisions That Will Provide Better Healthcare to All Nigerians* (self-published, 2018), 24, https://www.dropbox.com/s/g8a2m2n49w-lavui/Fixing%20Nigeria%20(2).pdf?dl=0.

[25] See "Africa: The Struggle for Development," *in Global Studies: Africa*, eds. R. C. Grote et al., 8th ed. (New York: McGraw-Hill, 1999), 3, 9.

[26] Aka et al., note 14, pp. 1, 23.

[...] without increasing the extent to which its health system relies on public revenue sources."[27] Contrary to this advice, in the 25-year period from 1995 to 2014, government spending on healthcare in Nigeria averaged US $118 per capital,[28] compared, for example, to smaller economies like Algeria at US $362,[29] and Botswana at US $358 per capita,[30] over the same period.

In 2011, Nigeria was among 27 countries assessed to be making insufficient progress toward meeting the funding target of the Abuja Declaration.[31] Most recently, in spring 2020, Nigeria placed an unimpressive fifth—after South Africa, Tunisia, Kenya, and Algeria, in this order—on a list of countries with improved healthcare in Africa.[32] The surveyors rationalized the country's ranking as mixed: while "[i]n general, the public healthcare system is of a low standard due to a lack of government funding and inadequate staffing levels[,]" "[p]rivate healthcare facilities in Nigeria are of high standards."[33]

Given these hard realities, the key to improving healthcare delivery in Nigeria is to improve the country's economic system by restructuring it.[34] Commenting on the suboptimal treatment cancer patients receive in Nigeria, one analyst opined that the country "cannot grow any sector, if [it] do[es]n't grow the healthcare sector."[35] He elaborated: "A farmer cannot farm if he is ill, an engineer cannot fix power if he is ill and there is not doctor or machine to treat him or her."[36] He observed that many

---

[27] Brown, note 24, quoting the WHO.
[28] *Public Financing for Health in Africa*, note 18, p. 71.
[29] Ibid., p. 38.
[30] Ibid., p. 41.
[31] Ibid., tbl. 1 (showing progress in health outcomes and health spending since 2001).
[32] Sebastiane Ebatamehi, "Top 10 Countries with Improved Healthcare System in Africa 2020," *African Exponent* (February 26, 2020), https://www.africanexponent.com/post/7167-top-10-african-countries-with-best-healthcare-system-2020. The other five countries were Egypt, Morocco, Rwanda, Tanzania, and Zambia. Ibid.
[33] Ibid.
[34] See Chap. 4 of this book (elaborating the modalities for that restructuring).
[35] Runice C.W. Chidiebe, "Cancer Patients Paying with Their Blood in Nigeria," *The Cable* (August 22, 2017), https://www.thecable.ng/cancer-patients-paying-blood-nigeriathe country's cancer.
[36] Ibid.

cancer survivors in Nigeria "received their treatment abroad,"[37] adding: "If truly health is a human right[,] [t]hen, let's give cancer patients the right to survive."[38] The surefire way to make health a human right for sufferers of cancer and other diseases in Nigeria, whether communicable or noncommunicable condition, is adequate funding of healthcare delivery anchored on a strong economy.

Nigeria's International Obligations Related to Healthcare

Nigeria is a state party to the International Covenant on Economic, Social, and Cultural Rights (ICESCR),[39] which it ratified on July 29, 1993.[40] The multilateral treaty guarantees for citizens of state parties the right to healthcare.[41] It enjoins state parties to "recognize the right of everyone" within their jurisdictions "to the enjoyment of the highest attainable standard of physical and mental health."[42] To minimize any possibility of ambiguity, the treaty indicates the steps state parties could take to achieve "the full realization of this right."[43] These include providing for the reduction of the stillbirth-rate and of infant mortality and for the healthy development of the child; improving "all aspects of environmental and industrial hygiene"; preventing, treating, and controlling epidemic, endemic, occupational, and other diseases; and creating "conditions which would assure to all medical service and medical attention in the event of sickness."[44] The guarantee of the right to healthcare

---

[37] Ibid.
[38] Ibid.
[39] See International Covenant on Economic, Social and Cultural Rights, Gen. Assembly Resolution 2200A (XXI) (adopted and opened for signature, ratification, and accession December 16, 1966, entry into force, January 3 1976) [hereinafter ICESCR].
[40] See "Ratification Status for Nigeria," Office of the UN High Commissioner for Human Rights, https://tbinternet.ohchr.org/_layouts/15/TreatyBodyExternal/Treaty.aspx?CountryID=127&Lang=EN.
[41] See generally ICESCR, note 39.
[42] ICESCR, note 39, art. 12.1.
[43] Ibid., art. 12.2.
[44] Ibid., art. 12.2(a)–(d).

elaborates and solidifies the language in the Universal Declaration of Human Rights (UDHR) of 1948 to the effect that "[e]veryone has the right to a standard of living adequate for the health and well-being of himself and of his family, including food, clothing, housing and medical care and necessary social services [....]."[45]

An applicable regional instrument here is the African Charter on the Rights and Welfare of the Child (ACRWC).[46] The multilateral treaty stipulates that "[e]very child shall have the right to enjoy the best attainable state of physical, mental and spiritual health."[47] It mandates state parties to the Charter to "undertake to pursue the full implementation of this right,"[48] through a variety of illustrative measures that includes: reduction of infant and child mortality rate,[49] provision of healthcare to children,[50] provision of adequate nutrition and safe drinking water,[51] combat of disease and malnutrition,[52] provision of healthcare for expectant and nursing mothers,[53] provision of preventive healthcare and family life education,[54] integration of basic healthcare into national development plan,[55] and inclusion of local communities and nongovernmental organizations in the design and implementation of basic healthcare services for children.[56]

Some of these measures, like clean drinking water and healthcare for expectant and nursing mothers, are social determinants not on the surface linked to health but without which it is hard to realize good health.

---

[45] Universal Declaration of Human Rights, G.A. Res. 217A, art. 25(1) (December 10, 1948).

[46] African Charter on the Rights and Welfare of the Child (ACRWC), OAU Doc. CAB/LEG/24.9/49 (1990) (entered into force in 1999), https://www.achpr.org/public/Document/file/English/achpr_instr_charterchild_eng.pdf. For a fact sheet on the Charter, see "African Charter on the Rights and Welfare of the Child," Health and Human Rights, https://www.who.int/hhr/African%20Child%20Charter.pdf.

[47] ACRWC, note 46, art. 14.

[48] Ibid.

[49] Ibid., art. 14(a).

[50] Ibid., art. 14(b).

[51] Ibid., art. 14(c).

[52] Ibid., art. 14(d).

[53] Ibid., art. 14(e).

[54] Ibid., art. 14(f).

[55] Ibid., art. 14(g).

[56] Ibid., art. 14(i).

The Charter "not[ed] with concern that the situation of most African children remains critical due to the unique factors of their socio-economic, cultural, traditional and developmental circumstances, natural disasters, armed conflicts, [as well as] exploitation and hunger[.]"[57] It mandated state parties "to support through technical and financial means, the mobilization of local community resources in the development of primary health care for children."[58] The instrument defined a "child" as persons below 18 years of age.[59] Nigeria made this treaty part of its domestic laws through ratification via the Child's Right Act (CRA) of 2003.[60]

However, the CRA does not apply throughout Nigeria.[61] This is because only 25 of the 36 states in Nigeria have adopted this law, while 11 states, all of them in Northern Nigeria, have yet to domesticate the law.[62] The issue of contention revolves around the definition of "children" as persons below 18 years of age.[63] Many northern legislators and the Sharia judges adjudge the CRA to be anti-culture, anti-tradition, and anti-religion.[64] Whereas the CRA mostly prohibits child betrothal and child marriage, this practice, particularly involving girls, remains prevalent in many northern states where, in some cases, children as young as ten years of age become betrothed or given out in marriage.[65] The result is that, while some have argued that other legal instruments, such as the constitution, protect children, minors in those northern states are still subject to practices like early marriage, female genital mutilation, and street begging.[66]

---

[57] Ibid., preamble.
[58] Ibid., art. 14(j).
[59] Ibid., art. 2.
[60] Child's Rights Act, Act No. 26 (2003), refworld.org/pdfid/5568201f.4.pdf ("An Act to Provide and Protect the Right of a Nigerian Child and other Related Matters").
[61] See Usang Maria Assim, "Why the Child's Rights Act Still Doesn't Apply Throughout Nigeria," *The Conversation* (September 24, 2020), https://theconversation.com/why-the-childs-rights-act-still-doesnt-apply-throughout-nigeria-145345.
[62] Ibid.
[63] Ibid.
[64] Ibid.
[65] Ibid.
[66] Ibid.

The Declaration of Alma-Ata, adopted by the WHO in 1978, stipulates that "[g]overnments have a responsibility for the health of their people which can be fulfilled only by the provision of adequate health and social measures."[67] The Declaration envisaged a "comprehensive national health[care] system" that national leaders strive to create by exercising political will, mobilizing resources, and making rational use of external resources.[68] None of these more or less healthcare commandments for citizens stands any reasonable chance of realization where allocation for healthcare delivery is paltry, sporadic, and inadequate, as is currently the case in Nigeria.

Several Recent Developments that Inspired this Research

Two major recent developments inspired this research and lent impetus to its message of improved healthcare delivery in Nigeria through economic restructuring. These developments, catalyzed by the healthcare debate in Africa, are the COVID-19 pandemic,[69] and an impending jettison of oil and gas as engine of the global economy.

---

[67] World Health Organization, Declaration of Alma-Ata, Int'l Conference on Primary Health Care, Alma-Ata, USSR (September 6–12, 1978), art. V, https://www.who.int/publications/almaata_declaration_en.pdf.

[68] Ibid., art. VIII.

[69] COVID-19 is a respiratory disease that can result in serious illness or death. It is caused by a new strain of coronavirus not previously identified in humans, which spreads from person-to-person through respiratory droplets produced when an infected person, within close proximity, coughs or sneezes. There is currently no effective antiviral treatment for the disease, though some vaccines believed to be generally effective have been developed to inoculate against the condition. The World Health Organization (WHO) declared the disease a pandemic on March 11, 2020. See "COVID-19: Frequently Asked Questions: Basics," Centers for Disease Control and Prevention [USA], https://www.cdc.gov/coronavirus/2019-ncov/faq.html; David J. Cennimo, "What is COVID-19?" *Medscape* (Updated January 4, 2021), https://www.medscape.com/answers/2500114-197401/what-is-covid-19.

The COVID-19 Pandemic

The first confirmed case of the COVID-19 pandemic in Africa involving Egypt was reported on February 14, 2020.[70] By May 13, 2020, all 54 countries in the region reported confirmed cases of the pandemic, the last being Lesotho.[71] As of October 28, 2020, the Nigeria Center for Disease Control reported that Nigeria itself recorded over 62,000 infections, with more than 1100 deaths.[72]

While, thus far, compared to other regions of the world, the pandemic has affected Nigeria and other African countries mildly in terms of the rates of infection and death,[73] nevertheless, its mayhem of infections and deaths portends new challenges on various fronts—socioeconomic consequences, food insecurity, and maintaining peace and security—that African leaders must respond to through creative

[70] United Nations Economic Commission for Africa, *Policy Brief: Impact of COVID-19 in Africa* (May 28, 2020), 6, https://www.uneca.org/sites/default/files/PublicationFiles/sg_policy_brief_on_covid-19_impact_on_africa_may_2020.pdf [hereinafter *Impact of COVID-19 in Africa*].

[71] Ibid.

[72] See "Nigeria's Economy Can't Afford Another Lockdown—Buhari," *Huhu Online* (October 29, 2020), https://huhuonline.com/index.php/home-4/huhuonline-more-news/13976-nigeria-s-economy-can-t-afford-another-lockdown-buhari.

[73] See *Impact of COVID-19 in Africa*, note 70, p. 1; see also Ahmed Mushfiq Mobarak and Rifaiyat Mahbub, "What the US Can Learn from How African Countries Handled COVID," *CNN* (November 3, 2020), https://www.cnn.com/2020/11/03/africa/africa-coronavirus-lessons-opinion-intl/index.html; and Cara Anna, "As US Struggles, Africa's COVID-19 Response is Praised," *AP* (September 22, 2020), https://apnews.com/article/virus-outbreak-ghana-africa-pandemics-donald-trump-0a31db50d816a463a6a29bf86463aaa9?campaign_id=9&emc=edit_nn_20210307&instance_id=27836&nl=the-morning&regi_id=124708682&segment_id=52986&te=1&user_id=3018d6faed4962db07930c7110d6aad4. But this statement risks being overstated, given that there are still some unknowns about this pandemic, especially as virulent strains of the disease emerge in parts of the world, including South Africa. See Patrick Gathara, "Charity Alone Will Not End the Calamity of COVID-19 in Africa," *Al Jazeera* (July 31, 2021), https://www.aljazeera.com/opinions/2021/7/31/accountability-is-africas-best-route-out-of-the-pandemic (counseling accountability, rather than charity, as Africa's "best route out of the pandemic"); Claire Felter, "How Dangerous Are New COVID-19 Strains?" Council on Foreign Relations (January 7, 2021), https://www.cfr.org/in-brief/how-dangerous-are-new-covid-19-strains?gclid=Cj0KCQiA1KiBBhCcARIsAPWqoSqLuooY_obXNC_aRxXuELh5kVnMYG8xr-NpA1rHgIvtD8sP0qVZHqwaAnzjEALw_wcB. One of the lessons of COVID-19 is the need to build stronger and more resilient healthcare systems in regions across the globe. See "Lessons from COVID-19: Building a Stronger Global Health System," *Foreign Policy* (May 26, 2020), https://foreignpolicy.com/events/fp-virtual-dialogue-lessons-from-covid-19/.

and human-right-compliant means.[74] These challenges include "tak[ing] measures to improve testing capacities, access to medical supplies, and participation in vaccine and treatment research; enhanc[ing] production and innovation through intra-African collaboration; expand[ing] deployment of community health workers, [...]; and boost[ing] medical personnel capacity [...]."[75] Consistent with the advice of the United Nations Economic Commission for Africa, these initiatives must be "part of a comprehensive effort to improve the resilience and preparedness of healthcare systems" in the region.[76]

Related to these challenges from COVID-19 have been appeals within Nigeria for private-sector contributions to healthcare funding. In one such appeal, Aliko Dangote, a business mogul, urged private companies to contribute 1 percent of their profits to fund the country's health sector.[77] He proposed that the money be used "to improve the country's health sector to better serve communities where infrastructure and personnel are almost non-existent in the wake of the COVID-19 pandemic that has stretched Nigeria's medical sector."[78] Dangote elaborated that the government alone cannot fund healthcare; instead, the private sector should contribute its share to health funding.[79] Commenting on the

---

[74] See *Impact of COVID-19 in Africa*, note 70. Instructively, the theme for 2020's Human Rights Day is "Recover Better—Stand Up for Human Rights." As the United Nations elaborates, the theme "relates to the COVID-19 pandemic and focuses on the need to build back better by ensuring Human Rights are central to recovery efforts" in that the world will "reach [its] common global goals only if" communities across the world "create equal opportunities for all, address the failures exposed and exploited by COVID-19, and apply human rights standards to tackle entrenched, systematic, and intergenerational inequalities, exclusion and discrimination." "Human Rights Day 10 December," United Nations, https://www.un.org/en/observances/human-rights-day#:~:text=2020%20Theme%3A%20Recover%20Better%20%2D%20Stand,are%20central%20to%20recovery%20efforts. The United Nations sets aside December 10 every year for commemoration as Human Rights Day.
[75] *Impact of COVID-19 in Africa*, note 70, p. 3.
[76] Ibid.
[77] "Dangote Seeks 1 [percent] Tax on Business Profits for Health Sector Funding," *The Will* (November 19, 2020), https://thewillnigeria.com/news/dangote-seeks-1-tax-on-business-profits-for-health-sector-funding/.
[78] Ibid.
[79] Ibid.

criticalness of the healthcare sector, he said there will be no "healthy economy" "without a healthy population."[80]

Imminence of Electric Cars

For over 135 years since the invention of the motor car,[81] oil and gas have been the engine of the global economy. With the invention and the rise of the electric car, that era of oil and gas is about to end. The electric car marks the antithesis of the gasoline-powered car, whose anticipated end the electric car presages. The impending jettison of oil and gas as engine of the global economy, the hypothesized end of the gasoline-powered car, aligns with the climate control and related clean-energy program of the US government under President Joseph R. Biden Jr.[82] In a meeting in August 2021 with executives of the three largest US auto manufacturers, President Biden praised electric vehicles as "a vision of the future that is now beginning to happen."[83] The impending move away from oil and gas reached a high point of crystallization with the announcement on January 28, 2021 by the giant US automaker, General Motors (GM), that it will cease manufacture of gas-powered cars, trucks, and sports utility vehicles

---

[80] Ibid.

[81] See, for example, Frank Coffey, *America on Wheels: The First 100 Years: 1896–1996* (Los Angeles, CA: General Publishing Group, 1998).

[82] See "Fact Sheet: President Biden Takes Executive Actions to Tackle the Climate Crisis at Home and Abroad, Create Jobs, and Restore Scientific Integrity Across Federal Government," White House (January 27, 2021), https://www.whitehouse.gov/briefing-room/statements-releases/2021/01/27/fact-sheet-president-biden-takes-executive-actions-to-tackle-the-climate--crisis-at-home-and-abroad-create-jobs-and-restore-scientific-integrity-across-federal-government/. See also Brook J. Detterman, "Biden Administration Rapidly Advances Climate Change Agenda," *National Law Review*, XI (58) (February 27, 2021), https://www.natlawreview.com/article/biden-administration-rapidly-advances-climate-change-agenda.

[83] "The Transition to Electric Vehicles," *New York Times The Morning* (August 6, 2021), https://outlook.live.com/mail/0/inbox/id/AQMkADAwATE2MTAwAC04NDcxLTY0YzEtMDACLTAwCgBGAAADmoSvjna2Kkmn8zqi9wi6ewcAnCBhZglRtU2kkOJpbeS6MQAAAgEMAAAAnCBhZglRtU2kkOJpbeS6MQAEku8U%2BAAAAA%3D%3D. The three largest auto companies are General Motors Co., Ford Motor Co., and Stellantis NV, a parent of Chrysler. See "Biden Seeks to Make Half of the New U.S. Auto Fleet Electric by 2030," *Reuters* (August 5, 2021), https://www.reuters.com/business/autos-transportation/biden-set-target-50-evs-by-2030-industry-backs-goal-2021-08-05/.

(SUVs) by 2035, among other clean-energy goals.[84] Chapter 4 elaborates the negative ramifications of the movement away from oil and gas toward electric energy for Nigeria's oil-based economy.[85]

Within the Context of the Debate on Healthcare in Africa

The preceding events are taking place within the context of a debate on healthcare in Africa.[86] It is a debate on health as an economic driver anchored on multiple themes, including efficiency and effectiveness as well as improved communication between finance and health ministries to ensure quality growth in healthcare delivery.[87] At a time when health-care systems in the region are enduring the "double burden" of noncommunicable diseases like hypertension, stroke, diabetes, and cancer, superimposed on the original communicable category like malaria, tuberculosis, and HIV/AIDS, half of the population of persons across the

---

[84] See Neal E. Boudette, and Coral Davenport, "G.M. Will Sell Only Zero-Emission Vehicles by 2035," *New York Times* (January 28, 2021), https://www.nytimes.com/2021/01/28/business/gm-zero-emission-vehicles.html. The announcement is elaborated in Chap. 4 (expounding the impact of the imminent shift to electric vehicles in the world on Nigeria's oil-based economy).

[85] See Chap. 4, notes 86–114 ("Impact of the Imminent Shift to Electric Vehicles on Nigeria's Oil-Based Economy").

[86] See, for example, Lily B. Clausen, "Taking on the Challenges of Health Care in Africa," *Stanford Business* (June 16, 2015), https://www.gsb.stanford.edu/insights/taking-challenges-health-care-africa (synthesizing the views of three health professionals—Abayomi Ajayi, Letitia Adu-Ampoma, and Azure Tariro Makadzange—who discussed the hurdles confronting African healthcare on a panel about healthcare in Africa at the Stanford Africa Business Forum); Anita Powell, "South Africa Debates Bill for National Health Care," Learning English, https://learningenglish.voanews.com/a/south-africa-debates-bill-for-national-heath-care/5127964.html (focusing on a proposal by the South African government designed to expand healthcare delivery in the land beyond the current 15 percent of South Africans with private health insurance coverage). Learning English is the Voice of America's (VOA's) multimedia source of news and information for English learners worldwide.

[87] ECA, "The Great Debate Focuses on How to Fix Africa's Healthcare" (February 12, 2019), https://uneca.org/stories/great-debate-focuses-how-fix-africa%E2%80%99s-healthcare.

region still lacks adequate health services.[88] The noncommunicable diseases typify middle-class lifestyles.[89]

To be sure, there is progress flowing to healthcare in Africa from the application of modern technology in healthcare delivery. For example, technology has afforded more people in the remote corners of the continent increased access to better healthcare hitherto unavailable, while the better access to data modern technology enables African doctors and policymakers to make more informed decisions about how to improve their healthcare systems.[90] However, across the region, healthcare systems still confront a range of challenges, including counterfeit medications, medical clinics in sweltering hot conditions without air-conditioners, and lack of medical equipment like Magnetic Resonance Imaging (MRI) machines, among other problems.[91] Even prior to the outbreak of COVID-19, many Africans ranked their health and healthcare among the lowest in the world.[92]

---

[88] See Clausen, note 86. The acronym HIV "stands for human immunodeficiency virus, [...] the virus that causes HIV infection." The acronym "can refer to the virus or to HIV infection." "HIV/ AIDS: The Basics," National Institutes of Health (last viewed September 24, 2020), https://hivinfo. nih.gov/understanding-hiv/fact-sheets/hivaids-basics#:~:text=HIV%20stands%20for%20 human%20immunodeficiency,stands%20for%20acquired%20immunodeficiency%20syndrome. The acronym AIDS "stands for acquired immunodeficiency syndrome. AIDS is the most advanced stage of HIV infection." Ibid. Here is the connection between HIV and AIDS. "HIV attacks and destroys the infection-fighting CD4 cells of the immune system. The loss of CD4 cells makes it difficult for the body to fight off infections and certain cancers. Without treatment, HIV can gradually destroy the immune system and advance to AIDS." Ibid.

[89] These are so called because these diseases can be prevented through modification of the common lifestyle causes of these conditions, such as unhealthy diet, physical inactivity, tobacco use, and excessive alcohol use. See *Global Action Plan for the Prevention and Control of Noncommunicable Diseases 2013–2020* (Geneva, Switzerland: World Health Organization, 2013), 3.

[90] Clausen, note 86.

[91] Ibid.

[92] See, for example, Angus S. Deaton and Robert Tortora, "People in Sub-Saharan Africa Rate Their Health and Healthcare Among the Lowest in the World," *Health Affairs*, 34(3) (March 2015), 3519–27 (March 2015); B. Rose Huber, "Sub-Saharan Africans Rate Their Health and Health Care Among the Lowest in the World," Woodrow Wilson School of Public & Int'l Affairs, Princeton University (February 25, 2015) (news story on the Deaton and Tortora research).

What this Book Is Not About

The argument of this book falls short of political restructuring of Nigeria. Since 2015, under retired General Muhammadu Buhari as president, Nigeria has been the scene of repeated debate for restructuring the country to better serve the social welfare needs of its teeming population.[93] These calls reached new heights with widespread protests in October 2020 by youth across the country against police brutality in an environment of lethargic performance by a government that operates with little regard for the ethnic pluralism and diversity of the country.[94]

In the aftermath of the demonstrations, Olisa Agbakoba, former President of the Nigerian Bar Association, and a human rights lawyer, proposed a "simple way to restructure Nigeria" embedded in devolution of political and governmental powers.[95] He reasoned that Nigeria's national government exercises exclusive power over 68 issue-areas of competency out of a total of 98 issue-areas under the Nigerian

---

[93] See, for example, Tolulope Ola-David, "The Need for Restructuring Nigeria's Political System," Oxford University Politics Blog (November 2, 2018), https://blog.politics.ox.ac.uk/the-need-for-restructuring-nigerias-political-system/; Philip C. Aka, "Why Nigeria Needs Restructuring Now and How It Can Peacefully Do It," *Denver Journal of International Law & Policy*, 46 (Winter 2017), 123–57 (marshaling numerous reasons "why Nigeria must be restructured now and present[ing] concrete proposals, embedded in constitutional democracy, for achieving that restructuring peacefully and nonviolently," using as context "the ongoing campaign for self-determination among the Igbo of Eastern Nigeria"); Ayobami Egunyomi, "Fifty-Seven Years After: The Case for Restructuring Nigeria," Council on Foreign Relations (posted November 8, 2017), https://www.cfr.org/blog/fifty-seven-years-after-case-restructuring-nigeria (among other things, arguing that restructuring "will silence the agitation of the unrelenting Biafra and Niger Delta movements by giving them a region with the autonomy they seek"); and Aka, "Bridging the Gap Between Theory and Practice in Humanitarian Action," note 21, pp. 24–30 ("Taking Political Restructuring Seriously").

[94] Nelly Ating, "Nigeria's Next-Generation Protest Movement," *Foreign Policy* (October 28, 2020), https://foreignpolicy.com/2020/10/28/nigerias-youth-protest-movement-end-sars/. See also Aina Ojonugwa, "Rtd. Col. Umar Dangiwa Says IPOB Threat Exaggerated and Buhari Has Mismanaged Nigeria's Diversity," *The Will* (Lagos) (July 7, 2021), https://thewillnigeria.com/news/rtd-col-umar-dangiwa-says-ipob-threat-exaggerated-and-buhari-has-mismanaged-nigerias-diversity/ (contending that "Buhari's government has so far exhibited poor skills in its management of [the country's] diversity"); Wole Soyinka, "Between Dividers-In-Chief and Dividers-In-Law," *Premium Times* (Abuja) (September 15, 2020), https://opinion.premiumtimesng.com/2020/09/15/between-dividers-in-chief-and-dividers-in-law-by-wole-soyinka/ (opining that Buhari does not "understand[] the minimal requirements for positioning [Nigeria] as a modern" state).

[95] "Agbakoba Writes Senate, Proposes 'Simple Way to Restructure Nigeria,'" *Elombah News* (last updated November 4, 2020), https://elombah.com/agbakoba-writes-senate-proposes-simple-way-to-restructure-nigeria/.

constitution.[96] This is in comparison to some 30 items on the concurrent list that the national government exercises in unison with the states.[97] However, the states may exercise power on the concurrent list only when the national government has not already preempted the states on any of the 30 functions or competency areas.[98] The overall result, he opined, is that "[i]n effect, State Governments really have no power" in Nigeria.[99] Agbakoba's solution was for a committee to "review the 98 items of power and assign what is best to Federal and what is best to the states, based on the principle of subsidiarity."[100]

The heated call for political restructuring has come with growing concerns about the dissipating unity of Nigeria under President Buhari. The commentaries of John Campbell, one-time US ambassador to Nigeria exemplifies this line of thinking. Campbell took the position that Nigeria is not a conventional nation-state, but instead a "prebendal archipelago."[101] In his elaboration, Nigeria is not a nation because "Nigerians are not united by language, religion, culture, or a common national story."[102] In the same vein, it is "not quite a state because the government is weak and getting weaker," to such an extent that "it fails to provide for the security of its citizens, the primary requirement of any state."[103] Campbell explains

---

[96] Ibid.

[97] Ibid.

[98] Ibid. In the lingo of constitutional law, preemption, "occupying the field," takes place when a "higher" level of government, whether national (central) or state, eliminates or reduces the authority of a "lower" level over a given issue, when the powers of the two authorities collide. "Preemption," Legal Information Institute, Cornell Law School, https://www.law.cornell.edu/wex/preemption#. Preemption may be either express or implied. Ibid. In the United States (US), preemption is *express* when Congress states clearly in a federal law that it intends to supersede (or occupy) related state laws. In such cases, the only remaining question is whether a particular state law is of the type that Congress may preempt. Ibid. Preemption is *implied* when a court decides that, even though federal law does not explicitly indicate that it occupies or covers a field, it nevertheless preempts state law, for example, when there is a conflict between a federal and state law. Ibid.

[99] "Agbakoba Writes Senate," note 95.

[100] Ibid.

[101] John Campbell, "Nigeria and the Nation-State," Council on Foreign Relations (November 16, 2020), https://www.cfr.org/teaching-notes/nigeria-and-nation-state ("Summary") (teaching notes from John Campbell, *Nigeria and the Nation-State: Rethinking Diplomacy with the Postcolonial World* (Lanham, MD: Rowman & Littlefield, 2020)).

[102] Ibid.

[103] Ibid.

that Nigeria is "prebendal" because the country's "corrupt elites appropriate public money for private purposes, but prevent the state from breaking apart due to ethnic and religious rivalries out of self-interest."[104] These elites "benefit from state preservation through access to revenue from state-owned oil, government contracts, and office, all of which require a formal state."[105] And it is an "archipelago" because "[s]imultaneously, the[se] elites keep the government weak so they are not challenged," with the result that "government[al] authority is restricted geographically to islands in a sea of ungoverned spaces"[106] in a manner that calls to mind the geographic imagery of an archipelago. More recently, Campbell observed that Nigeria's national government lacks the capacity to "tax the true wealth of the [country]," and depends heavily on income from oil and gas in a system where political corruption is endemic.[107] He urged the US government to deepen its engagement with Nigeria through internally led political reforms, using implements of "comfortable diplomacy," such as conferences, and technical recommendations, that empower nongovernmental organizations in the country to strengthen the country's democracy.[108]

These points are well taken. However, this book is limited to the narrower issue of restructuring Nigeria's oil-based economy to fund healthcare. While the authors are keenly aware that Nigeria may ultimately have to be restructured politically to better serve the felt needs of the Nigerian masses for a better healthcare system, their argument falls short of political restructuring. Rather than novel as such, views about the Nigerian state, such as Campbell expressed are gloss on an old theme. They call to mind the observations of Professors Jackson and Rosberg four decades ago regarding the juridical statehood of many African states

[104] Ibid.

[105] Ibid.

[106] Ibid.

[107] See John Campbell and Robert I. Rotberg, "The Giant of Africa is Failing," *Foreign Affairs* (May 31, 2021). Campbell and Rotberg noted that under Buhari, "a number of overlapping safety crises" across all regions of the country has moved it "from being a weak state to a failed one," whose corporate existence now stands severely threatened. Ibid. They urged the US and other partners of Nigeria to acknowledge this reality, given the populous size of the country and its strategic role in West Africa. Ibid.

[108] Ibid.

anchored on international relations, rather than empirical foundation embedded domestically in ability to perform the functions of modern states.[109] Equally, such views bring to mind Professor Joseph's concept of prebendal politics about the same time applied specifically to Nigeria.[110] What is different is that these features have lingered for long and that even states like Nigeria, with their comparative advantage in human and material resources, are not immunized from these attributes.

Yet, along with its argument focused on economic restructure, this book also inescapably delves into the influence of politics and its critically complementary role on healthcare funding. First, in Nigeria, like in many other societies, the economy is a proverbial handmaid susceptible to the dictates of the political system.[111] Secondly, no different from many other climes, politicians include access to healthcare among their many promises to the electorate when they run for office. [112] Thirdly, legislators have an important role not just in earmarking adequate revenue for healthcare, but also by ensuring that, within the best tradition of legislative oversight,[113] money voted for healthcare is actually used for the purpose. This is more so bearing in mind that, due to inefficiencies, in many countries, "between 20 [percent] and 40 [percent] of all health resources [are] wasted."[114] Increased use of public funds to finance universal healthcare in certain states in Africa has led to reduced out-of-pocket spending in

---

[109] Robert H. Jackson and Carl G. Rosberg, "Why Africa's Weak States Persist: The Empirical and the Juridical in Statehood," *World Politics*, 35(1) (October 1982), 1–24, http://www.jstor.org/stable/2010277.

[110] Richard A. Joseph (1983) Class, State, and Prebendal Politics in Nigeria, *The Journal of Commonwealth & Comparative Politics*, 21(3), 21–38 (1983), https://doi.org/10.1080/14662048308447434.

[111] See Will Kenton, "Political Economy," *Investopedia* (updated August 4, 2019), https://www.investopedia.com/terms/p/political-economy.asp (explaining that "[i]n a wider sense, political economy was once the common term used for the field we now call economics").

[112] With respect to Ghana, see Hassan Wahab and Philip C. Aka, "The Politics of Healthcare Reforms in Ghana under the Fourth Republic Since 1993: A Critical Analysis," *Canadian Journal of African Studies*, 55(1) (2021), 203; and Aka et al., note 13, pp. 1–65.

[113] For elaboration of this concept, see Chap. 5 (analyzing the influence of politics on healthcare in Nigeria).

[114] "Abuja Declaration: Ten Years On," note 9; World Health Organization, *The World Health Report: Health Systems Financing: The Path to Universal Coverage* (Geneva, Switzerland: World Health Organization, 2010), xvii.

those countries.[115] However, the main problem has been the manner in which public funding is allocated and used.[116] "Too often, public resources are fragmented, poorly distributed, and inefficiently used[,]" with the result that those resources "do not benefit the people who need them most."[117] As popular representatives of their people in the first branch of government, lawmakers can lead the way in minimizing these impediments.

Organization Of this Book

This book has six chapters. Chapter 1 sets the tone of the study with a concise statement of the problem, including its argument of improved healthcare through better economic health, and key recent developments that lent impetus to this research. Nigeria will be unable to realize the promise of universal healthcare for its teeming population, including pursuit of healthcare as human right, in the second quarters of this century, if it does not fix its dire healthcare funding problem. Awareness of the past history of a country is necessary "to fully understand the nature and issues of [its] contemporary politics," including the events "that have shaped the current patterns of politics."[118]

Guided by such wisdom, Chap. 2 provides a primer of factual background material necessary for proper understanding of Nigeria. It is a narrative built around the unrealized potentials of Nigeria as a "giant of Africa." The main takeaway is a distillation of four features, along with their ramifications for healthcare funding: demography, colonial history, federalism, and largest economy. Chapter 3 sketches the country's healthcare system. It identifies and discusses multiple characteristic elements that speak to the complexity of the healthcare system, including the high burden of diseases relative to resources, influence of private facilities relative to public initiatives, the continuing influence of traditional

---

[115] Kerry and Moeti, "Foreword," note 18, p. 5.

[116] Ibid.

[117] Ibid.

[118] Frank L. Wilson, *Concepts and Issues in Comparative Politics: An Introduction to Comparative Analysis* (Upper Saddle River, NJ: Prentice Hall, 1996), 17.

medicine, the privilege of curative healthcare over preventive medicine, and low public trust in the healthcare system, signified, for example, by medical tourism. The discussion includes an X-ray of the negative impact of long military rule in the country spanning nearly 30 years before 1999 on the healthcare system. The morale of the story is that maintenance of civil-democratic rule is desideratum for sustainable progress on healthcare and economic development in Nigeria.[119]

Chapter 4 elaborates the theme of economic restructure for better healthcare funding that drives this book. It is a theme built on the concept of the postindustrial economy. The trick is how to increase the contributions of the industrialization and service sectors of the Nigerian economy without undermining agriculture on which Nigerians depend for their food. The presentation is preceded by an overview of Nigeria's oil-based economy, analysis of the carcasses of development programs that dot the Nigerian geopolitical landscape, the impact of the imminent shift to electric vehicles on Nigeria's oil-based economy, diversification as tool for economic restructure, and the creative use of health services as diversification technique.

Chapter 5 builds on the theme of healthcare reform through economic restructure from a more tailored angle with its analysis on the influence of politics on healthcare in Nigeria. The focus is on the record of the Fourth Republic since 1999 with tailored suggestions on the possible role of the legislative branch using its power of oversight over the executive branch. The chapter reveals low awareness among Nigerian legislators related to healthcare and that what laws the lawmakers enacted in the field remain unimplemented many years after passage. Chapter 6 concludes the work in a statement that weighs in with a reflection on the comparative values of this book, including its contributions to comparative analysis, particularly comparative healthcare studies, and comparative human rights.

---

[119] See Aka, "Bridging the Gap Between Theory and Practice in Humanitarian Action," note 19, pp. 39–47 (highlighting maintenance of civilian rule among eight fateful steps to humanitarian wellness and integrity in Nigeria). See also Philip C. Aka, *Human Rights in Nigeria's External Relations: Building the Record of a Moral Superpower* (Lanham, MD: Lexington Books, 2017), 125–29 (discussing maintenance of civilian rule among seven steps to increased human rights in Nigeria).

Major features that set this book apart from comparable or similar works include its innovative perspective to healthcare reforms in Nigeria built on economic restructuring, and its contributions to the fields of comparative healthcare studies, and comparative human rights studies, using Nigeria as case in point and analytic window into the world.[120] This book coincides with back-and-forth debates on healthcare reforms in Nigeria, climaxed recently with the formation by President Muhammadu Buhari on September 6, 2021, of a Health Sector Reform Committee to review healthcare reforms adopted by the government in the past 20 years, under the Fourth Republic, including teachable lessons from those reforms.[121] The Committee, whose members include state governors and members of the National Assembly, is headed by Vice President Yemi Osinbajo and has been given six months to complete its work.[122]

"Performance is intrinsic to the vitality of a healthcare system."[123] However, to the extent it has evolved to this point, over 60 years since independence and over two decades under the Fourth Republic, the longest instalment of civilian rule in the country, Nigeria's *health*care system is still mostly sick care,[124] that, elsewhere, we analogized to a dying patient in need of shock intensive-care attention.[125] Thus, the suggestions for improvement advanced in this book are designed to help put more health in the purported healthcare system of Nigeria. Numerous studies and

---

[120] See Chap. 6 elaborating the nature of these contributions.

[121] "Buhari Sets Up Health Sector Reform Committee, Names Osinbajo Chairman," *Vanguard* (Lagos) (September 6, 2021), https://www.vanguardngr.com/2021/09/buhari-sets-up-health-sector-reform-committee-names-osinbajo-chairman/.

[122] Ibid.

[123] Aka, *Genetic Counseling and Preventive Medicine in Post-War Bosnia*, note 12, p. 45.

[124] See M. Joycelyn Elders, "Health Care vs. Sick Care: A Significant Difference," United Methodist News Service (June 25, 2009), https://pnhp.org/news/health-care-vs-sick-care/. See also Farshad Fani Marvasti, and Randall S. Stafford, "From 'Sick Care' to Health Care: Reengineering Prevention into the U.S. System," *New England Journal of Medicine* 367(10) (September 6, 2012), 889–91, https://doi.org/10.1056/NEJMp1206230. Both commentaries refer to the US healthcare system.

[125] See Joseph A. Balogun and Philip C. Aka, "Strategic Reforms to Resuscitate the Nigerian Healthcare System," in E. Ike Udogu, ed., *Nigeria in the Fourth Republic: Confronting the Contemporary Political, Economic and Social Dilemmas* (Lanham, Boulder, New York, and London: Lexington Books, forthcoming 2022).

policy statements, including materials we use in supporting our argument in this book, have commented on the need to diversify Nigeria's economy from oil and gas. What sets this book apart is that, in addition to sounding that urgency, it concretely points the way on means for achieving that diversification to the benefit of healthcare financing.

2

Primer on Nigeria, "Giant of Africa"

Abstract This chapter is a basic introduction to Nigeria, a historical background of sorts, wrapped around the more or less mythical status of the country as the "giant of Africa." Multiple issues covered in the discussion, more illustrative than exhaustive, and in no particular order, include the colonial roots of the country and achievements since independence, demographic features, as well as human and natural endowments, among others.

Keywords "Giant of Africa" • Demography and healthcare funding • Colonial history and healthcare funding • Federalism and healthcare funding • Concept of postindustrial economy • Relationship between largest economy and healthcare funding

Introduction

Pedagogically speaking, a primer is a penetrable material that serves to introduce a subject matter, especially to an uninitiated person not versed in the matter at issue, the same way, consistent with the etymology of the

© The Author(s), under exclusive license to Springer Nature Singapore Pte Ltd. 2022   **25**
P. C. Aka, J. A. Balogun, *Healthcare and Economic Restructuring*,
https://doi.org/10.1007/978-981-16-9543-8_2

word, a layer of paint operates as canvas underneath a topcoat. The material in this chapter takes the place of the usual historical background account, but without the depth usually associated with such chronicle. This presentation is justified by the wisdom that, to fully grasp "the nature and issues of [a country's] contemporary politics," including the events that shaped that politics, awareness of its history is necessary.[1] The ensuing discussion, more illustrative than exhaustive, bearing on the moniker of giant of Africa and more or less connected to healthcare funding, is organized around the four selective topics of demographic features, colonial history, political history across colonialism and independence embedded in federalism, as well as the complexities surrounding Nigeria's economic history and ambiguous status as the largest economy in Africa. Table 2.1 encapsulates these variables.

Table 2.1 Impact of Nigerian features on healthcare funding

Item No.	Feature	Ramifications for healthcare funding
1.	Demographic features	Large, diversified population, mostly youthful, with social welfare needs, including healthcare, that numerous governments since independence have been unable to meet
2.	Colonial history	Colonial rule was a rule of occupation and expropriation that did not attend to the healthcare needs of the "natives." British colonial rule set the tone for the underinvestment in social programs, including healthcare, that marked the period since independence.
3.	Federalism	The experience of federalism spanning colonial and post-independent periods did not provide good governance attentive to social welfare programs, including healthcare.
4.	Largest economy	Nigerian leaders have not used the resources of the country in a manner that afforded good health to the masses of ordinary Nigerians, most of who remained locked in poverty over 60 years since independence.

[1] Frank L. Wilson, *Concepts and Issues in Comparative Politics: An Introduction to Comparative Analysis* (Upper Saddle River, NJ: Prentice Hall, 1996), 17.

Demographic Features

Nigeria is a country in West Africa with a population of over 208 million people in 2020.[2] It is the most populous country in Africa and the seventh most-populous state in the world—after China, India, the United States (US), Indonesia, Pakistan, and Brazil, in this order.[3] Nigeria is a country with the largest population of people of African descent in the world.[4] Much of Nigeria's population is youthful: as of 2020, over 43 percent of the population were persons 14 years or below,[5] with 70 percent of the country under 30 years of age.[6]

Amplifying and solidifying this gigantic demographic feature, Nigeria boasts a vast Diaspora stretching out to several regions of the world that, besides every part of Africa, include Asia, Europe (especially the United Kingdom and Italy), the Middle East, and North America (especially Canada and the US).[7] In the US alone, Nigerians make up the largest African-born population, from where they "generate[] billions of dollars in annual remittance outflows" to their homeland.[8] According to one

---

[2] "Nigeria Population (Live)," *Worldometer*, https://www.worldometers.info/world-population/nigeria-population/.

[3] See "The World Population and the Top Ten Countries with the Highest Populations," *Internet World Stats*, https://www.internetworldstats.com/stats8.htm; "Countries in the World by Population (2020)," *Worldometer*, https://www.worldometers.info/world-population/population-by-country/.

[4] OECD, *Nigeria* (last updated September 2012), https://www.oecd.org/swac/publications/Nigeria_e-version_en_light.pdf ("One out of every four Africans and one out of every five persons of African origin is a Nigerian").

[5] See "Nigeria: Age Structure from 2010 to 2020," *Statista*, https://www.statista.com/statistics/382296/age-structure-in-nigeria/; Funke Fayehun, and Uche Charlie Isiugo-Abanihe, "EndSARS: How Nigeria Can Tap Into Its Youthful Population," *The Conversation* (October 25, 2020), https://theconversation.com/endsars-how-nigeria-can-tap-into-its-youthful-population-148319 (quoting UN figures).

[6] Fayehun and Isiugo-Abanihe, note 5.

[7] See "The Nigerian Diaspora," *Pilot Guides*, https://www.pilotguides.com/study-guides/the-nigerian-diaspora/#:~:text=The%20Nigerian%20diaspora%20is%20one,is%20very%20diffi-cult%20to%20estimate.&text=Nigerian%20Americans%20are%20notably%20distinct,recent%20immigrants%20from%20the%20country ("The modern Nigerian diaspora has major centers in the United States, the United Kingdom, Canada and Italy").

[8] Thomas F. Husted, and Lauren Ploch Blanchard, Nigeria: Current Issues and U.S. Policy, Congressional Research Service, RL 33964 (September 18, 2020), 1, https://fas.org/sgp/crs/row/RL33964.pdf.

estimate, Nigerian immigrants make up "about 0.6 percent of the United States' overall foreign-born population."[9] Many of these immigrants live in states like Maryland, New York, and Texas.[10] These human resources coupled with its vast reserve of oil and gas and other mineral resources, highlighted in Chap. 4 on the modalities for restructuring the Nigerian economy to generate revenue for healthcare funding, add up to give the country its celebrated moniker as "giant of Africa."[11]

Nigeria has an area of 923,769 square kilometers or 356,669 square miles.[12] This makes it No. 33 in the world, comparatively down the list in this attribute for a highly populous country.[13] With a population density of 571 people per mile,[14] more so in its tropical, non-Sahelian regions,[15] Nigeria is one of the most densely populated countries in the world.[16] To get a sense of the enormousness of that density, Nigeria is slightly more than twice the size of California, and about 36 percent larger than Texas, but with a population that, at over 208 million people, as indicated in the previous paragraph, dwarfs both of these large US states combined.[17]

---

[9] "The Nigerian Diaspora in the United States," *MPI* (revised June 2015), https://www.migrationpolicy.org/sites/default/files/publications/RAD-Nigeria.pdf (stating the "Nigerian immigrants account for about 0.6% of the United States' overall foreign-born population").

[10] Ibid.

[11] See Dave Ebi, "Why is Nigeria Called Giant of Africa," *Quora* (updated March 20, 2019), https://www.quora.com/Why-is-Nigeria-called-giant-of-Africa.

[12] See "Nigeria—Location, Size, and Extent," *Nations Encyclopedia*, https://www.nationsencyclopedia.com/Africa/Nigeria-LOCATION-SIZE-AND-EXTENT.html; "Nigeria Demographics," *Worldometer*, https://www.worldometers.info/demographics/nigeria-demographics/.

[13] "Country Comparison—Area," *C.I.A. World Factbook*, https://www.cia.gov/library/publications/the-world-factbook/rankorder/2147rank.html.

[14] "Nigeria Demographics," note 12.

[15] "Nigeria Population 2020 (Live)," *World Population Review*, https://worldpopulationreview.com/countries/nigeria-population.

[16] The population is unequally spread with much of the country's residents living in the southern regions of the country, particularly the south-east and south-west. See ibid.

[17] California has a population of approximately 39 million people within a land area of 155,779 square miles, while Texas has a population of approximately 27 million people within a land area of 261,232 square miles. See "U.S. States: Population, Land Area, and Population Density," *States101*, https://www.states101.com/populations. This is more so considering that with an urban population estimated at little over 51%, "Nigeria Demographics," note 12, many Nigerians live in rural areas mostly lacking in basic amenities like clean water and electricity. "Nigeria: Sanitation, Drinking-Water and Hygiene Status Overview," *UN-Water Global Analysis and Drinking Water (GLAAS)*, https://www.who.int/water_sanitation_health/monitoring/investments/nigeria-10-nov.pdf?ua=1.

Nigeria is bordered to the north by the French-speaking country Niger Republic,[18] to the northeast by Chad, to the east by Cameroon, and to the west by Benin Republic.[19] Its southern coast rests on the Gulf of Guinea in the Atlantic Ocean.[20]

A slight reshaping of Nigeria's borders took place soon after independence when, in a referendum in spring 1961, Northern Cameroon voted to join Nigeria, while Southern Cameroon voted to join French-speaking Cameroon. Before the referendum, Northern Cameroon was administered separately within Nigeria, while Southern Cameroon was part of Eastern Nigeria. More recently, the International Court of Justice heard a land and maritime dispute between Nigeria and Cameroon wherein it awarded ownership of the Bakassi Peninsula to Cameroon but a stretch of land in the area around Lake Chad to Nigeria.[21]

Altogether, there are over 250 ethnic groups in Nigeria.[22] Based on estimates as of 2018, the major ones, with their share of the population, are Hausa, about 30 percent, Yoruba 15.5 percent, Igbo 15.2 percent, Fulani 6 percent, Tiv 2.4 percent, Kanuri/Beriberi 2.4 percent, Ibibio 1.8 percent, and Ijaw/Izon 1.8 percent, with the rest constituting about 24.7 percent.[23] Nigeria is a country of immense religious pluralism, divided

---

[18] To the uninitiated, the name is confusedly similar to Nigeria. The two countries took their names after the River Niger which courses through their geopolitical landscapes. See "Niger River," *New World Encyclopedia*, https://www.newworldencyclopedia.org/entry/Niger_River. The confusion is needlessly amplified by some other facts, including that one of Nigeria's 36 states also goes by the name Niger, and that the national flag of Niger Republic has a green bar, compared to two green bars in Nigeria's.

[19] "Nigeria—Location, Size, and Extent," note 12.

[20] Ibid.

[21] See Philip C. Aka, *Human Rights in Nigeria's External Relations: Building the Record of a Moral Superpower* (Lanham, Boulder, New York, and London: Lexington Books, 2017), 1.

[22] See "Nigeria Fact Sheet," United States Embassy in Nigeria (January 2012), https://photos.state.gov/libraries/nigeria/487468/pdfs/Nigeria%20overview%20Fact%20Sheet.pdf.

[23] *Country Background Note: Nigeria* (London: UK Home Office, Updated December 5, 2019), https://assets.publishing.service.gov.uk/government/uploads/system/uploads/attachment_data/file/856368/Nigeria_-_Background_-_CPIN_-_v2.0__January_2020__gov.uk.pdf (quoting CIA *World Factbook* data on Nigeria).

almost equally between the Muslim and Christian faiths,[24] with a substantial sprinkling of traditional religions, particularly in the southern portions of the country. Taking the largest three ethnic groups as case in point, the Igbo in the East are predominantly Christians; Hausa-Fulani, two disparate groups characterized imprecisely at times as one, are predominantly Muslim; while the Yoruba in the West are divided between adherents of these two religions and adherents of traditional religion.[25] From an occupational standpoint, many Nigerian workers lucky to have a job are blue-collar workers,[26] a good number of them self-employed subsistence farmers.[27] In 2020, Nigeria's GDP per capital was a little over US$ 2273, placing it at 18 percent, squarely within the last quantile, of the world's average.[28] More discussion on economic issues is saved for the section below on Nigeria's status as Africa's largest economy.

As immutable attributes, ethnicity and religion and their intersections exert a negative influence on Nigerian politics when these variables are opportunistically activated to achieve parochial ends as is often the case. This effect is discussed in the section on federalism where it more properly belongs. For Nigeria, the relationship between healthcare funding and demography in the sense we define it here is that the country is home to a large number of citizens of diverse ethnicity and religion, among other immutable attributes, whose legitimate need for affordable healthcare services that, in the period since independence more than 60 years ago, their governments repeatedly have been unable to fill.

---

[24] John Paden, "Religion and Conflict in Nigeria," United States Institute of Peace, Special Report No. 359 (February 2015), https://www.usip.org/sites/default/files/SR359-Religion-and-Conflict-in-Nigeria.pdf.

[25] See "Nigeria Religious Records," *FamilySearch*, https://www.familysearch.org/wiki/en/Nigeria_Religious_Records#:~:text=In%20terms%20of%20Nigeria's%20major,Ijaw%20(south)%20were%2098%25; "Nigeria—Religions," *Nations Encyclopedia*, https://www.nationsencyclopedia.com/Africa/Nigeria-RELIGIONS.html.

[26] See, for example, "Unemployment Crisis: More Nigerians Dump White[-]Collar Jobs for Blue[-]Collar Jobs," *The Nation* (July 29, 2018), https://thenationonlineng.net/unemployment-crisis-more-nigerians-dump-white-collar-jobs-for-blue-collar-jobs/.

[27] See Kenneth Obunadike, "[Seven] Most Common Jobs in Nigeria," *LA-Job Portal* (August 17, 2020), https://latestjobsinnigeria.com.ng/7-most-common-jobs-in-nigeria/.

[28] "Nigeria GDP Per Capita," *Trading Economics*, https://tradingeconomics.com/nigeria/gdp-per-capita#:~:text=GDP%20per%20capita%20in%20Nigeria%20is%20expected%20to%20reach%202300.00,according%20to%20our%20econometric%20models.

Wholesale Creature of British Colonialism in Africa

Nigeria is a wholesale creature of British colonial overlords who, in 1914, merged two previously separate "protectorates," along with the colony of Lagos, to form the country.[29] These three entities encompass numerous ethnic groups, some of them identified in the previous section that, before 1914, had no history of living together.[30] Some of these were kingdoms, others acephalous (or kingless) communities, while yet others combined these two features.[31] British occupation of the territory that became Nigeria was a direct result of the Berlin Conference of 1883–1884 and a so-called general act emerging from that conference, part of the "scramble for Africa" among major European powers, which allocated the area to Britain for "pacification."[32] The term was a deceptive misnomer. For, contrary to the connotation of peace, pacification was a thoroughgoing machine of violence that was anything but peaceful.[33]

---

[29] See Philip C. Aka, "The 'Dividend of Democracy': Analyzing U.S. Support for Nigerian Democratization," *Boston College Third World Law Journal* 22(2) (2002), 225, 228–29; "History," in *Nigeria: A Country Study*, ed. Helen Chapin Metz (Washington, DC: GPO for the Library of Congress, 1991). Like some countries in the world, Nigeria is a state that does not exist in history. An analogy is Iraq. Like Nigeria, Iraq was created in 1917 by the UK, after nearly 400 years as a region of three provinces (Mosul, Baghdad, and Basra) under the Ottoman Empire. Britain exercised control over the country, after World War I as a League of Nations mandate, until the country's independence in 1932. "Iraq Profile—Timeline," *BBC News* (October 3, 2018), https://www.bbc.com/news/world-middle-east-14546763. For a history of the country, see Charles R.H. Tripp, A *History of Iraq* (New York: Cambridge University Press, 2002).

[30] Aka, "Dividend of Democracy," note 29, p. 229. Pre-1914, the areas that became Nigeria were known as the Slave Coast, in notorious testament to the commerce in humans that went on there before the abolition of the slave trade in 1807. See Kathleen Sheetz, "Slave Coast," *Encyclopedia Britannica*, https://www.britannica.com/place/Slave-Coast.

[31] "History," in *Nigeria: A Country Study*, note 29.

[32] See Sybil E. Crowe, *The Berlin West African Conference, 1884–1885* (New York: Longmans, Green, 1981, originally published in 1942).

[33] See Philip C. Aka, "The Military, Globalization, and Human Rights in Africa," *New York Law School Journal of Human Rights*, 18 (3) (2002), 379 ("[t]he entire architecture of colonial rule, like that of military rule down the road in [Africa], was built and maintained solely and completely on naked force designed to crush any and every 'native' resistance to external domination").

The creation and colonization of the country was a "white man's bur-den," a presumed duty to civilize,[34] that, in retrospect, British colonial authorities did not handle well. First, for no reason than financial consid-erations, they lumped the Northern Protectorate that lacked the resources to cater to its administrative needs into the more buoyant Southern Protectorate.[35] In so doing, as the reasoning goes, British colonizers "free[d] the British treasury of the financial responsibility for Northern Nigeria,"[36] but cobbled together two incompatible entities that going back at least to 1906 had been governed separately. This was mistake number one.

A second mistake compounding the first and magnifying it was that "British colonial authorities made little attempt to create a coherent country out of these disparate groups."[37] Instead, through their practice of "indirect rule," the British colonial office insulated the Islamic North from the supposed material "corruption" of the South.[38] Indirect rule was a style of administration by which British colonizers governed their colo-nies, including Nigeria, through the use of traditional political institu-tions and rulers.[39] And in the lead up to independence, northern leaders strove hard to maintain the advantages from British rule that included assignment of 50 percent of the seats in the national legislature and a separate public service, concessions codified in the 1954 constitution, to the detriment of national integration and nation-building.[40]

Thus, as one Nigerian constitutional law scholar aptly characterized it, the forced creation of Nigeria in 1914 was an "amalgamation without

---

[34] The proclaimed duty are justifications for colonial control, based on poems by Rudyard Kipling (1865–1936), the English journalist and writer, published between 1899 and 1902. See Stuart Creighton Miller, *Benevolent Assimilation: The American Conquest of the Philippines, 1899–1903* (New Haven, CT: Yale University Press, 1982), 5.

[35] See J.A.A. Ayoade, "Nigeria: Positive Pessimism and Negative Optimism: A Valedictory Lecture," Nigerian Voice (September 17, 2010), 2, http://www.thenigerianvoice.com/print/34992/1/nigeria-positive-pessimism-and-negative-optimism-a.html.

[36] Ibid.

[37] Aka, *Human Rights in Nigeria's External Relations*, note 21, p. 70.

[38] Ibid.

[39] See, for example, Michael Crowder, "Indirect Rule: French and British Style in Africa," *Journal of the International African Institute*, 34(3) (July 1964), 197–205; Ralph J. Bunche, "French and British Imperialism in West Africa," *The Journal of Negro History*, 21(1) (January 1936), 31–46.

[40] Ayoade, note 35, p. 2.

integration" that invokes the analogy of a "prisoner pa[ying] for his own handcuffs."[41] Nigeria won political independence from the United Kingdom (UK) in October 1960 after 46 years of colonial rule.[42] It was decolonization without revolution, one devoid of "a nationwide independence movement that crossed ethnic divisions," where, instead, the nationalist leaders simply stepped into the shoes of the departing British colonial authorities.[43] Nigeria became a republic in 1963, in a move that eliminated residues of British control emblematized by the station in the new country of a governor-general who functioned as representative of the British Crown.[44] But the damage to nation building had been done and it would take a long time to repair it, if ever.[45]

This brings us to the connection between colonial history and healthcare funding. The Igbo have a saying to the effect that a person drenched by rain will not dry until he acknowledged at what point the rain started beating him. The nature of that connection is that, in many respects, British rule in Nigeria supplied that rain-drench point: It was a period of expropriation that set the tone, nay the foundation, for the

---

[41] Ibid.

[42] See Nigeria Independence Act 1960, 1960 CH. 55 8 & 9 ELIZ. 2 (July 29, 1960), https://www.legislation.gov.uk/ukpga/1960/55/pdfs/ukpga_19600055_en.pdf ("An Act to make provision for, and in connection with, the attainment by Nigeria of fully responsible status within the Commonwealth").

[43] See John Campbell, "Nigeria and the Nation-State," Council on Foreign Relations (November 16, 2020), https://www.cfr.org/teaching-notes/nigeria-and-nation-state ("Main Takeaways") (teaching notes from John Campbell, *Nigeria and the Nation-State: Rethinking Diplomacy with the Postcolonial World* (Lanham, MD: Roman & Littlefield, 2020). In one of the most fawning speeches to a former colonial authority on Independence Day, Sir Abubakar Tafawa Balewa, first Prime Minister of Nigeria, intoned: "We are grateful to the British officers whom we have known, first as masters, and then as leaders, and finally as partners, *but always as friends.*" Speech of Sir Abubakar Tafawa Balewa, October 1, 1960, reprinted in *Blackpast* (August 20, 2009), https://www.blackpast.org/global-african-history/1960-sir-abubakar-tafawa-balewa-independence-day/. Emphasis added.

[44] Nigeria Republic Act 1963, 1963 CH. 57 (December 18, 1963), https://www.legislation.gov.uk/ukpga/1963/57/enacted ("An Act to make provision as to the operation of the law in relation to Nigeria as a Republic within the Commonwealth"). For example, § 2 of the Nigerian Independence Act stipulated that "[n]o Act of the Parliament of the United Kingdom passed on or after [October 1, 1960] shall extend, or be deemed to extend, to Nigeria or any part thereof as part of the law thereof, and as from that day." However, the same law also indicated in § 1 that from October 1, 1960, the supposedly independent country "shall […] constitute part of Her Majesty's dominions under the name of Nigeria." Republican status eliminated the seeming contradiction.

[45] See Campbell, note 43 ("Summary") (dubbing modern-day Nigeria a "prebendal archipelago," rather than a nation-state).

underinvestment in healthcare and other social programs that marked the period since independence in 1960. Chapter 3, focusing on the features of Nigeria's healthcare system, elaborates this position.

The Experience of Federalism in Nigeria

Federalism is "a constitutional division of government[al] power between a central or national government and a set of regional units."[46] Features of a federal system include that both the national and regional governments have some independent as well as some shared powers over their citizens; that neither government owes its legal existence to the other; and that, as a matter of law, neither may dictate to the other(s) regarding structural organization, fiscal policies, or definition of essential functions.[47] Under a federal system, both the national government and its regional components have sovereignty in the sense that each level can exercise governmental powers directly over citizens.[48]

Federalism came to Nigeria in 1954 under the Lyttelton Constitution, named after Oliver Lyttelton, Secretary of State for the Colonies from 1951 until the period the constitution was adopted. This was six years before the country's independence in 1960. Federalism came to Nigeria in the aftermath of the large-scale killings in 1953 of Igbo residents in Kano, a metropolitan city in northern Nigeria, along with equally large-scale destruction of Igbo property, in the heels of an earlier attack seven years earlier in Jos, in Nigeria's so-called middle belt region.[49] The orchestrated attacks convinced British colonial authorities that Nigeria, "if it [were] to be a nation, must be a federation, with as few subjects reserved for the Central Government as would preserve national unity."[50] Thus,

---

[46] Michael E. Milakovich, and George Gordon, *Public Administration in America*, 10th ed. (Belmont, CA: Wadsworth Publishing, 2009), 109.

[47] Ibid.

[48] Ibid.

[49] See Herbert Ekwe-Ekwe, "The Igbo Genocide and Its Aftermath," *Pambazuka News* (February 21, 2012), https://www.pambazuka.org/human-security/igbo-genocide-and-its-aftermath.

[50] A.H.M. Kirk-Greene, *Crisis and Conflict in Nigeria: A Documentary Sourcebook, Vol. 1* (London: Oxford University Press, 1971), 10 (quoting the diary of British Colonial Secretary, Oliver Lyttelton).

from a federation of one national government and three regions under Nigeria's 1954 Constitution, Nigeria today has 36 states and a federal capital territory based in Abuja.[51]

Starting at independence with a parliamentary system of government modeled after the UK, since 1979, Nigeria adopted a presidential system of government patterned after the US where, however, unlike the US, as indicated earlier in Chap. 1, too many powers are assigned to the national government.[52] Also, unlike the US, under Nigeria's current constitution, power is divided among three levels of government.[53] In contrast, in the US, only the national and state governments share power.[54] There, under the principle of Dillon Rule, named after Iowa State Supreme Court Justice John F. Dillon, who articulated this doctrine in an 1868 case, local governments are "creatures of the states."[55] Nigeria has a multiplicity of 776 local governments with very little functional role under the constitution.[56] Coupled with the economic non-viability of many of the country's 36 states,[57] this situation by default leaves many powers in the hands of

[51] Aka, *Human Rights in Nigeria's External Relations*, note 21, p. 134. See also *Dele Babalola, The Political Economy of Federalism in Nigeria* (London: Palgrave Macmillan, 2019), 27–56.

[52] See Chap. 1, notes 95–100.

[53] Constitution of the Federal Republic of Nigeria, 1999, http://www.nigeria-law.org/ConstitutionOfTheFederalRepublicOfNigeria.htm#StatesOfTheFederation. An appendix to this document, denominated "First Schedule," contains a list of the 30 states in alphabetical order, including local governments of each state and capital city. First Schedule, ibid.

[54] Robert Longley, "What Is Federalism? Definition and How It Works in the US," *Thoughtco* (updated August 2, 2020), https://www.thoughtco.com/federalism-powers-national-and-state--governments-3321841#:~:text=In%20the%20case%20of%20the,and%20the%20individual%20state%20governments ("[T]he U.S. Constitution establishes federalism as the sharing of powers between the U.S. federal government and the individual state governments").

[55] Travis Moore, "Dillon Rule and Home Rule: Principles of Local Governance," *LRO Snapshot* (Nebraska Legislature), https://nebraskalegislature.gov/pdf/reports/research/snapshot_local-gov_2020.pdf. For more on the status of local governments in the US federal system, see, for example, "The American State and Local Government," *The USA Online*, https://www.theusaonline.com/government/state-local-government.htm.

[56] See Aka, *Human Rights in Nigeria's External Relations*, note 21, p. 134.

[57] For a sample of numerous commentaries on the non-viability of many Nigerian states, see Johnbosco Agbakwuru, "Only [Six] States Viable, as Katsina Made N8bn but Got N136bn Federal Allocation," *Vanguard* (Lagos) (July 27, 2020), https://www.vanguardngr.com/2020/07/only-6-states-viable-as-katsina-made-n8bn-but-got-n136bn-federal-allocation/; "Do We Need Unviable [Thirty-Two] States?" *Guardian* (Lagos) (November 19, 2019) (Editorial Commentary), https://guardian.ng/opinion/do-we-need-unviable-32-states/; Gabriel Ewepu, "Nigeria: 2020 Budget—Only [Four] States Are Viable in Nigeria—Report," *Guardian* (Lagos) (October 23, 2019),

the national government. In Nigeria, traditionally local authority like law enforcement is lodged in the national government based in Abuja.

Still on the key distinctions between federalism in Nigeria and the US, in America, "[p]residents compete with numerous actors [...] for influence over public policy, including Congress, the courts, interest groups, political appointees in the departments and agencies, and career civil servants."[58] There, "[t]he president must rely on his informal ability to convince other political actors [that] it is in their interest to go along with him, or at least not stand in his way."[59] Conversely in Nigeria, the president is a political overlord who exercises oversized influence on public policy.[60]

The centralization and over-concentration of powers in the national government at Abuja have reached new heights under General Muhammadu Buhari since 2015.[61] This is contrary to the recommendation of the colonial authorities for a central government with few powers necessary to preserve national unity, one made after the try-out of a centralized unitary formula for 40 years from the setup of the country in 1914. The over-centralization also works against the very definition of federalism as a political arrangement where both national government and its constituent units exercise powers directly over their citizens. There

---

https://allafrica.com/stories/201910240037.html; and "Nigeria: Only [Ten] States Economically Viable, [Seventeen] Insolvent—Viability Index Report," *PM News* (May 13, 2019), https://www.pmnewsnigeria.com/2019/05/13/nigeria-only-10-states-economically-viable-17-insolvent-viability-index-report/.

[58] David Leonhardt, "The Morning: The Transition Begins," *New York Times* (November 24, 2020) (quoting Matt Glassman, a Georgetown University political scientist).

[59] Ibid. This wisdom calls to mind the power of the US president as being mostly "the power to persuade." Richard E. Neustadt, *Presidential Power: The Politics of Leadership* (Hoboken, NJ: Wiley, 1960), 10–11, 30–32. As Harry Truman, 33rd President of the US from 1945 to 1953 famously put it, "I sit here all day trying to persuade people to do the things they ought to have sense enough to do without my persuading them. [...]. That's all the powers of the President amount to." See "Harry S. Truman," *Independent* (London) (January 20, 2009), https://www.independent.co.uk/news/presidents/harry-s-truman-1451147.html.

[60] See Obi Nwakanma, "The President's Power is Tyrannical Power in Nigeria," *Vanguard* (Lagos) (March 26, 2017), https://www.vanguardngr.com/2017/03/presidents-power-tyrannical-power-nigeria/ ("[T]he president of Nigeria functions more as a monarch rather than the president in a republic").

[61] See Wole Soyinka, "Lessons for Nigeria's Militarized Democratic Experiment," *New York Times* (October 9, 2020), https://www.nytimes.com/2019/10/09/opinion/nigeria-militarized-democratic-experiment.html.

is little sovereignty left for subnational governments in a setting like Nigeria where an all-powerful national government exercises expansive powers that extend into characteristically local issues like law enforcement, which in the US, where Nigeria draws its model, are entrusted to local authorities.

One notable feature of Nigeria's federal system of government is the huge influence of religion in politics, particularly when linked with ethnicity, whose salience appears to increase with time, rather than abate. "While fundamentalism is a problem for all religions in Nigeria, Islamic extremism is particularly troubling because of the intertwining of Islam and ethnicity in northern Nigeria."[62] There are two testaments of the increased salience of religion in Nigeria's contemporary politics that bear indication here. The first is the upgrading of sharia law into criminal code by 12 states in northern Nigeria, at the dawn of the Fourth Republic, beginning with Zamfara State, in October 1999.[63] The 12 states, in alphabetical order, are: Bauchi, Bornu, Gombe, Jigawa, Kaduna, Kano, Katsina, Kebbi, Niger, Sokoto, Yobe, and Zamfara.[64] The adoption of sharia law as criminal code has resulted in the creation of *hisbah* organization (sharia police) in these states charged with responsibility for prosecuting a range of offenses, including "social vices" like prostitution, mixing of the sexes, and drinking in public places.[65] Taken together, these actions have had the effect of restoring sharia law in northern Nigeria, until 2000, private personal law, "to a state of completeness and a degree of autonomy" never seen before in the country "for over a century."[66]

---

[62] Aka, *Human Rights in Nigeria's External Relations*, note 21, p. 137.

[63] See ibid., p. 138.

[64] See "Nigeria Sharia Architect Defends Law," *BBC News*, http://news.bbc.co.uk/2/hi/africa/1885052.stm. The map accompanying this story mistakenly leaves out Kaduna State.

[65] Aka, *Human Rights in Nigeria's External Relations*, note 21, p. 138.

[66] Philip Ostien, and Albert Dekker, "Sharia and National Law in Nigeria," *in Sharia Incorporated: A Comparative Overview of the Legal Systems of Twelve Muslim Countries in Past and Present*, ed. Jan Michiel Otto (Leiden, Netherlands: Leiden University Press, 2010), 567. See also "Nigeria Looks Back on [Twenty] Years of Sharia Law in the North," *DW* (October 27, 2019), https://www.dw.com/en/nigeria-looks-back-on-20-years-of-sharia-law-in-the-north/a-51010292 (reflecting on the negative effects adoption of Sharia law has wrought in the country).

The second testament to the increased salience of religion in Nigerian politics is the terrorist group Boko Haram.[67] The insurgency group works overdrive to turn Nigeria into an Islamic state in the mode of theocratic Iran on the theory that "Western education is a sin."[68] Driven by this proposition, since 2009, the group has ceaselessly waged war on any person or institution that it assesses as an insignia of Western education, "using every terroristic tool of violence within its reach, including arson, fire-bombing, suicide bombing, kidnapping, raping, and maiming."[69] The tragic result is that "[i]t has killed tens of thousands of people, maimed an untold number, engaged in incalculable destruction of private and public property, and rendered millions of citizens homeless both within [its] area of operation in northeastern Nigeria and beyond."[70] According to one conflict tracker, as of September 2021, Boko Haram has killed about 350,000 people, displaced 3 million, and turned 310,000 people into refugees.[71]

Federalism affords a laboratory for experimentation where subnational entities compete among themselves, and even with the center, in formulating and implementing a slate of policies and social programs for the people that includes healthcare.[72] Federalism came late to Nigeria under British colonial rule. The connection of federalism to healthcare funding is that, to the extent this system of government has been practiced in the post-independence period, no such experimentation beneficial to

---

[67] Aka, *Human Rights in Nigeria's External Relations*, note 21, p. 138.

[68] Ibid. For an overview of the Iranian government and political system, see "The Structure of Power in Iran," *Frontline* (PBS), https://www.pbs.org/wgbh/pages/frontline/shows/tehran/inside/govt.html (pointing out that an obvious difference between the religion-based presidential system of government in Iran and a secular presidential system, such as the US's, is that in Iran, "one man, the Supreme Leader, exerts ideological and political control over a system dominated by clerics who shadow every major function of the state"). See also Greg Bruno, "Religion and Politics in Iran," Council on Foreign Relations (June 19, 2008), https://www.cfr.org/backgrounder/religion-and-politics-iran.

[69] Aka, *Human Rights in Nigeria's External Relations*, note 21, p. 138.

[70] Ibid.

[71] "Global Conflict Tracker," Council on Foreign Relations (last updated September 1, 2021), https://www.cfr.org/global-conflict-tracker/conflict/boko-haram-nigeria.

[72] See Bradley A. Blakeman, "States Are the Laboratories of Democracy," *The Hill* (May 7, 2020), https://thehill.com/opinion/judiciary/496524-states-are-the-laboratories-of-democracy (citing the dissenting opinion of Louis Brandeis, then Associate Justice of the US Supreme Court, in *New State Ice Co. v. Liebmann*, 285 U.S. 262 (1932)).

healthcare took place. This suboptimal operation of the country's federal system, with negative ramification for healthcare and other social programs, was the reason why one instructive study of the political system from 1960 until 1996 assessed the country as a "crippled giant."[73]

Largest Economy in Africa

Nigeria is home to the largest economy in Africa.[74] But, this is a status that, like the "giant of Africa" myth, conceals more than it informs.[75] Using the concept of postindustrial economy as model, three components of a modern economy are agriculture, industrialization (or industry), and services.[76] Developed economies tend to have more of the mainstays of their economies in the service sector,[77] while developing countries tend to focus on the agricultural sector, with middle-income economies straddling agricultural and industrial production. Take Japan

---

[73] See generally Eghosa E. Osaghae, *The Crippled Giant: Nigeria since Independence* (Bloomington and Indianapolis: Indiana University Press, 1998). This somewhat dated study traced the political history of the country up to 1996 under the military regime of General Abacha (1993–1996) before the inauguration of the Fourth Republic in 1999.

[74] Prinesha Naidoo, "Nigeria Tops South Africa as the Continent's Biggest Economy," *Bloomberg* (March 3, 2020, updated March 4, 2020), https://www.bloomberg.com/news/articles/2020-03-03/nigeria-now-tops-south-africa-as-the-continent-s-biggest-economy; Kate Whiting, "[Five] Facts to Know About Africa's Powerhouse—Nigeria," *World Econ. Forum* (August 9, 2019), https://www.weforum.org/agenda/2019/08/nigeria-africa-economy/#:~:text=Last%20year%2C%20Nigeria's%20economy%20was,2%20million%20barrels%20each%20day; and "Africa's New Number One," *Economist* (April 12, 2014), https://www.economist.com/leaders/2014/04/12/africas-new-number-one.

[75] See, for example, "Five Things About Nigeria: The Superpower with No Power," *BBC News* (February 4, 2019), https://www.bbc.com/news/world-africa-47217557 (one of the five being the irony of "little electricity" in the country for a land with "lots of oil").

[76] See Ashley Crossman, "Post-Industrial Society in Sociology," *Thoughtco* (updated May 30, 2019), https://www.thoughtco.com/post-industrial-society-3026457 (defining a postindustrial society as "a stage in a society's evolution when the economy shifts from producing and providing goods and products to one that mainly offers services[,]" elaborating that in such society, "technology, information, and services are more important than manufacturing actual goods"). As this source indicates, instructively shedding needed light on the connection between economy and society, "[a] post-industrial society not only transforms the *economy*; it alters society as a whole." Ibid. Emphasis added.

[77] Ibid. ("Post-Industrial Society: Timeline") (citing Europe, Japan, and the US as examples of postindustrial economies and societies).

as example. In 2015, services accounted for 70.9 percent of the labor force in the country, industry 26.2 percent, and agriculture 2.9 percent.[78] These numbers mimic the contributions of these sectors to the GDP with services contributing over 71 percent, industry over 27 percent, and agriculture 1 percent.[79]

After over one hundred years, including the 60 years since independence, Nigeria's economy remains steeped in the mold of agricultural production with little traction toward industrial production, much less postindustrial services. Before independence in 1960 and for many years after self-rule, the engine of the Nigerian economy revolved around production of agricultural goods that the country exported to the world market: palm oil in the east, cocoa in the west, and groundnuts (peanuts) in the north.[80] The picture seemingly changed with expanded export of oil products in the early 1970s following the discovery of oil and gas in commercial quantities more than one decade earlier.[81] "With [eighteen] operating pipelines and an average daily production of over two million barrels in 2019, Nigeria [became] the eleventh largest oil producer worldwide."[82] Due to the export of oil in commercial quantity, crude oil

---

[78] "Labor Force—By Occupation—Service (%) 2020 Country Ranks, by Rank," *Countries of the World*, https://photius.com/rankings/2020/economy/labor_force_by_occupation_services_2020_0.html; "Labor Force—By Occupation—Industry (%) 2020 Country Ranks, by Rank," *Countries of the World*, https://photius.com/rankings/2020/economy/labor_force_by_occupation_industry_2020_0.html; "Labor Force—By Occupation—Agriculture (%) 2020 Country Ranks, by Rank," *Countries of the World*, https://photius.com/rankings/2020/economy/labor_force_by_occupation_agriculture_2020_0.html.

[79] See Benjamin Elisha Sawe, "The Economy of Japan," *World Atlas* (August 21, 2019), https://www.worldatlas.com/articles/the-economy-of-japan.html. Japan's main exports include motor vehicles, auto parts, power-generating machinery, iron and steel products, semiconductors, and plastic materials. Ibid.

[80] See Sylvester Okotie, "The Nigerian Economy Before the Discovery of Crude Oil," in *The Political Economy of Oil and Gas Activities in the Nigerian Aquatic Ecosystem*, ed. Prince E. Ndimele (Cambridge, MA: Academic Press, 2017), 71–81 ("There is an urgent need for diversification of the Nigerian economy from its present crude oil–dependent system[,]" such that sectors of the economy like "agriculture and manufacturing" are afforded the opportunity "to thrive and support revenue from petroleum…") (abstract).

[81] See Jedrzej Georg Frynas, *Oil in Nigeria: Conflict and Litigation Between Oil Companies and Village Communities* (Münster-Hamburg-Berlin-Wi, Germany: Lit Verlag, 2000), 8–41 (discussing the making of Nigeria's oil industry from discovery to the country's petroleum policy up to the 1990s).

[82] Simona Varrella, "Oil Industry in Nigeria—Statistics and Facts," *Statista* (November 6, 2020).

"account[ed] for about nine percent of Nigeria's GDP and for over 90 percent of all export value."[83]

Henceforth, however, Nigeria turned into a mono-product economy that supplied crude oil to the world economy and little else. It retained its position as a proverbial hewer of wood and drawer of water to the world economy, only now as an exporter of crude oil, rather than agricultural exports the era before.[84] The high dependence on crude oil creates a problem for the country because it makes its economy vulnerable to fluctuations in oil prices and production.[85] The structure of the country's economy remained that of an underdeveloped country where agriculture continued to play a major role.[86] Chapter 4 on our proposals for restructuring Nigeria's oil-based economy to raise enough money for healthcare elaborates this line of argument.

This is not to suggest that there was no growth in the non-agriculture sectors of the economy, for there was. Aided by the launch of multiple national development plans,[87] Nigerian industrialization sired a simulacrum of processed and manufactured goods.[88] Similarly, the service sector, also elaborated upon in Chap. 4, witnessed an uptick. However, though important, these spurts of growth in the industrialization and

---

[83] Ibid. Oil started yielding windfall revenue back to 1964 before the civil war and there was expectation in some quarters during the civil war from 1967 to 1970 that oil revenue will propel postwar reconstruction and recovery. See Kairn A. Klieman, "U.S. Oil Companies, the Nigerian Civil War, and the Origins of Opacity in the Nigerian Oil Industry," *Journal of American History*, 99(1) (June 2012), 155, 157–58, https://doi.org/10.1093/jahist/jas072 (discussing "[t]he Oil Boom of 1964–1965").

[84] On the analogy to hewers of wood and drawers of water, see generally John James Quinn, *Global Geopolitical Power and African Political and Economic Institutions: When Elephants Fight* (Lanham, MD: Lexington Books, 2017); and Immanuel Wallerstein, *The Modern-World System* (Cambridge, MA: Academic Press, 1974) (analyzing dependency theory that focuses on the peripheral location of developing economies in the global economic system). The concept itself came originally from Joshua 9: 21–27. See *Holy Bible, New Int'l Version*, p. 27 ("That day [Joshua] made the Gibeonites woodcutters and water carriers for the assembly, to provide for the needs of the altar of the Lord at the place the Lord would choose. And that is what they are to this day").

[85] "Nigeria: Economic and Political Overview," *Nordea* (updated October 2020), https://www.nordeatrade.com/no/explore-new-market/nigeria/economical-context.

[86] L.N. Chete et al., *Industrial Development and Growth in Nigeria: Lessons and Challenges* (Washington, DC: Brookings Institution, 2016–2017), 1, https://www.brookings.edu/wp-content/uploads/2016/07/l2c_wp8_chete-et-al-1.pdf.

[87] See Table 4.2 in Chap. 4 of this book.

[88] Chete et al., note 86, p. 1 (abstract).

service wings of the Nigerian economy were not enough to decisively change the essentialist mono-culture status of the Nigerian economy embedded in agriculture, in the expansive sense the term is used here. This assessment remains tenable despite the fact that Nigeria achieved its status as largest economy in Africa by rebasing its GDP calculation in April 2014 to give more credit to services.[89] Due to rebasing, Nigeria became the largest economy in Africa, overtaking South Africa, which previously held the prize.[90] Following the rebasing, Nigeria had an economy worth approximately US$ 510 billion as of 2013.[91] Yet, in the instructive observation of one source, Nigeria's being Africa's largest economy is a confounding occurrence, viewed against the background of the country's dire economic situation dating to the time of the rebasing, evident in an "abject decline in [...] real GDP, income, employment, manufacturing, and retail sales."[92] Put simply, in many respects, the emergence of Nigeria as largest economy in Africa is an event more apparent than real.

Nothing speaks to the ambiguous status of Nigeria as the giant of Africa than its lackluster capacity to project its power. Power projection is the ability of a country to exert influence, including deploying and sustaining military forces, outside its geographic borders, whether regionally or globally.[93] An important work by Jakkie Cilliers and his colleagues

---

[89] "Africa's New Number One," note 74; "Five Things about Nigeria," note 75 (commentary on the country's then upcoming general elections in spring 2019). Nigeria's National Bureau of Statistics conducted the rebasing exercise. The rebasing was consistent with the standard practice of the International Monetary Fund, which permits countries to update their GDP numbers every five years to reflect changes in their economic structure. Erick Oh, Nigeria's Services Economy: The Engine for Future Growth, U.S. International Trade Commission (USITC) (Executive Briefings on Trade) (March 2017), 1, n.2, https://www.usitc.gov/publications/332/executive_briefings/nige-ria_srv_ebot_oh-final.pdf. Until then, Nigeria had not updated its GDP numbers since 1990. Ibid.

[90] Oh, note 89.

[91] PharmaAccess Foundation, Nigerian Health Sector: Market Study Report (Pietersbergweg and Amsterdam, Netherlands, March 2015), 9, https://www.rvo.nl/sites/default/files/Market_Study_Health_Nigeria.pdf.

[92] "Nigeria Needs Industrialization Now," Forbes Africa (May 1, 2017), https://www.forbesafrica.com/investment-guide/2017/05/01/nigeria-needs-industrialization-now/.

[93] See US Dept. of Defense, The Dictionary of Military Terms (New York: Skyhorse Publishing, 2013).

sheds some helpful light on this problem as it relates to Nigeria.[94] The study explored the changing power capabilities of five big African countries, including Nigeria, over a 25-year period up to 2040.[95] The others were Algeria, Egypt, Ethiopia, and South Africa.[96]

The five countries were found to have the largest current or forecasted capabilities.[97] The study gauged capabilities using governance indicators like domestic security, government capacity, and inclusiveness,[98] specifically micro indexes like demographics, economic size and military might, international interactions, and technology on the Hillebrand-Herman-Moyer Index (HHMI) scale, a measure of relative national power.[99] Of the five countries, Nigeria and Ethiopia were the two Cilliers and his colleagues predicted would increase their power capabilities, while the other three, namely, Algeria, Egypt, and South Africa, were expected to stagnate or decline.[100] Although Nigeria was hypothesized to increase its power capabilities, Ethiopia was the country currently punching above its weight, while Nigeria was not.[101]

Moving from potential to power projection, the study found that "South Africa and Ethiopia do a good job of punching above their current power capabilities," that "Algeria and Nigeria [...] punch below their weight in Africa and the world," and that "Egypt punches above its weight internationally but below its weight in Africa."[102] The study noted,

---

[94] Jakkie Cilliers et al., *Power and Influence in Africa: Algeria, Egypt, Ethiopia, Nigeria, and South Africa*, Africa Futures Paper No. 14 (Denver, CO: Institute for Security Studies, March 2015), https://issafrica.s3.amazonaws.com/site/uploads/AfricanFuturesNo14-V2.pdf.   "The African Futures Project is a collaboration between the Institute for Security Studies (ISS) and the Frederick S. Pardee Center for International Futures at the Josef Korbel School of International Studies, University of Denver. The African Futures Project uses the International Futures (IFs) model to produce forward-looking, policy-relevant analysis based on exploration of possible trajectories for human development, economic growth and socio-political change in Africa under varying policy environments over the next four decades." Ibid., book back cover.

[95] Cilliers et al., note 94.

[96] Ibid.

[97] Ibid.

[98] See ibid. ("An Overview of Africa's Big Five").

[99] Ibid.

[100] Ibid. ("Summary").

[101] Ibid.

[102] Ibid. ("From potential to power projection in Africa").

instructive here for us in this book, "[i]f Nigeria were able to take the necessary steps that would see far-reaching changes to the governance issues and social challenges that currently beset the country, it could become Africa's lone superpower."[103] This point lends significance for this book: how to increase the ability of Nigeria to punch within its weight in economic development beyond dependence on oil and gas in a manner that is beneficial to healthcare delivery to its teeming population.

Under its Fourth Republic since 1999, Nigeria continues to derive most of its foreign exchange from the sale of crude oil products, during which period the four administrations that have governed the country did little to diversify the economy and minimally funded healthcare.[104] This book contributes ideas that could change this negative equation to the benefit of healthcare delivery in the country. The connection of the myth of largest economy in Africa to healthcare funding is a negative one represented in the reality that Nigerian leaders have not used the resources of the country in a manner that afforded good health to the masses of ordinary Nigerians, most of whom remained locked in poverty over 60 years since independence.

Conclusion

This chapter is a historical background account designed to introduce Nigeria to an uninitiated reader while simultaneously providing material that informs the argument of this book to the reader already familiar with the basic history of the country. The narrative revolves around the threadbare imagery of the country as the giant of Africa. Several provocative questions follow, some of which this book raises and others which it resolves. Since the production of oil in commercial quantity in the

---

[103] Ibid. ("Summary").

[104] The four administrations are Olusegun Obasanjo (1999–2007), Umaru Musa Yar'Adua (2007–2010), Goodluck Jonathan (2010–2015), and Muhammadu Buhari (2015 to present). Justin Findlay, "Presidents and Military Leaders of Nigeria Since Independence," *World Atlas* (August 1, 2019), https://www.worldatlas.com/articles/nigerian-presidents-and-military-leaders-since-independence.html (including pre-1999 leaders).

country in the early 1970s, Nigeria has received billions, if not trillions of US dollars in royalties from the export of oil alone, not counting other mineral resources. First, why, therefore, has a country so hugely endowed with natural and human resources, since independence 60 years ago, been unable to provide its citizens affordable healthcare? Put differently, why have Nigerian leaders, since independence, repeatedly been unable to improve access to healthcare for the masses of their citizens, using the windfall income from oil and gas?

Secondly, given the known negative influence of out-of-pocket expenses or user fees on access to healthcare for poor people,[105] why have these leaders failed to use the tool of affordable healthcare to minimize poverty in the country? In May 2018, Nigeria notoriously displaced India as the country with the highest number of extremely poor people in the world.[106] Thirdly, is a country now home to these many abjectly poor persons in a position to provide universal safe and affordable healthcare for the masses of its citizen? Wealth is needed to provide people with access to health-enhancing services, such as housing, clean water, nutritious foods, and healthcare itself. However, lack of access to education and affordable healthcare makes it difficult for many Nigerians to create the wealth they need to deal effectively with poverty. Only healthy persons, for example, participate in wealth-creating activities.

Fourthly, how then can extremely poor people avail themselves of necessary healthcare services so that they can remain healthy enough to participate gainfully and effectively in wealth-creating economic activities? And how can Nigeria remove this vicious cycle? Because poor people are

---

[105] See Chap. 1, note 19, and accompanying text.

[106] Nigeria is reported to have a population of about 87 million extremely poor people, defined as persons who live on an income of less than US$2 a day, out of a population of about 200 million people, compared to India, with a population of about 73 million extremely poor people, out of a population of nearly 1.4 billion people. Looking beyond Nigeria, increases in the number of people living in extreme poverty is a problem in Africa that unfortunately Nigeria with its wealth of natural resources is not immunized from. A study by the Kamla Foundation, a charity based in the UK, revealed that "14 out of 18 countries in the world where the number of extreme poor is rising are in Africa," and projects that, based on current trends, Africans will account for 90 percent (nine-tenths) of abjectly poor people by 2030. "World Poverty Clock," Kamla Foundation, https://kamlafoundation.org/wp-content/uploads/2019/01/World-Poverty-Clock.pdf.

unlikely to have the initial resources to pay for access to the healthcare services that they need to improve their health and become more productive, they may be relegated to a trap of underdevelopment that, without resolution, could lock them out for generations. The possible solution then becomes for the governments to provide free healthcare to its citizens, especially those who are on the margins of the economic system.[107] Doing so can lead to better educational outcomes for these citizens and subsequently more participation in the economy—as employees and entrepreneurs. Herein lies the timeliness and significance of this book: it deals with a policy issue central to Nigeria's efforts to fight poverty.

Fifthly, what is the relationship among conflicts, poverty alleviation (through wealth creation), and healthcare? Under the Fourth Republic since 1999, a generation of young people with no memory of the civil war has been up in arms against Nigeria's national government, using radical ideologies, religious and secular, in an attempt to upstage it.[108] The religion-based movements are typified by Boko Haram while the secular-based ones are exemplified by different groups seeking to resurrect the campaign for Biafra that was supposed to have been put to rest by the civil war from 1967 to 1970. Stated differently, what precisely is the nature of the negative influence of conflict, of the type Nigeria has endured under the Fourth Republic since 1999, on healthcare? Last but not least, what individual and cumulative effects have factors like the civil war, environmental damage from oil exploration in the Niger Delta, and military intervention into Nigerian politics had on healthcare delivery and enjoyment in Nigeria?

---

[107] See Amartya Sen, "Universal Healthcare: The Affordable Dream," *Vanguard* (London) (January 6, 2015), https://www.theguardian.com/society/2015/jan/06/-sp-universal-healthcare-the-affordable-dream-amartya-sen.

[108] A well-known name among the Igbo is *azi-ka-iwe*, meaning the youth are more prone to anger than older persons because of a built-in comparative advantage indicated by an ability to hold more grudge that can be more toxic for society—because they are younger and have more time to draw a pound of blood from detractors with their grudge. Instructively, Azikiwe is the last name of Nnamdi Azikiwe, a foremost figure in the decolonization movement in the country and beyond, whom many, in veneration of his pan-African ideals, have dubbed "Zik of Africa." Azikiwe was Nigeria's governor-general (1960–1963) and president (1963–1966). See, for example, "Azikiwe, Nnamdi, 1904–1996," *Encyclopedia* (Updated June 11, 2018), https://www.encyclopedia.com/people/history/historians-miscellaneous-biographies/nnamdi-azikiwe.

These are the illustrative questions this book tackles more or less. As the social scientist Karl Marx (1818–1883) once famously advised, analysis should be the springboard to remedial action.[109] In obedience to this wisdom, to change the way Nigerians fund their healthcare, we must first provide a portraiture of the Nigerian healthcare system. That is the object of Chap. 3.

---

[109] "Theses on Feuerbach, Thesis 11 (1845)," in *Selected Works, Vol. 1*, Marx Engels (Moscow: Foreign Languages Publishing House, 1950), 13–15 (stating "the philosophers have only interpreted the world, in various ways; the point is to change it"); Whittaker Chambers, *Witness* (New York: Random House, 1952), 9 (citing Karl Marx for the proposition that "[p]hilosophers have explained the world; it is necessary to change the world"). See also Karl Marx and Friedrich Engels, *The German Ideology, Including Theses on Feuerbach* (Amherst, NY: Prometheus, 1998), Chap. 3 ("One of the most difficult tasks confronting philosophers is to descend from the world of thought to the actual world. […] Just as philosophers have given thought an independent existence, so they were bound to make language into an independent realm").

3

Features of Nigeria's Healthcare System

Abstract This chapter highlights several features, more illustrative than exhaustive, of Nigeria's healthcare system: a huge burden of diseases relative to resources, influence of private facilities relative to public initiatives, continuing influence of traditional medicine, privileging of curative over preventive medicine, and low public trust in the healthcare system, evident in medical tourism. The discussion is crowned with comments, central to these features, on the negative legacy of long military rule on healthcare delivery in the country.

Keywords Healthcare system • Burden of disease • Private versus public healthcare facilities • Traditional medicine • Curative versus preventive medicine • Medical tourism

Introduction

A healthcare system comprises any collection of people and material resources of varying degree of integration and coordination, including monies, focus of this book, and information technology, designed to

© The Author(s), under exclusive license to Springer Nature Singapore Pte Ltd. 2022
P. C. Aka, J. A. Balogun, *Healthcare and Economic Restructuring*,
https://doi.org/10.1007/978-981-16-9543-8_3

49

maintain or promote health.[1] This composite includes formal healthcare services like the delivery of personal medical attention by a doctor, whether dispenser of traditional or allopathic medicine; taking care of the sick at home; activities designed to prevent diseases and promote good health; and interventions designed to improve good health, such as road safety and environmental safety campaigns.[2] Still other activities outside this formal boundary, yet germane to health, are increased school enroll-ment for girls, and changing the educational curriculum to make stu-dents better future caregivers and consumers of healthcare.[3]

Multiple features that influence a country's healthcare system include the unique history and culture of its society, priorities accorded to certain ethical values (such as autonomy of patients and healthcare providers), and, again consistent with the theme of this book, the level of economic resources available for healthcare.[4] It is these unique features, including how Nigeria funds its healthcare delivery, that underlie this sketch of Nigeria's healthcare system. In Nigeria, responsibility for healthcare deliv-ery tracks the country's three levels of government. Under the fragmented arrangement, local governments are responsible for primary care, such as dispensaries;[5] state governments for secondary care, such as general hos-pitals; while the national government is responsible for tertiary care, such as running Federal Medical Centers, coordinating university teaching hospitals, developing national policy, as well as formulating and implementing regulations.[6] Of an estimated 23,640 health facilities in

[1] See Philip C. Aka, *Genetic Counseling and Preventive Medicine in Post-War Bosnia* (Gateway East, Singapore: Palgrave Macmillan, 2020), pp. 31–2.
[2] Ibid., p. 32.
[3] Ibid.
[4] Ibid.
[5] These are health posts, many nominally, that provide basic, first-aid-like curative services. See *Country Policy and Information Note: Nigeria: Medical and Healthcare Issues, Version 3.0* (London, UK: Home Office, January 2020), 8, https://assets.publishing.service.gov.uk/government/uploads/system/uploads/attachment_data/file/857358/NGA_-_Medicalissues_-_CPIN_-_v3.0.finalG.pdf. [hereinafter *Country Policy and Information Note: Nigeria*].
[6] PharmaAccess Foundation, *Nigerian Health Sector: Market Study Report* (Pietersbergweg and Amsterdam, Netherlands, March 2015), 10, https://www.rvo.nl/sites/default/files/Market_Study_Health_Nigeria.pdf; Francis Koce et al., "Understanding Healthcare Self-Referral in Nigeria from the Service Users' Perspective: A Qualitative Study of Niger State," *BMC Health Services Research*, 19(209) (April 2, 2019), 2 (fig. 1), https://doi.org/10.1186/s12913-019-4046-9.

Nigeria in 2005, nearly 86 percent were primary, 14 percent secondary, and 0.2 percent tertiary.[7]

While the division of healthcare labor rings ideal, in practice, many things fall into the crack. First, the referral is not often followed in the sense that "[a]ilments that are supposed to be managed at the primary level are often managed at the tertiary level."[8] The reason for this occurrence is "because the other levels, especially the primary level[,] [are] very weak," with manifest deficiencies that include inadequate infrastructure, and a shortage of healthcare personnel.[9] To cite a related example, local governments are governments closest to the people. Yet, these units are the least funded and organized level in Nigeria's healthcare system, an occurrence that renders them "a very weak base for the [...] system."[10]

A similar division of labor tracks the distribution of pharmaceutical products in the country.[11] Under the arrangement, the national government stocks medications in a central location in Lagos, from where these products are then "transported to different states."[12] Equally, states "have their State Medical Stores, where [these products] are stored and transported to local government stores. From the local government stores, drugs are taken to the health facilities."[13] But here too there is a coordination problem, one notably evident in the massive "circulation of fake, substandard, and adulterated pharmaceutical products" estimated to be anywhere from 15 to 75 percent of total drug circulation.[14]

There are six interrelated aspects to the ensuing discussion: (i) a high burden of disease relative to resource allocations, (ii) predominant influence of private facilities relative to public initiatives, (iii) continuing

---

[7] *Country Policy and Information Note: Nigeria*, note 5, p. 8.

[8] *Country Policy and Information Note: Nigeria: Medical and Healthcare Issues, Version 2.0* (London: UK Home Office, Updated August 28, 2018), 6, https://www.justice.gov/eoir/page/file/1094261/download (citing Project MedCoI, June 2017). MedCOI is an information outfit that collects medical information on countries to assist the UK government with accurate information that will form the basis for informed decision on asylum applications.

[9] Ibid.

[10] PharmaAccess Foundation, note 6, p. 10.

[11] *Country Policy and Information Note: Nigeria*, note 5, p. 11.

[12] Ibid.

[13] Ibid.

[14] Ibid.

influence of traditional medicine, (iv) privileging of curative healthcare over preventive medicine, (v) low public trust in Nigeria's healthcare system indicated by medical tourism, and (vi) a reflection on the deleterious legacy of long military rule on the healthcare system. These features are illustrative rather than exhaust the possibilities for a country the size of Nigeria.[15]

The Huge Burden of Diseases Relative to Resources

Every healthcare system has a disease burden it carries relative to available resources. Nigeria is no different. Ten current leading causes of morbidity (disease) and mortality (death) in the country, in order of severity, are: neonatal disorder, lower respiratory infections, malaria, diarrheal diseases, HIV/AIDS, meningitis, tuberculosis, protein-energy malnutrition, dietary iron deficiency, and measles.[16] A less current but still valid breakdown with number attached to each source is as follows: malaria (20 percent), lower respiratory infection (19 percent), HIV/AIDS (9 percent), diarrheal diseases (5 percent), road injuries (5 percent), protein

---

[15] See Joseph A. Balogun and Philip C. Aka, "Strategic Reforms to Resuscitate the Nigerian Healthcare System," in *Nigeria in the Fourth Republic: Confronting the Contemporary Political, Economic and Social Dilemmas,* ed. E. Ike Udogu (Lanham, Boulder, New York, and London: Lexington Books, forthcoming 2022) (analyzing ten steps for energizing Nigeria's healthcare system). These reform measures, some of which parallel the ones presented in this chapter are: (i) Nigeria's leaders should recommit themselves to the Abuja Declaration on optimal budgetary allocation; (ii) these leaders should promote increased participation in the country's National Healthcare Insurance Scheme; (iii) they should expand access to essential medicines and vaccines; (iv) strengthen the health information system; (v) tackle the shortage of healthcare workers (HCWs); and (vi) improve the conditions of Service for these workers. Ibid. Other measures are: (vii) minimize corruption in the healthcare industry; (viii) update the healthcare education curricula; (ix) address the public health consequences of political violence; and (x) promote research and development within the healthcare system. Ibid. The features take the form of an appeal to effect reforms to give more life form to a dying system, whereas the discussion here is more broad-based.

[16] "Main Causes of Death and Disability in Nigeria in 2017," *Statista,* https://www.statista.com/statistics/1122916/main-causes-of-death-and-disability-in-nigeria/. Cf. "Global Health—Nigeria," Centers for Disease Control and Prevention, https://www.cdc.gov/globalhealth/countries/nigeria/default.htm (ranking those causes as (1) lower respiratory infections, (2) neonatal disorders, (3) HIV/AIDS, (4) malaria, (5) diarrheal diseases, (6) tuberculosis, (7) meningitis (8) ischemic heart disease, (9) stroke, and (10) cirrhosis).

energy malnutrition (4 percent), cancer (3 percent), meningitis (3 percent), stroke (3 percent), and tuberculosis (2 percent).[17]

Scrutiny of the breakdown uncovers several uncontradicted facts. First, three diseases—malaria, lower respiratory infection, and HIV/AIDS—account for nearly half the disease burden. Take malaria as example. The disease is viewed as the gravest public health challenge Nigeria faces.[18] There are "over 100 million cases per year [of the disease] and about 300,000 deaths."[19] The disease is responsible for 60 percent of outpatient visits to health facilities, 30 percent of childhood deaths, 11 percent of maternal deaths, and work absences due to the condition cost the country about US$ 8.4 million per annum.[20] Second, some conditions on the list, such as road injuries, and protein energy malnutrition, are not really diseases in the strict sense of the term. Instead, one, road injuries, speaks to the suboptimal level of infrastructural development in the country, resulting many a time in avoidable deaths in an environment of inadequate medical attention, while the other, malnutrition in protein energy, mirrors the insufficient economic development in the land, analyzed shortly. Between them, these two conditions account for nearly one-tenth of the country's disease burden.

Third is the "dual burden" of infectious diseases, such as malaria, along with noninfectious diseases like heart attacks, diabetes, stroke, and cancer.[21] The combination confounds and complicates the disease burden and puts the country in the worst of both worlds: While it has not eradicated traditional diseases like malaria, it is now faced with lifestyle

---

[17] "Nigeria Report 2013," Centers for Disease Control and Prevention, https://www.cdc.gov/globalhealth/countries/nigeria/why/default.htm (last visited June 17, 2016).

[18] PharmaAccess Foundation, note 6, p. 11.

[19] Ibid.

[20] Ibid.

[21] See ibid.; "Opportunities for Private Companies in Nigeria's Health Care Sector, and Efforts to Improve Provision," Oxford Business Group, https://oxfordbusinessgroup.com/overview/opportunities-private-companies-nigerias-health-care-sector-and-efforts-improve-provision [hereinafter "Opportunities for Private Companies in Nigeria's Healthcare Sector"].

diseases.[22] Take cancer as example, referenced earlier in Chap. 1.[23] Nigeria has a dubious record as the country with the highest rate of cancer deaths in Africa.[24] About four out of every five cancer patients in the country die from the condition, a rate considered "one of the worst in the whole world."[25]

There are three illnesses that barely made the lists not because they are unimportant but because there is only so much a composite, unsegregated, list can cover. Because of their high prevalence and overall impact on the disease burden in Nigeria, these three illnesses deserve some comments here. The first is child mortality. Nigeria has an infant mortality of approximately 55 infant deaths per 1,000 live births with deaths for children below 5 years of age of little over 90 per live births.[26] The second is maternal mortality. As of 2017, the date for which information is available, Nigeria had a maternal mortality rate of 917 per 100,000 live births.[27] This is by far one of the highest in the world. To put the matter in comparative perspective, in 2020, Nigeria made up approximately 3 percent of the world's population of approximately 8 billion people,[28] but

---

[22] Noninfectious diseases are called "lifestyle" illness because many of these diseases are preventable. They are caused by lifestyle choices like tobacco use (smoking), alcohol abuse, unhealthy diet (e.g., foods with too much sugar, salt, or fat), and physical inactivity. See "Noncommunicable Diseases," World Health Org., https://www.who.int/health-topics/noncommunicable-diseases#tab=tab_1. Many noninfectious diseases are associated with economic development, one reason some commentators call them "diseases of the rich." See "NCDs and Development (Chap. 2)," World Health Org., https://www.who.int/nmh/publications/ncd_report_chapter2.pdf (pointing out that, although noncommunicable diseases "are fundamentally a development and socioeconomic issue" that afflict both rich and poor, poor people in all countries bear the brunt of the health consequences arising from these diseases).

[23] See Chap. 1, notes 35–38, and accompanying texts.

[24] Sanni Onogu, "The Burden of Cancer in Nigeria," *Vanguard* (Lagos) (August 27, 2016), https://www.vanguardngr.com/2016/08/burden-cancer-nigeria/.

[25] Ibid.

[26] "Nigeria Demographics," *Worldometer*, https://www.worldometers.info/demographics/nigeria-demographics/.

[27] "Nigeria Maternal Mortality Rate 2000-2020," *Macro Trends*, https://www.macrotrends.net/countries/NGA/nigeria/maternal-mortality-rate. The rate is calculated based on the number of women who die from pregnancy-related causes while pregnant or within 42 days of pregnancy. More concretely, "the data are estimated with a regression model using information on the proportion of maternal deaths among non-AIDS deaths in women ages 15-49, fertility, birth attendants, and GDP." Ibid.

[28] "Nigeria Population 2020 (Live)," *World Population Review*, https://worldpopulationreview.com/countries/nigeria-population.

accounted for nearly one-fifth of global maternal deaths.[29] This dismal statistics explains why, in 2020, Nigeria had a life expectancy of approximately 55 years,[30] at a time when life expectancy has doubled in every region of the world, including Africa, where, in 2019, the number stood at 63 years.[31]

Last but not least is mental illness. This condition includes anxiety, depression, schizophrenia, bipolar disorder, and eating disorder.[32] About 50 million Nigerians live with some form of mental illness.[33] A World

---

[29] See, for example, "Maternal Health in Nigeria: Generating Information for Action," World Health Organization, https://www.who.int/reproductivehealth/maternal-health-nigeria/en/#:~:text=Spotlight%20on%20Nigeria&text=Nigeria%20is%20also%20the%20country,all%20global%20maternal%20deaths%20happen.&text=In%20fact%2C%20a%20Nigerian%20woman,risk%20is%201%20in%204900. Key drivers of these maternal deaths include the fact that many women in Nigeria, especially in rural communities, still deliver their babies at home without antenatal attention. See Bolaji Aregbeshola, "Health Care in Nigeria: Challenges and Recommendations," Social Protection (February 7, 2019), https://socialprotection.org/discover/blog/health-care-nigeria-challenges-and-recommendations.

[30] See "Nigeria Life Expectancy 1950-2020," *Macro Trends*, https://www.macrotrends.net/countries/NGA/nigeria/life-expectancy#:~:text=The%20current%20life%20expectancy%20for,a%20020.58%25%20increase%20from%202018. Life expectancy "refers to the number of years a person can expect to live[,]" and is, "[b]y definition [...] based on an estimate of the average age that members of a particular population group will be when they die." Esteban Ortiz-Ospina, "'Life Expectancy'—What Does This Actually Mean?" *Our World in Data* (August 28, 2017), https://ourworldindata.org/life-expectancy-how-is-it-calculated-and-how-should-it-be-interpreted. To put the matter simply, for a specific year, life expectancy is "the age a person born in that year would expect to live if the average age of death did not change over their lifetime." Ibid. The measurement is a key metric, over and above the much narrower indicator of infant and child mortality (focusing on mortality at a young age), for assessing population health, given that it "captures the mortality along the entire life course," specifically "the average age of death in a population." Max Roser et al., "Life Expectancy," *Our World in Data* (first published 2013, last revised October 2019), https://ourworldindata.org/life-expectancy#twice-as-long-life-expectancy-around-the-world.

[31] See Roser et al., note 30.

[32] Hannah Ritchie, and Max Roser, "Mental Health," *Our World in Data* (April 2018), https://ourworldindata.org/mental-health. See also *WHO-AIMS Report on Mental Health System in Nigeria: A Report of the Assessment of the Mental Health System in Nigeria Using the World Health Organization Assessment Instrument for Mental Health Systems* (WHO-AIMS) (Geneva, Switzerland: World Health Organization, and Abuja, Nigeria: Federal Ministry of Health, 2006), 17, https://www.who.int/mental_health/evidence/nigeria_who_aims_report.pdf. (providing a breakdown of the various categories of mental illness in Nigeria).

[33] Socrates Mbamalu, "Nigeria Has a Mental Health Problem," *Al Jazeera* (October 2, 2019), https://www.aljazeera.com/economy/2019/10/2/nigeria-has-a-mental-health-problem (citing WHO). According to this news story, one in four Nigerians, or about 25 percent of the populace, suffers from mental illness. Ibid. See also Dauda Eneyamire Suleiman, "Mental Health Disorders in Nigeria: A Highly Neglected Disease," *Annals of Nigerian Medicine*, 10(2) (2016), 47–8 [Editorial], https://www.anmjournal.com/article.asp?issn=0331-3131;year=2016;volume=10;is

Health Organization Assessment Instrument for Mental Health Systems (WHO-AIMS) on Nigeria, published in 2006, concluded that "there is considerable neglect of mental health issues in the country."[34] The report enumerated multiple factors impeding mental integrity and wellness in the country, including the absence of an updated mental health policy, lack of essential medications, the absence of any designated desk on mental health issues in government ministries, and an inadequate budgetary appropriation amounting to 4 percent of government expenditures for mental health.[35] By 2016, ten years later, the situation remained essentially unchanged.

A perceptive commentary in a Nigerian medical journal assessed the condition of mental healthcare in the country as "highly negligent," elaborating that attention to mental health disorders in the land "is at best, fleeting; the level of awareness of the Nigerian public on mental health issues […] poor, [while] the misconceptions regarding mental health have continued to flourish."[36] It added its voice to past recommendations for mental health to be treated as a legitimate issue of primary care in the country, and advised Nigerian governments to lead the fight against mental disorders through various means, including educating the public to recognize mental health disorders as a disease, and eschewing stigmatization of people suffering from these disorders.[37]

Supply of mental health services in Nigeria falls severely below demands for these services. Eight psychiatric centers spread across the country plus the psychiatric units attached to the medical schools of twelve major universities render the bulk of the mental health services in the country.[38]

---

sue=2;spage=47;epage=48;aulast=Suleiman#ref1 (putting the number as 20–30 percent of the population). To put the matter in comparative perspective, in 2017, an estimated 792 million people worldwide, representing nearly 11 percent of the world's population, lived with some form of mental disorder. Ritchie and Roser, note 32.

[34] *WHO-AIMS Report on Mental Health System in Nigeria*, note 32, p. 4. This report was an exploratory study conducted in 2005–2006 based on six states comprising Nigeria's six geopolitical zones, specifically six out of the eight federally funded psychiatric hospitals in the country. See ibid., pp. 5, 8, 33, 36.

[35] Ibid., pp. 4–5, 36.

[36] Suleiman, note 33.

[37] Ibid.

[38] See *WHO-AIMS Report on Mental Health System in Nigeria*, note 32, pp. 5, 8, 33, 36.

Several general hospitals also contribute with provision of mental health services.[39] This is barely enough for a country the large size of Nigeria with a sizable number of people living with mental illnesses.[40]

Other problems that Nigeria's healthcare system faces include a severe shortage of doctors, low pay and other unattractive working conditions for healthcare workers, and a poor system of collecting healthcare data and record keeping.[41] The doctor–patient ratio in the country is about 1 doctor per 5,000 patients, well below the WHO recommendation of 1 doctor per 600 patients.[42] The shortage is compounded by the equally low ratio of paramedical personnel in the country, such as psychologists, and social workers.[43] For example, the ratio of psychologists and social workers is about 2 of these professionals to 100,000 clients or service recipients.[44] Next to working conditions for healthcare workers, gross underpayment of these workers is linked to a range of negative outcomes that include unabated strikes, and exodus of many health workers,

---

[39] See Richard Uwakwe, "Mental Health Service and Access in Nigeria: A Short Overview," *International Journal of Global Social Work*, 2(103) (2018), 3, https://doi.org/10.15344/ijgsw/2018/103 (pointing out that additional to the eight psychiatric centers, "teaching hospitals and Federal Medical Centers also provide some mental health services in most of the thirty[-]six states of the federation").

[40] See note 33 and accompanying text.

[41] See Akindare Okunola, "[Five] Facts Every Nigerian Should Know About Our Health Care," *Global Citizen* (September 9, 2020), https://www.globalcitizen.org/en/content/health-care-facts-nigeria-covid-19/?utm_source=paidsearch&utm_medium=usgrant&utm_campaign=verizon&gclid=Cj0KCQiAtqL-BRC0ARIsAF4K3WGZxHt-Yz41A7pIT75mK9ftJcCI-GjctLUo_rcIqLU_7fEgaOJGkZgaAry7EALw_wcB

[42] See Chukwuma Muanya, and Adaku Onyenucheya, "Bridging Doctor-Patient Ratio Gap to Boost Access to Healthcare Delivery in Nigeria," *Guardian* (Lagos) (February 4, 2021), https://guardian.ng/features/health/bridging-doctor-patient-ratio-gap-to-boost-access-to-healthcare-delivery-in-nigeria/. The Nigerian Medical Association estimates that there are about 600 consultant pediatricians to manage and care for the nation's 70 million children. PharmaAccess Foundation, note 6, p. 15.

[43] "Nigeria," Global Health Workforce Alliance, https://www.who.int/workforcealliance/countries/nga/en/ (Nigeria "has densities of nurses, midwives and doctors that are still too low to effectively deliver essential health services (1.95 per 1,000)"). The Global Health Workforce Alliance (The Alliance) was created in 2006 as a common platform for action to address the crisis of healthcare delivery in Nigeria. The Alliance is a partnership of national governments, civil society, international agencies, finance institutions, researchers, educators and professional associations dedicated to identifying, implementing and advocating for solutions. "About the Alliance," https://www.who.int/workforcealliance/about/en/.

[44] Uwakwe, note 39, p. 3.

especially physicians, to other countries in search of the proverbial greener pastures.[45] The situation complicates the already low ratio of physicians to patients in the country.[46]

Nigerian healthcare law requires healthcare providers to "establish and maintain a health information system as part of the national health information system."[47] Despite this mandate, data collection and record keeping in many hospitals and other healthcare centers in Nigeria are still mostly undigitized, sometimes resulting in lost patient data, duplicate record keeping, and, in some cases, misdiagnosis.[48] Moreover, the country lacks a unified database of health indicators, an occurrence that impedes tracking within the system.[49] Given this void, much "data compiled on Nigeria's health care system are done by global organizations like UNICEF, international nonprofits, and the WHO."[50] Going further, "[t]here are also no comprehensive medical equipment registries and blood bank data is limited."[51]

---

[45] Okunola, note 41; Koce et al., note 6, p. 2.

[46] Okunola, note 41.

[47] See National Health Act, 2014, Act No. 8, Federal Republic of Nigeria Official Gazette, 145(101) (October 27, 2014),§38(1)(a), https://www.ilo.org/dyn/natlex/docs/ELECTRONIC/10415 7/126947/F-693610255/NGA104157.pdf.

[48] Okunola, note 41.

[49] Ibid.

[50] Ibid. UNICEF is the acronym for the United Nations International Children's Emergency Fund. The agency was established on December 11, 1946, to meet the emergency needs of children in postwar Europe and China. In 1950, its mandate was broadened to address the long-term needs of children and women in developing countries everywhere. In 1953, it became a permanent part of the UN system and its name was shortened to the United Nations Children's Fund. However, the agency chose to retain its original acronym (rather than go by the abbreviation UNCF). See "What Does the Acronym UNICEF Stand For: Frequently Asked Questions," UNICEF, https://www. unicef.org/about-unicef/frequently-asked-questions#1

[51] Okunola, note 41. Okunola points out that "[w]hile there are startups like Helium Health and LifeBank attempting to use technology to change this situation, adoption and scale is quite slow." Ibid. Both companies were formed in 2016 and, speaking to the unequal distribution of healthcare facilities that mark the Nigerian healthcare system, both companies are based in Lagos. Helium Health works to create "a connected healthcare ecosystem across Africa that simplifies health access, making it easy for patients to get the care they need when they need it." "About Us," Helium Health, https://heliumhealth.com/about.html. LifeBank delivers "an average of 300 imperial pints (170 l) of blood a month to more than 170 hospitals across" Nigeria. Saminu Machung, "How LifeBank is Solving the Problem of Blood Scarcity—One Hospital at a Time," The Cable Lifestyle (November 9, 2016), https://lifestyle.thecable.ng/lifebank-solving-problem-blood-scarcity-one-hospital-time/. To help increase the supply of blood, working with the Lagos State Government, the company runs blood drives across the state. Osarumen Osamuyi, "LifeBank Will Hold the Largest-Ever Blood Drive in Lagos, on February 13, 2016" TechCabal (February 4, 2016), https://techcabal. com/2016/02/04/lifebank-will-hold-the-largest-ever-blood-drive-in-lagos-on-february-13-2016/.

Add to this mix the low rate of health insurance in Nigeria, the huge out-of-pocket expenditure, and the unabated single-digit budgeting for healthcare and a clear picture emerges on why, as we elaborate shortly, many Nigerians lack trust in their own healthcare system. A key indicator of access to healthcare services is health insurance.[52] The National Health Act (NHA) of 2014 created a National Council on Health that it charged with responsibility for "ensur[ing] the widest possible catchments for the health insurance scheme throughout the" country.[53] As of that date, about 5 million Nigerians, about 3 percent of the country's population, had health insurance.[54] As we show in Chap. 5, several years later, the situations remained unchanged, if not worse, as many provisions of the NHA remains unimplemented.

Related to the absence of health insurance, Nigeria has a high patient out-of-pocket expenses estimated by the UN at 77 percent of healthcare spending that effectively limits access to quality healthcare for the poor.[55] Equally, Nigeria is notorious for an unabated low budget for its healthcare system "financially and managerially overwhelmed by" a heavy disease burden,[56] recounted in the preceding discussion. Yet, despite the

---

[52] Health coverage helps protect the patient from high, unexpected costs. If an individual unexpectedly gets sick or injured, health insurance exists to help cover costs that the individual may not afford to pay on their own. See "What is Health Insurance and Why Is It Important," Virginia Premier, https://www.virginiapremier.com/what-is-health-insurance-and-why-is-it-important/ ("Health Insurance as a Safety Net"), ("medical bills aren't the sort of thing [a person] want[s] to be dealing with while ill, injured, in a hospital bed or the emergency room. It's smart to make difficult financial decisions ahead of time, by getting health insurance before [a person] get[s] sick"). Additionally, health insurance makes it easier for a person to keep from staying sick in the first place, meaning it promotes preventive medicine, through means like annual checkups, and blood tests and lab work, as well as scans and screenings. Ibid.

[53] See National Health Act, 2014, note 47, § 40.

[54] "History of Health Insurance in Nigeria," Health Insurance, https://www.ehealthinsurance.com.ng/history-of-health-insurance-in-nigeria/#:~:text=Health%20insurance%20in%20Nigeria%20has,NHIS)%20Act%2035%20of%201999.&text=The%20Nigerian%20healthcare%20system%20is,and%20public%20managed%20medical%20facilities. Though still low, the percentage was an improvement from an estimated 150,000 people, or about 0.1% of the total population in 2004. Ibid.

[55] Okunola, note 41.

[56] Olanrewaju Tejuoso et al., "Health and the Legislature: The Case of Nigeria," *Health Systems & Reform*, 4(2) (2018), 62-4, doi: 10.1080/23288604.2018.1441622.

glaring funding need, and oblivious to the commitment in the Abuja Declaration for an allocation of 15 percent,[57] since 2012, "the budget allocation to health has fallen every year, from 6.2 [percent] of the total budget in 2015 to a proposed 3.9 [percent] for 2018."[58] The picture remained unchanged for the 2020 budget.[59] To make matters worse, about three-fifths of this low budgetary outlay goes to personnel over-heads, "leaving little for infrastructural development, expansion, acquisition of new equipment and scaling up of services[,]" resulting in run-down hospitals and fueling the lack of participation in the healthcare system that marks the phenomenon of medical tourism,[60] elaborated upon shortly.

Perceptive observers of Nigeria's healthcare system, such as the US and Australian diplomatic missions in Nigeria, equally comment on its sub-optimal features. The US Embassy and Consulate in Nigeria assessed the quality of Nigeria's healthcare providers as "rang[ing] from poor to fair[,]" based on US standards of training;[61] opined that Nigeria experiences

---

[57] See Chap. 1, notes 9–10, and accompanying texts.

[58] Tejuoso et al., note 56. Mathematically speaking, in 2018, Nigeria spent about 2 cents per person on healthcare, compared to $33 per person in the US. Okunola, note 41.

[59] "Could COVID Reduce Medical Travel from Nigeria?" *International Medical Travel Journal* (October 2, 2020), https://www.imtj.com/news/could-covid-reduce-medical-travel-nigeria/ ("Nigeria's national budget for healthcare in 2020 works out at just US$ 5.40 for each Nigerian"). In this budget speech, President Muhammadu Buhari identified the top four priorities of his government as fiscal consolidation, investment in critical infrastructure, incentivizing private sector investment, and enhancing social investment programs. "Top Four Priorities of the 2020 Budget," Channels Television (Updated October 8, 2019), https://www.channelstv.com/2019/10/08/top-four-priorities-of-the-2020-budget/. Healthcare was missing in action. His budget bears comparison with that of Rwanda, considered by many a bellwether in healthcare reforms in Africa. The Rwandan government's top four priority goals were "*strengthening the health system,* increasing agri-culture and livestock productivity, scaling up social protection coverage, and creation of employment opportunities through investment in public works and support to micro, small, medium and large enterprises affected by COVID-19." "Rwandan Government Proposes to Prioritize Health, Agriculture in Budget for Next Fiscal Year," *Xinhuanet* (May 21, 2020), http://www.xinhuanet.com/english/2020-05/21/c_139075836.htm#:~:text=%22Key%20priorities%20for%20the%20 2020,by%20COVID%2D19%2C%22%20said. Emphasis added.

[60] PharmaAccess Foundation, note 6, p. 16.

[61] "Medical Assistance," U.S. Embassy and Consulate in Nigeria, https://ng.usembassy. gov/u-s-citizen-services/local-resources-of-u-s-citizens/doctors/. It elaborated that recent graduates of Nigerian medical institutions "lack experience with modern equipment and sophisticated pro-cedures." Ibid.

severe shortages of medical and pharmaceutical equipment impelling it to fill its needs abroad, to the detriment of "medical practice, research, and training" in the country;[62] and took the view that Nigeria's blood supply is unsafe, marked by "[b]lood-banking services [that] are unacceptable by U.S. standards."[63] Finally, based on US standards, US diplomats in Nigeria rank Nigeria's capabilities in disaster and emergency response as well as in the management of national disaster as below par.[64] In their elaboration, the abilities of the civilian sector to manage disaster "are poor to nonexistent[,]"[65] and, although the military is able to provide crowd control during disasters, it lacks systematic medical response and currently lacks resources for mass casualty response.[66] In the opinion of the Australian Department of Foreign Affairs and Trade, "Nigerians have poor access to health care and poor health outcomes, particularly outside major urban centers."[67] In Nigeria, it said, "demand for public health care significantly exceeds supply[,]"[68] and, although healthcare services "are the responsibility of all levels of government[,]" access to quality medical services and the availability of these services, remain "inadequate, with most Nigerian unable to afford health care."[69]

To be sure, since the return to civilian rule under the Fourth Republic in 1999, some Nigerian states, such as Ekiti, Enugu, Jigawa, Kaduna, Kano, Lagos, Niger, Ondo, and Osun, have occasionally extended free healthcare to low-income or economically marginal groups like children, pregnant women, disabled persons, elderly people, displaced persons, the unemployed, and retirees.[70] However, these exemptions do not always work, because they are often "politically motivated, [...] poorly implemented," and short-lived.[71] In a word, those exemptions embed some

---

[62] Ibid.
[63] Ibid.
[64] Ibid.
[65] Ibid.
[66] Ibid.
[67] *Country Policy and Information Note: Nigeria*, note 5, p. 6.
[68] Ibid.
[69] Ibid.
[70] Aregbeshola, note 29.
[71] Ibid.

degree of out-of-pocket that render them alienable in short order by the givers, inconsistent with health as human right, when the wind of politics changes direction.[72]

Influence of Private Facilities Relative to Public Initiatives

In his work *The Wealth of Nations,* published in 1776, the arch-capitalist Adam Smith (1723–1790) conceded that the government must provide the infrastructure of roads, bridges, ports, and other investments that lay the groundwork for capitalist initiatives.[73] Contrary to this wisdom, private investments dwarf public initiatives in Nigeria's healthcare system. In Nigeria the government assumes a more limited role in the country's healthcare system than Smith formulated or would have imagined. Private healthcare facilities are an integral part of the three-tier healthcare system in Nigeria comprising the national, state, and local governments.[74] And as the US Embassy in Nigeria assessed, "[t]he best health care in Nigeria is available in private and nonprofit medical facilities," compared to government-owned medical facilities, whose quality it considers "unacceptable by U.S. standards."[75]

Private initiatives account for about 70 percent of healthcare services in the country.[76] Private-sector healthcare services in Nigeria include private hospitals owned by qualified medical practitioners; licensed pharmacists; the minimally trained and sometimes unlicensed chemist shop owners that dot the country's healthcare arena; drug peddlers; traditional drug hawkers, such as those who sell their wares in commercial buses

---

[72] Ibid.

[73] See generally Adam Hayes and Michael Boyle, "Adam Smith and 'The Wealth of Nations,'" *Investopedia* (Updated April 28, 2021), https://www.investopedia.com/updates/adam-smith-wealth-of-nations/.

[74] See Koce et al., note 6, fig. 1.

[75] "Medical Assistance," note 61. Instructively, the Embassy observed that, even with their higher quality, private healthcare facilities in Nigeria "typically fail to meet U.S. standards." Ibid.

[76] *Country Policy and Information Note: Nigeria,* note 5, p. 8. Compare "Opportunities for Private Companies in Nigeria's Healthcare," note 20 (stating that private facilites account for 62 percent of all healthcare delivery in the country, compared to 38 percent for the public sector).

wishing commuters good health; herbal healers; and other forms of health providers like spiritual homes and churches.[77] Over the years, major cities, such as Abuja, Enugu, Kano, Lagos, and Port Harcourt have witnessed noticeable growth in the number of private facilities.[78] Overall, private healthcare delivery in Nigeria is better managed and funded, compared to public healthcare delivery but, also on the average, more expensive.[79]

Because of this cost factor, private-sector healthcare services tend to cater to middle-class persons,[80] more able economically than poor people to afford these services. The dominance of private facilities over public initiatives betrays the Nigerian governments' relative inattention to healthcare delivery that includes inadequate funding. Despite official promises of expanded healthcare, a marked difference exists "in the availability and quality of services between private and public facilities [as well as] between urban and rural areas."[81]

Access to private healthcare serves to increase the overall quantum of medical services beyond what it would be without private healthcare while giving citizens more choice. A testament to the important role of private facilities in the Nigerian healthcare system is the public–private partnership that the national and state governments are adopting in an attempt to improve the quantity and quality of healthcare services in the country. Nigerian officialdom appreciates that "private[-]sector participation" in the healthcare system "can help resolve some of the inadequacies of the public health system as well as help relieve funding pressures."[82] Although the strategy in the partnership encompasses multiple models, the most common arrangement is one in which the "government solely

---

[77] Alex E. Asakitikpi, "Healthcare Coverage and Affordability in Nigeria: An Alternative Model to Equitable Healthcare Delivery" (June 3, 2019) [open-access peer-reviewed chapter], https://www.intechopen.com/books/universal-health-coverage/healthcare-coverage-and-affordability-in-nigeria-an-alternative-model-to-equitable-healthcare-delive. From *Universal Health Coverage*, ed. Aida Isabel Tavares (London, UK: IntechOpen), doi 10.5772/intechopen.85978.

[78] PharmaAccess Foundation, note 6, p. 12.

[79] *Country Policy and Information Note: Nigeria*, note 5, pp. 8, 9.

[80] Asakitikpi, note 77.

[81] "Opportunities for Private Companies in Nigeria's Healthcare Sector," note 21.

[82] Ibid.

finances the infrastructure and contracts a private entity to operate the facility."[83]

Like the Nigerian public healthcare sector but for a different reason, private healthcare in the country is also highly fragmented, comprising small medical centers owned by individual healthcare practitioners.[84] And for all its huge contributions, private healthcare in Nigeria "remains underregulated and underutilized for the control of infectious diseases like tuberculosis, HIV, and AIDS and for the provision of effective interventions such as family planning/child spacing."[85] Historically, the national Ministry of Health focuses its activities and regulations mostly on the public health sector and pays little attention to the private sector.[86] Finally, private healthcare in Nigeria is both predominately urban-centered and marked by regional disparities. "The health *workforce* is concentrated in urban tertiary health care services delivery in the southern part of the country, particularly in Lagos."[87]

Similarly, most "healthcare *infrastructure* is confined to major cities, with people living in urban areas getting four times as much access to healthcare as those living elsewhere."[88] Next to regional disparities, on average, private health facilities are concentrated in the southern portions of the country, while public health facilities dominate service provision in the northern portions.[89] Distribution of available medical services is equally skewed, with many supply points found in the southern portions of the country with the western part having more hospitals, followed by the eastern region.[90]

Private-sector participation in Nigeria's healthcare system predates the birth of the country. Portuguese navigators made their appearance in the coast of what later became Nigeria in 1472, bringing along with them

---

[83] *Country Policy and Information Note: Nigeria*, note 5, pp. 8–9.
[84] Ibid., p. 8.
[85] Tejuoso et al., note 56.
[86] See ibid.
[87] "Nigeria," Global Health Workforce Alliance, note 43. Emphasis added.
[88] *Country Policy and Information Note: Nigeria*, note 5, p. 8. Emphasis added.
[89] See ibid., pp. 7–8.
[90] Ibid., p. 8. See ibid. (noting that about 60 percent of the public primary healthcare facilities are found in the northern part of the country).

European medicine.[91] However, their motivation was a desire to satisfy their own healthcare needs, rather than those of the local people they met in their navigational journey.[92] Next came the missionaries. Different missionaries operated in different areas of what became Nigeria. In 1880, the Church Missionary Society (CMS) opened a dispensary in Obosi, what later became Eastern Nigeria.[93] This was followed by the Roman Catholic Mission, which, in 1895, established the Sacred Heart Hospital in Abeokuta, today Western Nigeria.[94] In the northern portions, the Sudan United Mission, and the Sudan Interior Mission, sponsored mission hospitals, respectively, in the Middle Belt and the Islamic north.[95] "Together [these two missions] operated twenty-five hospitals or other facilities […] [m]any of [which] […] hospitals remained important components of the health care network in the north in 1990."[96]

In the 1870s, prelude to the formal birth of Nigeria in 1914, "[t]he British colonial government began providing formal medical services with the construction of several clinics and hospitals in Lagos, Calabar, and other coastal trading centers."[97] Unlike the missionary healthcare centers, these healthcare facilities were initially solely designed to serve Europeans, but later extended their services to African employees of European businesses.[98] The expansion of healthcare facilities to other areas of the country coincided with European commercial activities within the country.[99] Thus, the Jos hospital was founded in 1912 following the introduction of tin mining there.[100]

---

[91] Ajayi Scott-Emuakpor, "The Evolution of Health Care Systems in Nigeria: Which Way Forward in the Twenty-First Century," *Nigeria Medical Journal*, 51(2) (2010), 53–65.

[92] Ibid.

[93] Ibid.

[94] "More About Sacred Heart Hospital[,] Lantoro," Sacred Heart Hospital, Lantoro, Abeokuta, https://www.sacredhearthospitallantoro.org/about.php; "Health," *in Nigeria: A Country Study*, ed. Helen Chapin Metz (Washington, DC: GPO for the Library of Congress, 1991)

[95] See "Nigeria: History of Modern Medical Services," *Photius Courtsoukis* (June 1991), https://photius.com/countries/nigeria/society/nigeria_society_history_of_modern_me~10005.html.

[96] Ibid.

[97] Ibid.

[98] Ibid.

[99] Ibid.

[100] Ibid.

Events after World War II lent added impetus to the expansion of healthcare facilities in Nigeria. Those events were driven by animated campaigns against colonial rule that were encouraged by perceptions of a decline of British powers occasioned by economic and other devastations the UK endured during the war.[101] In 1946, the colonial government announced a ten-year health development plan.[102] A highlight of the plan was the establishment of the Ministry of Health charged with responsibility for coordinating health services throughout the country, both those provided by the government and the private sector, including missionaries.[103] This was followed in 1948 by the formation of the University of Ibadan with ancillary institutions, including the University College Hospital, the first such full faculty of medicine and university hospital in the country.[104] A number of nursing schools were established, as were two schools of pharmacy; by 1960 there were 65 government nursing or midwifery training schools.[105]

Continuing Influence of Traditional Medicine

A third feature of Nigeria's healthcare system is the continuing influence that traditional medicine continues to exert over healthcare delivery in the country. Traditional medicine "is the sum total of the knowledge, skill and practices based on the theories, beliefs and experiences indigenous to different cultures, whether explicable or not, used in the maintenance of health as well as in the prevention, diagnosis, improvement or

---

[101] See John Darwin, "Britain, the Commonwealth[,] and the End of Empire," *BBC* (last updated March 3, 2011), http://www.bbc.co.uk/history/british/modern/endofempire_overview_01.shtml ("1960s: Loss of the Colonies") ("[t]o avoid being trapped in a costly struggle with local nationalist movements, Britain backed out of most of the remaining colonies with […] haste").

[102] "Nigeria: History of Modern Medical Services," note 95. This was one of two development plans unveiled during the course of British colonial rule in Nigeria. The other was unveiled in 1951, meaning that the 1946 plan lasted below the projected 10-year period.

[103] "Nigeria: History of Modern Medical Services," note 95.

[104] Ibid.

[105] Ibid.

treatment of physical and mental illness."[106] In Nigeria and many other African countries, traditional healing comprises various elements that include herbs, animal products, healer advice, and spiritual technique (usually embedded in God as creator and supreme being), designed holistically to heal mind, body, and spirit.[107] Therefore, a traditional healer is "a person [...] recognized by the community [...] as someone competent to provide health care by using plant, animal and mineral substances and other methods based on social, cultural and religious practices."[108]

Practitioners of traditional medicine are among the healthcare providers that the international health community indicated should work as a "health team [...] to respond to the expressed health needs of the community."[109] At a summit of the Organization of African Unity (OAU) in 2001, African leaders declared 2001–2010 the Decade of African Traditional Medicine, reasoning that traditional medicine is "the most affordable and accessible system of health care for the majority of the African rural population" that they aim to make "safe, efficacious, quality, and affordable [...] to the vast majority of the people."[110] In an attempt to meet this goal, since 2003, these leaders have set aside August 31 as African Traditional Medicine Day.[111]

Depending on the illness involved, many patients in Africa adopt a dual healthcare mindset whereby, in seeking medical attention, these patients consult a traditional healer first before an allopathic doctor.[112]

---

[106] *Global Report on Traditional and Complementary Medicine* (Geneva, Switzerland: World Health Organization, 2019) ("Glossary").

[107] See Mmamosheledi E. Mothibe, and Mncengeli Sibanda, *African Traditional Medicine: South African Perspective* (London: IntechOpen, 2019), https://www.intechopen.com/books/traditional-and-complementary-medicine/african-traditional-medicine-south-african-perspective ("Overview of African Traditional Medicine Practice").

[108] Quoted in ibid.

[109] World Health Organization, Declaration of Alma-Ata, Int'l Conference on Primary Health Care, Alma-Ata, USSR (September 6–12, 1978), https://www.who.int/publications/almaata_declaration_en.pdf, art. VII.7.

[110] Anju Sharma, "African States Confirm Support for Traditional Medicine," *Sci. Dev. Net.* (September 3, 2004), https://www.scidev.net/global/news/african-states-confirm-support-for-traditional-med/.

[111] See ibid.

[112] See Mothibe and Sibanda, note 107 ("Utilization and Prevalence of Traditional Medicine in South Africa").

Given this occurrence, there remains a need for traditional medicine, especially in view of the inadequate access to conventional Western healthcare in Africa. In the face of the interlacing between traditional medicine and allopathic medicine, some commentators have thoughtfully observed that "[a] respectful attitude of open exchange and information is essential for successful collaboration" between practitioners of the two fields.[113] The continuing influence of traditional medicine in Nigeria's healthcare system also points to the inadequacy of Western medicine for a populous state like Nigeria with a high burden of disease. In Nigeria, "many people […] continue to consult traditional healers because of the absence of adequate Western medicine."[114] Compared to allopathic medicine, traditional medicine is more within the reach of many poor people.[115]

Traditional medicine has a long history among the numerous communities that make up present-day Nigeria and forms a necessary part of the precolonial order.[116] Long before Europeans made their ways into Africa, traditional doctors performed circumcision on boys in many parts of Africa.[117] Similarly, traditional midwives and other birth attendants provide(d) care and advice to expectant mothers during and immediately after pregnancy.[118] Nigeria's national government accepts and regulates three systems of health care delivery: orthodox, alternative, and

---

[113] Ibid. ("Collaboration between African Traditional Medicine Practice and Conventional Research").

[114] "Medical Assistance," note 61.

[115] See Mothibe and Sibanda, note 107 (positing that traditional medicine "is physically, socially[,] and culturally more available than allopathic treatment"); and "Is There a Role for Trado-Medicine in the Nigerian Health Sector?" *Nigeria Health Watch* (October 4, 2018), https://nigeriahealth-watch.medium.com/is-there-a-role-for-trado-medicine-in-the-nigerian-health-sector-d824d13a47e8 (stating that traditional medicine is cheaper because there are no testing and medication fees for patients using this medicine).

[116] Ali Arazeem Abdullah, "Trends and Challenges of Traditional Medicine in Africa," *African Journal of Traditional Complementary and Alternative Medicines*, 8(5 Suppl.) (2001), 115–23 (portraying traditional medicine as "the oldest form of health care system that has stood the test of time," as well as "an ancient and culture-bound method of healing that humans have used to cope and deal with various diseases that have threatened their existence and survival"). As this source elaborated, "different societies," including communities in Africa "have evolved different forms of indigenous healing methods […] captured under the broad concept of" traditional medicine. Ibid.

[117] Mothibe and Sibanda, note 107 ("Overview of African Traditional Medicine Practice").

[118] See ibid.

traditional.[119] This is the way to go from a practical standpoint. However, while traditional medicine potentially can contribute to good health and promote economic development, it is still little regulated and users have little protection from potential misuse of traditional medicine.[120] Nigeria satisfies most of its medical and pharmaceutical supply needs from imports primarily from European countries.[121] In 2019, pharmaceutical products ranked eighth of ten top imports by Nigerians and amounted to US$ 1.5 billion.[122] That is a gap with negative ramifications for "medical practice, research, and training" in the country,[123] that more improved traditional medicine can fill.

Privileging of Curative Healthcare Over Preventive Medicine

Prevention, as one adage goes, is better than cure. Against the grain of this wisdom, Nigeria's healthcare system appears, like that of some other climes, to privilege curative healthcare over preventive medicine.[124] Preventive medicine is quality medical attention short of complex diagnoses and treatment, motivated by the need to remove the causes of ill-health, rather than addressing their symptoms, often embedded in primary health.[125] Progressive healthcare systems today stress primary

---

[119] "Nigeria," Global Health Workforce Alliance, note 43.

[120] See Yusuf Abdul Azeez, "Alternative Medicine in Nigeria: The Legal Framework," Int'l Conf. on Language, Literature, Culture, and Education, April 25–6, 2015, pp. 62,70, https://icsai.org/procarch/2icllce/2icllce-90.pdf (stating that it is "hard to conclude that" Nigerian law has a regulatory body tasked with responsibility for regulating traditional medicine in the country).

[121] See "Medical Assistance," note 61.

[122] Daniel Workman, "Nigeria's Top [Ten] Imports," World's Top Exports, http://www.worldstopexports.com/nigerias-top-10-imports/.

[123] "Medical Assistance," note 61.

[124] The concept of preventive medicine calls to mind the children's animal song about five little monkeys that jumped on the bed. Each of the five bumped its head, and on each occasion, mama monkey dutifully called the doctor who in each instance administered a preventive medicine: no more monkeys jumping on the bed. Intriguingly, each of the five ignored the advice, whereupon, with the fifth also—predictably—bumping its head, the doctor advised that all five monkeys be put to bed. Preventive medicine seems so basic, yet, for some reason, it is easily overlooked.

[125] See Aka, *Genetic Counseling and Preventive Medicine in Post-War Bosnia*, note 1, pp. vii, 3–5.

healthcare, revolved around keeping people healthy, over curative medicine. They "make disease unacceptable instead of building ever larger infrastructure to accommodate it."[126]

Preventive medicine spells holistic wellness campaigns that "involve not only medical staff, but also officials dealing with agriculture, transportation, law enforcement, water and sanitation, food security and housing."[127] It also encompasses well-targeted education designed "to prevent [people] from developing chronic diseases in the first place[,]" while providing patients with chronic conditions effective techniques for "manag[ing] their health[.]"[128] In the US, the Affordable Care Act (ACA) under then-president Barack Obama was predicated largely on preventive medicine.[129]

A shift of emphasis to preventive medicine will conserve resource and help to rationalize access to healthcare for a country with limited resources. However, Nigeria has yet to make that shift. Take the National Health Insurance Scheme (NHIS), a putative monument of Nigeria's national healthcare under the Fourth Republic, as example. The scheme is an attempt by Nigeria's national government to make healthcare more affordable for ordinary citizens.[130] The expectation was that this scheme would provide increased access to healthcare for ordinary people, particularly children, pregnant women, disabled persons, elderly people, displaced persons, the unemployed, retirees, and other vulnerable groups within the society, most of whom live in rural communities where access

---

[126] "The Future of Healthcare in Africa," Economist Intelligence Unit (London), 10 (2014), 17, http://www.economistinsights.com/sites/default/files/downloads/EIU-Janssen_HealthcareAfrica_Report_Web.pdf. (quoting Dr. Ernest Darkoh, founding partner of BroadReach Healthcare, a healthcare services company). According to Dr. Darkoh, the most successful outcome for a healthcare system in Africa should be defined as never needing to see the inside of a hospital. In his view, the continuous need to build more hospitals and clinics should be considered a sign of failure. Ibid.

[127] Ibid.

[128] Ibid.

[129] Aka, *Genetic Counseling and Preventive Medicine in Post-War Bosnia*, note 1, p. 108.

[130] See Chima Onoka et al., "Why are States Not Adopting the Formal Sector Program of the NHIS and What Strategies Can Encourage Adoption?" Alliance for Health Policy and Systems Research, Policy Brief (October 2012), https://www.who.int/alliance-psr/projects/alliancehpsr_nigeriapolicybriefstates.pdf?ua=1).

to basic healthcare services is limited.[131] The program was established in 1999,[132] but was not formally launched until 2005.[133] The scheme was preceded by many unsuccessful attempts dating back to the country's independence in 1960 to introduce expanded healthcare.[134]

But the program is also a poster child of the Nigerian government's incompetence in healthcare administration. Many years after its inauguration, the program only succeeded in enrolling and covering less than 5 percent of the population, most of them employees of the national government.[135] Thus, despite the introduction of the measure, quality healthcare remained unaffordable to many poor or economically vulnerable groups. In retrospect, discussing the privilege of curative treatment over preventive medicine rings premature in a healthcare system like Nigeria's marked by a huge burden of disease relative to available resources where, as a result, private facilities predominate over public initiatives and, for the same reason, a continuing role remains for traditional medicine.

Low Public Trust in Nigeria's Healthcare System Evident in Medical Tourism

The result of all the features above is a healthcare system many Nigerians put small trust in. Nigerians lack trust in their own healthcare system. Trust in a healthcare system exists when patients have confidence that they will receive the correct treatment for their conditions; that the care they receive will be delivered by healthcare professionals with requisite competence, among others, backed by adequate monitor, indicated by governmental regulation.[136] To the contrary, in opinion surveys, nine out

---

[131] Aregbeshola, note 29.

[132] National Health Insurance Scheme No. 35 (1999), http://www.nigeria-law.org/National%20 Health%20Insurance%20Scheme%20Decr... (last visited November 8, 2016).

[133] Aregbeshola, note 29.

[134] Ibid.

[135] Ibid. The appellation less than 5 percent is justified because the enrollment figure varies, at times 3 percent or 4 percent, depending on what year of Nigeria's ever-growing population the researcher used in calculation. But so far, less than 5 percent is indicated.

[136] See "Restoring Trust to Nigeria's Healthcare System," PwC, https://www.pwc.com/ng/en/assets/ pdf/restoring-trust-to-nigeria-healthcare-system.pdf.

of every ten Nigerians perceive their healthcare system to be "low quality."[137] Low trust in Nigeria's healthcare system is a perception built on the composite of personal experience and those of others, as well as news reports and the state of disrepair in healthcare infrastructure care users visualize when they contemplate their healthcare system.[138] There is little patient protection in the Nigerian healthcare system, and regulation of clinical practice is modest, in some cases, nonexistent, with minimal accreditation or quality-control standards in place.[139] Moreover, because the Nigerian legal and judicial systems create little space for tort account-ability, patients and their survivors have little opportunity to hold health tortfeasors accountable through medical malpractice lawsuits when things go wrong.[140]

The net effect of all these is an unwholesome practice that, because of the access it gives only to government officials and private citizens who can afford it to the exclusion, nay the expense, of ordinary Nigerians, many Nigerians refer to derisively as "medical tourism" or "medical

---

[137] See ibid.

[138] Ibid.

[139] Ibid.

[140] See ibid., p. 5. See also Oluwakemi Mary Adekile, "Compensating Victims of Personal Injuries in Tort: The Nigerian Experience in Fifty Years," *SSRN* (2013), 33, https://doi.org/10.2139/ ssrn.3111539 (contending that Nigeria's tort system needs restructuring by legislation to extend protection to victims presently unprotected, such as unemployed persons, nonindustrial workers, criminal injury sufferers, sufferers of natural or manmade disasters, victims of no-fault personal injury, victims of unidentified or untraced torts or crimes, persons living with disability, and vic-tims of accidental injury, guided by the experience of other countries within the tenets of compara-tive law). Finally, Nigerian governments should be able to hold pharmaceutical companies liable for marketing products that bring harm to the population, as is the case in the US. See Katie Dwyer, "[Six] Critical Risks Facing the Pharmaceutical Industry," *Risk & Insurance* (June 29, 2018), https://riskandinsurance.com/6-critical-risks-facing-pharmaceuticals/ (including "Legal Liability for Opioid Addiction" among the six). Recently the consulting giant Kingsley & Company settled a lawsuit brought against it by 43 states, the District of Columbia and three US territories over its role in the country, including these 47 jurisdictions, in epidemic related to opioid addictions that resulted in 450,000 overdose deaths from 1999 to 2018. The lawsuit alleged that the firm's aggres-sive marketing of OxyContin, a painkiller, helped fuel the epidemic. See Nate Raymond, "McKinsey to Pay $573 Million to Settle Claims Over Opioid Crisis Role: Source," Reuters (February 3, 2021), https://www.reuters.com/article/us-usa-mckinsey/mckinsey-to-pay-573-million-to-settle-claims-over-opioid-crisis-role-source-idUSKBN2A405Q. For a case in Oklahoma involving Johnson and Johnson in the lead up to this lawsuit, see Jan Hoffman, "Johnson & Johnson Ordered to Pay $572 Million in Landmark Opioid Trial," *New York Times* (August 26, 2019, updated August 30, 2019), https://www.nytimes.com/2019/08/26/health/oklahoma-opioids-johnson-and-johnson.html.

vacation."[141] Average Nigerians believe that their healthcare system is substandard and something to be avoided whenever an alternative can be found.[142] Nigerians still go to their local doctor for primary healthcare needs and routine medical attention because of the proximity of services, "but whenever advanced medical care is required, the first option is to reach for their passports and head to foreign lands."[143] This is especially the case with the cream of Nigerian elite that tend to seek medical treatment abroad when confronted with serious medical conditions.[144] Destinations of these medical journeys include Dubai, Germany, India, Saudi Arabia, South Africa, Turkey, the UK, and the US.[145] The Nigerian Medical Association (NMA) estimates that over 5,000 Nigerians travel out to these countries monthly for medical treatment.[146] Nigeria spends about US$ 1 billion every year receiving treatment abroad that they would have received at home.[147] In material terms alone, this amount translates into a loss of about 3.7 million patients per year who would have received treatment in Nigeria.[148] Key healthcare services sought in these tours are cardiology, oncology, and orthopedic surgeries.[149]

The National Health Act of 2014 provides that no national government official "shall be sponsored for medical check-up, investigation[,] or treatment abroad at public expense," except in exceptional circumstances, subject to the recommendation of a medical board and approval by the Minister of Health.[150] Yet, medical tourism is one issue where, like the use of public office for private ends, which defines political corruption,

---

[141] "Restoring Trust to Nigeria's Healthcare System," note 136, p. 5; Conor Gaffey, "Nigeria's President Buhari Didn't Get the Memo About Health Tourism," *Newsweek* (August 25, 2017), http://www.newsweek.com/nigeria-president-muhammadu-buhari-health-tourism-655006.

[142] "Restoring Trust to Nigeria's Healthcare System," note 136, p. 4.

[143] Ibid.

[144] Ibid.

[145] PharmaAccess Foundation, note 6, p. 15; "Could COVID Reduce Medical Travel from Nigeria?" note 58.

[146] "Buhari's Medical Tourism in London," *Huhu Online* (March 31, 2021) [Editorial], https://huhu-online.com/index.php/home-4/opinions/14460-editorial-buhari-s-medical-tourism-in-london.

[147] See "Could COVID Reduce Medical Travel from Nigeria?" note 59.

[148] "Restoring Trust to Nigeria's Healthcare System," note 136, p. 4.

[149] PharmaAccess Foundation, note 6, p.15.

[150] National Health Act, 2014, note 47, §46 ("Medical Treatment Abroad").

some Nigerian rulers have failed to lead by example. Since taking office in May 2015, Nigeria's current leader, Muhammadu Buhari has traveled to the UK thrice for medical treatment, both for disclosed and undisclosed conditions.

The first, for an ear infection, was in June 2016,[151] just months after the President indicated that he would not support medical treatment abroad for federal government workers.[152] The second was for an extended period in 2017, beginning February of that year for 154 days, for an undisclosed illness.[153] The third, most recently, was in March, 2021, when the President insensitively traveled to London for medical checkup two days before Nigerian doctors went on strike over unsatisfactory work conditions, including unpaid salaries.[154] Buhari indulged in this non-exemplary conduct despite the relative plenitude in access to medical

---

[151] See "Nigeria's Buhari 'Broke Promise to End Medical Tourism,'" *BBC News* (June 7, 2016), https://www.bbc.com/news/business-36468154. This news story included a statement from one Dr Enabulele, Vice-President of the Commonwealth Medical Association, who remarked that it was a "national shame" that Mr Buhari went to the UK for treatment when Nigeria had more than 250 ear, nose and throat (ENT) specialists, as well as a National Ear Centre. Ibid. He advised Mr Buhari to lead by example by using Nigerian doctors and facilities, and ensuring that government officials do not go abroad on "frivolous" medical trips. Ibid. In the era of COVID-19, this is analogous to leaders advising their citizens to maintain social distancing, wash their hands, and wear face covers in an attempt to curtail the spread of Coronavirus without doing these same things.

[152] During an address in April 2016 at an annual meeting of the Nigeria Medical Association (NMA) in Sokoto in northwestern Nigeria, Buhari stated that his administration will not encourage expending the nation's resources on any government official seeking medical care abroad especially when treatment is available in Nigeria. See Haruna Gimba, "Nigeria Lost $[US]1 b[illion] to Medical Tourism," *Health Reporter* (April 27, 2016), http://healthreporters.info/2016/04/27/nigeria-lost-1b-to-medical-tourism-buhari/.

[153] Yomi Kazeem, "Nigeria's President is Back Home after 104 Days of Medical Vacation in London," *Quartz* (August 19, 2017), https://qz.com/africa/1057953/nigerias-president-buhari-will-return-home-after-104-days-in-london-on-medical-leave/. The 104 days in this story does not include 50 days from February of the same year, also spent in London, receiving treatment. Ibid. Regarding expense, the government spent about US $4,000 per day for many days to park the presidential jet while the president received treatment. "Presidential Plane Parked in London since May," *Vanguard* (Lagos) (July 10, 2017) [Editorial], https://www.vanguardngr.com/2017/07/presidential-plane-parked-london-since-may/.

[154] Anthony Osae-Brown, "Nigeria's Buhari Takes Medical Trip Abroad Before Doctor Strike," *Bloomberg* (March 30, 2021), https://www.bloomberg.com/news/articles/2021-03-30/nigeria-s-buhari-takes-medical-trip-abroad-before-doctor-strike. See also Aina Ojonugwa, "Go Home, Protesting Nigerians Boo Buhari in UK," *The Will* (April 2, 2021), https://thewillnigeria.com/news/go-home-protesting-nigerians-boo-buhari-in-uk/.

attention in State House Medical Center, the presidential clinic.[155] His predecessor, Umaru Musa Yar'Adua, set the tone for this practice when, in November 2009, he traveled to Saudi Arabia where he spent three months undergoing medical treatment for a heart condition.[156]

Negative Legacy of Long Military Rule on Nigeria's Healthcare System

There is an Igbo saying to the effect that an individual drenched by rain will not dry from his wetness unless he pinpoints where the rain started beating him. Colonialism impacted healthcare negatively as we broached in Chap. 2 and elaborated above in the section on the influence of private over public spending on healthcare. For nearly 30 years from 1966 until 1998 with a brief pause under the Second Republic from 1979 to 1983, Nigerians lived under more or less repressive military dictatorships. Many of the country's major policies, such as the division of the country into 36 states, the move to a new national capital, and the controversial Land Use Decree, among numerous other policy initiatives, took place during military rule.[157]

Repressive military rule in Nigeria cast a negative shadow over many aspects of the country's national life whose effects, onto the present period, are still keenly felt. Testament to those lingering effects is the domination of the Fourth Republic by former military generals who packaged themselves as "converted democrat[s],"[158] but still govern more

---

[155] Based on press reports, in 2016, the national government invested more money in the health facility than it did in the country's 16 teaching hospitals. See "Aso Rock Clinic Gulps ₦9.17bn in Four Years," *Sahara Reporters* (January 7, 2019), http://saharareporters.com/2019/01/07/aso-rock-clinic-gulps-n917bn-four-years%E2%80%8B. More on this point later in Chap. 5 on the influence of politics on healthcare in Nigeria. Aso Rock refers to the workplace and official residence of the Nigerian president, in the same way the White House is the official residence and office of the US president.

[156] Mark Tran, "President Umaru Yar'Adua Returns to Nigeria," *Guardian* (London) (February 23, 2010), https://www.theguardian.com/world/2010/feb/24/president-yaradua-back-in-nigeria.

[157] See Philip C. Aka, *Human Rights in Nigeria's External Relations: Building the Record of a Moral Superpower* (Lanham, MD: Lexington Books, 2017), 126.

[158] See Alexis Akwagyiram, "Muhammadu Buhari: Nigeria's Converted Democrat Comes Back from the Brink," Reuters (February 26, 2019), https://www.reuters.com/article/us-nigeria-election-buhari-newsmaker/muhammadu-buhari-nigerias-converted-democrat-comes-back-from-the-brink-idUSKCN1QF2SN.

or less as dictators in a civilian dispensation.[159] Two of them—Olusegun Obasanjo, 1999–2007 and Muhammadu Buhari, 2015–2023—won two terms in office, accounting for 16 of the 24 years of the Fourth Republic by May 2023 when Buhari completes his second term in office. The 16 years represent two-thirds of the Fourth Republic. To seal the domination by former military rulers, Obasanjo handpicked the two non-former military leaders, Umaru Musa Yar'Adua (2007–2010), and Goodluck Jonathan (2010–2015), sandwiched between these two retired generals.[160]

A substandard healthcare system ranks among the negative bequeaths and legacies of long military rule in Nigeria. First, military rule laid the notorious foundation for the alignment of national priorities in favor of guns (defense) over butter (social programs),[161] which explains, but does not justify, the low funding for healthcare that has marked the Fourth Republic. Second, many of the ills that currently bedevil healthcare delivery in Nigeria, including repeated strikes among health workers, ill-equipped laboratories, ill-stocked pharmacies, dilapidated hospital buildings, unsanitary hospital environments, and poor remuneration of health workers, are carryovers from the era of military rule.[162]

Military dictatorship and proper management of any economy are two oxymoronic phenomena that do not go together.[163] In its compositeness,

---

[159] See John Campbell, and Matthew T. Page, *Nigeria: What Everyone Needs to Know* (New York: Oxford University Press, 2018), 1 (pointing out that even though Obasanjo's presidency was ostensibly civilian, "his [governance] style was that of a military ruler"). For example, Obasanjo did not enforce court judgments that he did not like. Ibid., pp. 1–2. See also Wole Soyinka, "Lessons from Nigeria's Militarized Democratic Experiment," *New York Times*, Op-Ed. (October 19, 2019); Etim O. Frank, and Wilfred I. Ukpere, "The Impact of Military Rule on Democracy in Nigeria," *Journal of Social Sciences*, 33(3) (2012), 285–92, https://www.researchgate.net/publication/261672856_The_Impact_of_Military_Rule_on_Democracy_in_Nigeria.

[160] See Aka, *Human Rights in Nigeria's External Relations*, note 157, p. 82; and Michelle Gavin, "The Post-Presidential Legacy of Nigeria's Goodluck Jonathan," Council on Foreign Relations (July 16, 2019), https://www.cfr.org/blog/post-presidential-legacy-nigerias-goodluck-jonathan.

[161] For an elaboration of the guns-over-butter dichotomy, see Alan Farley, "What Does 'Guns and Butter' Refer To?" *Investopedia* (updated February 11, 2020), https://www.investopedia.com/ask/answers/08/guns-butter.asp.

[162] See, for example, Dennis A. Ityavyar, "The State, Class[,] and Health Services in Nigeria," *Africa Spectrum*, 22(3) (1987), 285–314, https://www.jstor.org/stable/40174297.

[163] See Annalisa Merelli, "No Benevolent Dictators: 150 Years of Data Proves It: Strongmen are Bad for the Economy," *Quartz* (August 19, 2019), https://qz.com/1688397/data-proves-it-authoritarian-leaders-are-bad-for-the-economy/

development is "a big cultural moment, a complex process [...] entail[ing] changes in people's minds as well[,]"[164] that rarely occurs under military rule. Broadly speaking, this supports the seminal position of the political scientist Claude Ake who portrayed authoritarian political conditions in Nigeria and other Africa countries as the greatest impediment to development in these countries, an occurrence that he traced back to colonial rule in these lands.[165] The moral of this commentary is that maintenance of civilian rule, even if low quality, is desideratum for lasting progress in healthcare and repairing the suboptimal relationship between poverty and access to healthcare in Nigeria.

Conclusion

Nigerian healthcare legislation stipulates that "all citizens shall be entitled to a basic minimum package of health services."[166] Similarly, these laws prescribe a heavy penalty, including a term of imprisonment for any healthcare provider, worker or clinic which "refuse[s] a person emergency medical treatment for any reason."[167] Yet, even on their faces, none of these laws makes adequate provisions to fund healthcare.[168] And as we show in Chap. 5, which details the influence of politics on healthcare in Nigeria, many of these provisions remained unimplemented many years after the passage of the law.

In the final analysis, given the features outlined in this chapter, healthcare in Nigeria amounts to little more than a misnomer for a sick care

---

[164] See Philip C. Aka, "The Senegambia Confederation in Historical Perspective," in *African Intellectuals and the State of the Continent: Essays in Honor of Professor Sulayman S. Nyang*, eds. Olayiwola Abegunrin and Sabella Abidde (Newcastle upon Tyne, UK: Cambridge Scholars Publishing, 2018), 37, 50. As this piece elaborated, political culture consists of basic attitudes about political life that are widely shared within a particular community. These shared values are divisible into the three clusters of: attitudes toward authority, attitudes toward society, and attitudes toward politics, especially the state. Ibid., p. 51.

[165] See generally Claude Ake, *Democracy and Development in Africa* (Washington, DC: Brookings Institution Press, 1996).

[166] National Health Act, 2014, note 47, §15(3).

[167] National Health Act, 2014, note 47, §20 ("Emergency Treatment").

[168] See Chap. 1, notes 1–6, and accompanying texts.

system. Using the same treatment analogy, we likened the healthcare system elsewhere as a patient in life support needing medical intervention of the kind necessary to resuscitate a dying patient in an ICU.[169] Health is the mother of socioeconomic human rights.[170] Healthy citizens are more productive workers, if nothing else, because they post fewer sick days.[171] They are the secret to the durable workforce that a country needs to create wealth and maintain a strong modern economy.[172] In turn, strong health systems are a marker of a fair and just society, and the healthcare system of a country influences its ability to participate effectively in the global economy.[173] In obedience to the proposition about analysis as a guide and springboard to remedial action,[174] the challenge Nigeria's latest experiment in civilian rule faces is how to put *health* into a more or less sick care system. Restructuring the economy to find revenue for healthcare is the viable and sustainable way forward. Chapter 4 tackles that issue.

[169] See Balogun and Aka, "Strategic Reforms to Resuscitate the Nigerian Healthcare System," note 15.

[170] Aka, *Genetic Counseling and Preventive Medicine in Post-War Bosnia*, note 1, p. 47.

[171] See Lauren Weber, "Healthier Workers Are More Productive, Study Finds," *Wall Street Journal* (August 8, 2017), https://www.wsj.com/articles/healthy-workers-are-more-productive-study-finds-1502219651.

[172] See, for example, Chris Orchard, "The Business Benefits of a Healthy Workforce," Harvard School Public Health, https://www.hsph.harvard.edu/ecpe/the-business-benefits-of-a-healthy-workforce/#:~:text=Thats%20in%20part%20because%20the,reflected%20in%20health%20care%20costs; and Special Committee on Health, Productivity, and Disability Management, "Healthy Workforce/Healthy Economy: The Role of Health, Productivity, and Disability Management in Addressing the Nation's Health Care Crisis: Why an emphasis on the Health of the Workforce is Vital to the Health of the Economy," *Journal of Occupational and Environmental Medicine*, 51(1) (January 2009), 114–19, doi: 10.1097/JOM.0b013e318195dad2.

[173] See, for example, *Health and Human Development in the New Global Economy: The Contributions and Perspectives of Civil Society in the Americas*, eds. Alexandra Bambas et al. (Geneva, Switzerland: World Health Organization, 2000).

[174] See Chap. 2, note 109, and accompanying text.

4

Restructuring the Nigerian Economy to Generate Revenue for Healthcare Funding

Abstract This chapter explores more or less pragmatic measures, revolved around the concept of a postindustrial economy, for restructuring the Nigerian economy to generate revenue for healthcare funding. The trick is to increase the contributions of the *industrialization* (industry) and *service* components of the Nigerian economy without compromising *agriculture*, emblematized by the ability of the country to feed itself. The discussion is preceded by a range of threshold issues, namely: an overview of Nigeria's oil-based economy; layout of failed development programs going back to the period of political independence in 1960; the impact of the imminent shift to electric vehicles on Nigeria's oil-based economy; the utility of diversification as a tool for restructuring an economy; and the exploration of health services in their own right as diversification technique, nay a source of funding.

Keywords Mainstays of Nigeria's economy • Impact of impending shift to electric vehicles on Nigeria's economy • Applying the concept of postindustrial economy to Nigeria • Diversification as tool for economic restructuring • Health services as diversification technique • Harmonizing the rate of population growth with supply of healthcare and other social services

© The Author(s), under exclusive license to Springer Nature Singapore Pte Ltd. 2022
P. C. Aka, J. A. Balogun, *Healthcare and Economic Restructuring*,
https://doi.org/10.1007/978-981-16-9543-8_4

Introduction

This chapter unearths more or less pragmatic measures, revolved around the concept of a postindustrial economy, broached in Chap. 2,[1] as tool for restructuring the Nigerian economy in an attempt to generate revenue for healthcare services. The modest technique this book adopts, nothing of a grand theory,[2] involves a shift in the economy from agriculture, expansively defined, through manufacturing, ultimately to production of services. The trick is to increase the contributions of the industrialization and service components of the Nigerian economy without compromising agriculture, symbolized by the ability of the country to feed itself, such as by maintaining a balance between economic growth and the rate of population growth. The discussion is preceded by a range of threshold issues, namely: an overview of Nigeria's oil-based economy; layout of the carcasses of development programs that, since independence, have dotted Nigeria's geopolitical landscape; the impact of the imminent shift to electric vehicles on Nigeria's oil-based economy; diversification as a tool for restructuring the Nigerian economy; and a proposal for the application of health services in their own right as diversification technique, nay a source of funding, independent of the general service sector.

Overview of Nigeria's Economy

In 2017, Nigeria's GDP in purchasing power parity (PPP) was about US$ 1.121 trillion.[3] The figure placed Nigeria at No. 25 out of 228 economies in the world, in a survey where China ranked first with US$ 25.36

---

[1] See Chap. 2, notes 76–7.

[2] A grand theory is a highly abstract formulation where, supposedly, every phenomenon under investigation is slotted into "a wider theoretical scheme," such that everything is explained and nothing is left out. C. Wright Mills, *The Sociological Imagination* (New York: Oxford University Press, 1959); Derek Gregory, "Grand Theory," in *The Dictionary of Human Geography*, 5th ed., eds. D. Gregory et al. (London: Wiley-Blackwell Publishing, 2009), 315–16.

[3] Ibid.; "GDP—Purchasing Power Parity 2020 Country Ranks, by Rank," *Countries of the World*, https://photius.com/rankings/2020/economy/gdp_purchasing_power_parity_2020_0.html. PPP is a well-known metric in macroeconomics used to compare economic productivity and standards

trillion, followed by the European Union as one entity at US$ 20.85 trillion, and the US at $19.49 trillion.[4] In 2017, Nigeria had a GDP per capita of US$ 5900, which figure placed it at No. 147 out of 181 countries in the world in a survey where Liechtenstein came first (as of 2009) with US$ 139,100,[5] and Burundi last at US$ 700.[6] By comparison, the US ranked No. 19 in the world with $59,800.[7] A monoculture economy of the kind that Nigerian leaders since independence unwittingly developed is a monumental developmental crisis.[8] That is not all. Under the Buhari administration since 2015, the Nigerian economy has taken a hit across all sectors that the damage from COVID-19 has compounded. A recent report released by the World Bank projects that, by the end of 2021, Nigeria will lose a full decade of economic growth.[9] The report elaborated that the country's GDP will approach its 2010 level by the end of 2021, thus reversing a full decade of economic growth.[10] It noted that under Buhari, Nigeria endured two record-breaking recessions in 2016 and 2020, which it blamed on the government's fiscal policies, taking the position that what reforms the government implemented to correct the problem were incoherent and inadequate.[11]

---

of living between countries. Under this concept, two currencies are in equilibrium or at par when a basket of goods is priced the same in both countries, taking into account the exchange rates. For an explanation of this concept, including the formula for calculating it, see "What Is Purchasing Power Parity (PPP)?" *Investopedia* (Updated August 19, 2020), https://www.investopedia.com/updates/purchasing-power-parity-ppp/.

[4] "GDP—Purchasing Power Parity 2020 Country Ranks," note 3.

[5] Liechtenstein is a German-speaking micro state in central Europe with an area of 62 square miles and a population of little over 38,000 people in 2020. See "Liechtenstein Population (Live)," *Worldometer*, https://www.worldometers.info/world-population/liechtenstein-population/.

[6] "GDP—Per Capita (PPP) 2020 Country Ranks, by Rank," *Countries of the World*, https://photius.com/rankings/2020/economy/gdp_per_capita_2020_0.html.

[7] Ibid.

[8] See Toyin Falola, *Understanding Modern Nigeria: Ethnicity, Democracy, and Development* (New York: Cambridge University Press, 2021), 285–331 (classifying "the political economy of oil" among the "development crises" Nigeria endures, with corruption featured on pp. 269–284 of the work).

[9] "Nigeria [Wi]ll Lose Ten Years of Economic Gain Under Buhari's Administration—World Bank," *Economic Confidential* (June 24, 2021), https://economicconfidential.com/2021/06/nigeria-economic-gain-buhari-administration/.

[10] Ibid.

[11] Ibid.

Survey of the Non-Petroleum Sectors Based on Share of the Labor Force

Table 4.1 presents information on the composition of the Nigerian economy, based on the share of agriculture, industry, and services in the entire
labor force and the contribution of these sectors to the GDP vis-à-vis
petroleum. In 2017, Nigeria had a labor force of about 60.08 million
workers,[12] with an unemployment rate of about 16.5 percent,[13] a public
debt of about 21.8 percent of the GDP,[14] and a population below poverty
line of 70 percent (as of 2010).[15] Classified based on share of the labor
force, *agriculture* formed 70 percent of Nigeria's labor force.[16] The number placed the country at No. 20 out of 146 economies in the world in a
survey where Tonga ranked first with 100 percent (as of 2006),[17] and

Table 4.1 Mainstays of Nigeria's economy

Item no.	Sector	Contribution to government revenue in percentage	Share of labor force in percentage	Contribution to GDP in percentage
1.	Petroleum	65–70	N/A	9–10
2.	Agriculture	N/A	70	21.1
3.	Industrialization	N/A	10	22.5
4.	Services	N/A	20	56.4

Key: NA is abbreviation for Not Applicable
Table created by authors, based on information from multiple sources identified
in this book, including "Nigerian Economy 2020," *Countries of the World*,
https://theodora.com/wfbcurrent/nigeria/nigeria_economy.html

---

[12] "Nigerian Economy 2020," *Countries of the World*, https://theodora.com/wfbcurrent/nigeria/
nigeria_economy.html.

[13] Ibid.

[14] Ibid.

[15] Ibid.

[16] Ibid.; "Labor Force—By Occupation—Agriculture (%) 2020 Country Ranks, by Rank,"
Countries of the World, https://photius.com/rankings/2020/economy/labor_force_by_occupation_
agriculture_2020_0.html [hereinafter "Labor Force by Agriculture"].

[17] Tonga is an archipelago of 176 islands with only 36 that are inhabited. It is located in Oceania in
the South Pacific Ocean, south of Western Samoa. The microstate has an area of 278 square miles
(about four times the size of Washington, DC) and a population of approximately 106,000 people
in 2020. See "Tonga Population (Live)," *Worldometer*, https://www.worldometers.info/world-
population/tonga-population/#:~:text=Tonga%202020%20population%20is%20
estimated,of%20the%20total%20world%20population.

Burundi second at 93.6 percent (as of 2002), with Monaco last at 0 percent (as of 2017).[18] In 2017, *industry* comprised 10 percent of Nigeria's labor force.[19] The number placed Nigeria at No. 112 out of 135 countries in the world, in a survey where North Korea ranked first at 63 percent (as of 2008) and Gibraltar last at 1.8 percent (as of 2014).[20] Based on data gathered in 1999, as of 2017, *services* constitute 20 percent of Nigeria's labor force, a number which placed the country at No. 155 out of 164 countries in the world in a survey where Tonga ranked first with a perfect score, followed by Gibraltar at 98.2 percent (as of 2014), with Burundi last at 4.1 percent (as of 2002).[21]

Survey of the Non-Petroleum Sectors Based on Contribution to the GDP

In 2016, *agriculture* contributed 21.1 percent to Nigeria's GDP.[22] The figure placed the country at No. 40 out of 148 countries surveyed, with Sierra Leone placing first at 60.7 percent (as of 2017), and Macau 0 percent (as of 2016).[23] By comparison, Japan ranked 138 with 1.1 percent (as of 2017) and the US 140 with 0.9 percent (also as of 2017).[24] Over the same period, *industry* contributed about 22.5 percent to Nigeria's GDP,[25] ranking the country as No. 106 out of 177 countries in the world,

---

[18] "Labor Force by Agriculture," note 16.

[19] "Nigerian Economy 2020," note 12. "Labor Force—By Occupation—Industry (%) 2020 Country Ranks, by Rank," *Countries of the World*, https://photius.com/rankings/2020/economy/labor_force_by_occupation_industry_2020_0.html [hereinafter "Labor Force by Industry"].

[20] "Labor Force by Industry," note 19. Gibraltar is a British Overseas Territory located at the southern tip of the Iberian Peninsula and bordered to the north by Spain. It is a microstate with an area of 2.6 square miles and a population of approximately 34,000 people in 2020. See "Gibraltar Population (Live)," *Worldometer*, https://www.worldometers.info/world-population/gibraltar-population/.

[21] "Labor Force by Industry," note 20.

[22] "Nigerian Economy 2020," note 12. "GDP—Composition, by Sector of Origin—Agriculture (%) 2020 Country Ranks, by Rank," *Countries of the World*, https://photius.com/rankings/2020/economy/gdp_composition_by_sector_of_origin_agriculture_2020_0.html [hereinafter "GDP Composition by Agriculture"].

[23] "GDP Composition by Agriculture," note 22.

[24] Ibid.

[25] "Nigerian Economy 2020," note 12; "GDP Composition by Agriculture," note 22.

in a survey where Angola came first with 61.4 percent (as of 2011) and Gibraltar last, meaning 0 percent contribution (as of 2016).[26] By comparison, Japan ranked 64 with a score of 30.1 percent (as of 2017), while the US drew with Pakistan at No. 123 with a score of 19.1 percent (as of 2009, but Pakistan as of 2016).[27] The seemingly low ranking of the US, complete with the draw with Pakistan, may be due to the phenomenon of outsourcing, involving the siting of US firms in countries, mostly in Asia, with relatively low labor costs.[28] Last but not least is *services*. In 2017, this sector contributed 56.4 percent to Nigeria's GDP.[29] The number placed Nigeria at No. 120 out of 186 countries in the world, in a survey where Gibraltar ranked first with a perfect score as of 2016 while Angola placed last with a score of 28.4 percent (as of 2011).[30] By comparison, the US placed No. 28 with a score of 80, while Japan ranked 66 with a score of 68.7 percent.[31]

Elements of the Non-Petroleum Sectors

Agriculture

The list of Nigerian agricultural products is broad-ranging and as of 2018 included cassava (manioca, tapioca), yam, cowpea, and taro, in which crops Nigeria ranked as the largest producer in the world; okra, and sorghum, where it ranked second-largest producer after India in the case of

---

[26] "GDP—Composition, by Sector of Origin—Industry (%) 2020 Country Ranks, by Rank," *Countries of the World*, https://photius.com/rankings/2020/economy/gdp_composition_by_sector_of_origin_industry_2020_0.html [hereinafter "GDP Composition by Industry"].

[27] Ibid.

[28] Alexandra Twin, and Margaret James, "Outsourcing," *Investopedia* (updated July 5, 2020), https://www.investopedia.com/terms/o/outsourcing.asp (explaining the term).

[29] "GDP—Composition, by Sector of Origin—Services (%) 2020 Country Ranks, by Rank," *Countries of the World*, https://photius.com/rankings/2020/economy/gdp_composition_by_sector_of_origin_services_2020_0.html [hereinafter "GDP Composition by Services"].

[30] Ibid.

[31] Ibid.

okra and the US in the case of sorghum; ginger, peanuts, and sweet potato where it ranked third in the world, after India and China in the case of ginger; China and India in peanut production; and China and Malawi in the production of sweet potato. In the same vein, Nigeria ranked fourth in the world in cocoa beans, palm oil, millet, and sesame seed, after Côte d'Ivoire, Ghana, and Indonesia in cocoa production; Indonesia, Malaysia, and Thailand in palm oil; India, Niger, and the Sudan in millet production; and the Sudan, Myanmar, and India in the production of sesame seeds. Similarly, Nigeria was the fifth-largest producer of plantain in the world after Cameroon, Ghana, Uganda, and Colombia; sixth-largest producer of papaya in the world after India, Brazil, Mexico, Dominican Republic, and Indonesia; and in 2019 eighth-largest producer of pineapple in the world after Costa Rica, the Philippines, Brazil, Indonesia, China, India, and Thailand. Other agricultural products Nigeria produces in sizable quantities include cotton, rubber, timber, corn, rice, beans, soybeans, cocoyam, maize, tomato, sugarcane, mango and guava, cashew nuts, banana, onion, green pepper, livestock (cattle, sheep, goats, pigs, and chicken), and fish.[32]

Nigeria produces these food items both for export and domestic consumption. Different regions of the country specialize in the production of these crops with yam, rice, maize, and fish products coming mostly from the southern and central regions of the country, while sorghum, millet, rice, and livestock come from the north.[33] Nigerian agriculture is mostly subsistence. About 70 percent of agricultural activities in the country is unmechanized, with agricultural holdings generally small and scattered.[34] Because of the continued reliance on antiquated methods of production, Nigeria's agricultural sector suffers from low productivity. We return to this point later in this book.

---

[32] Based on multiple sources, including "Nigerian Economy 2020," note 12.

[33] See ibid.

[34] "Nigeria—Agriculture," *Nations Encyclopedia*, https://www.nationsencyclopedia.com/economies/Africa/Nigeria-AGRICULTURE.html.

Industrialization

Elements of Nigeria's industry include oil refining, coal, tin, columbite, rubber, plastic materials, beverages, tobacco, pharmaceutical products, electrical and electronic products, iron and steel, motor assembly, wood, pulp paper products, chemicals, ceramic products, hides and skins, textiles, apparel, footwear, cement, building materials and construction, food processing, chemicals, fertilizer, printing, and ceramics, among others.[35] The largest industries within this sector are petroleum, agriculture, mining, and tourism.[36] The feature on this list of natural resource items like oil, coal, tin, columbite, and rubber, speaks to the small traction in Nigerian industrialization.

Services

Elements of Nigeria's service sector include banking and finance, insurance, real estate, transportation, telecommunication or information and communication technology (ICT), wholesale and retail trading, restaurants and hospitality services, motion pictures (Nollywood) and entertainment, education, and tourism.[37] Of these service elements, the entertainment industry signified by Nollywood deserves some more elaborate discussion, given the place of importance it has assumed in the

---

[35] "Nigerian Economy 2020," note 12.

[36] "The Economic Context of Nigeria," Nordea (October 2020). Nordea (in full Nordea Bank Abp) is a European financial services group operating in northern Europe and based in Helsinki, Finland.

[37] See "Nigerian Employment in Services (% of Total Employment)," *Trading Economics* (February 2021), https://tradingeconomics.com/nigeria/employment-in-services-percent-of-total-employment-wb-data.html#:~:text=Employment%20in%20services%20(%25%20of%20total%20employment)%20(modeled%20ILO%20estimate,compiled%20from%20officially%20recognized%20sources (actual values, historical data, forecasts and projections were sourced from the World Bank in February 2021); Abiodun Moses Adetokunbo, and Ochuwa Priscillia Edioye, "Response of Economic Growth to the Dynamics of Service Sector in Nigeria," *Future Business Journal*, 6(27) (2020), https://fbj.springeropen.com/articles/10.1186/s43093-020-00018-9; and "The Economic Context of Nigeria," note 36.

repertoire.[38] Nollywood resulted in the export of Nigerian music and entertainment to many parts of the globe.[39]

In prolific-ness, Nollywood is reputed to be the second-largest film industry in the world after Hollywood in the US, and Bollywood in India.[40] Nollywood produces about 2500 films a year under more exacting circumstances than in India, talk less the US.[41] In 2014, Nollywood alone accounted for little over 1 percent of Nigeria's GDP.[42] True to its name, the service sector complements the other two sectors, beginning with industrialization, given that activities in these two sectors "rely majorly on the service sector to supply needed functions[,] such as banking, accountancy, information, and technology."[43] Such is the interrelatedness of the sectors that an activity like tourism features in both the industrialization and service sectors.

Factoring in the Ambiguous Role of Petroleum

Back to Table 4.1, petroleum is not a sector in the strict sense of the word. Oil and gas dominate the mainstays of Nigeria's economy, to such high extent that some scholars liken the country's entire economic system to

---

[38] The term *Nollywood* is an adaption of Hollywood in the US and Bollywood in India. The term is believed to have been coined in 2002 by Norimitsu Onisha, reporter for the *New York Times*. Charles Igwe, "How Nollywood Became the Second[-]Largest Film Industry," British Council (November 6, 2015), https://www.britishcouncil.org/voices-magazine/nollywood-second-largest-film-industry#:~:text=The%20term%20'Nollywood'%20was%20coined,and%20Bollywood%20in%20India's%20Bombay.

[39] See "Five Things About Nigeria: The Superpower with No Power," *BBC News* (February 14, 2019), https://www.bbc.com/news/world-africa-47217557 ("Afrobeats—One of [Nigeria's] Greatest Exports"); Erick Oh, "Nigeria's Film Industry: Nollywood Looks to Expand Globally," US International Trade Commission (USITC) (Executive Briefing on Trade) (October 2014), https://www.usitc.gov/publications/332/erick_oh_nigerias_film_industry.pdf.

[40] See Alyssa Maio, "What Is Nollywood and How Did It Become the [Second]-Largest Film Industry," Studio Binder (December 5, 2019), https://www.studiobinder.com/blog/what-is-nollywood/ (account on the history and evolution of the industry).

[41] Ibid.

[42] Erick Oh, "Nigeria's Services Economy: The Engine for Future Growth," U.S. International Trade Commission (USITC) (Executive Briefings on Trade) 1, n.1 (March 2017), https://www.usitc.gov/publications/332/executive_briefings/nigeria_srv_ebot_oh-final.pdf.

[43] Adetokunbo and Edioye, note 37.

an "oil economy."[44] Here is why. Nigeria is the ninth-largest producer of oil in the world, after Saudi Arabia, Russia, Iraq, Canada, United Arab Emirates, Kuwait, Iran, and the US, in this order.[45] The country boasts an oil reserve estimated at about 35 billion barrels.[46] Oil was discovered in Nigeria in commercial quantity in 1956 in Oloibiri in present-day Bayelsa State,[47] the country's southernmost state close to the Atlantic Ocean. Production peaked in the 1970s, when the country started pumping about 2 million barrels of oil per day into the world market.[48] This high-point coincided with Nigeria's membership in the Organization of the Petroleum Exporting Countries (OPEC) in 1971,[49] and the formation six years later of the Nigerian National Petroleum Corporation (NNPC), charged with responsibility for overseeing the country's expansive oil

---

[44] See J.K. Onoh, *The Nigerian Oil Economy: From Prosperity to Glut* (New York: Routledge, 2018; first published 1983 by Croom Helm Ltd.), esp. 66–85 (discussing the impact of oil on the Nigerian economy).

[45] Alexandra Twin, "World's Top 10 Oil Exporters," *Investopedia* (updated October 23, 2019), https://www.investopedia.com/articles/company-insights/082316/worlds-top-10-oil-exporters.asp. In 2018, oil ranked as the leading exported product in the world, accounting for nearly 6% of all exports. Ibid. Based on projection by the International Energy Agency, by 2024, the US, currently ranked eighth-largest exporter of world, will sprint to No. 2. Ibid.

[46] "The Economic Context of Nigeria," note 36.

[47] See "History of the Nigerian Petroleum Industry," Nigerian National Petroleum Corporation, http://www.nnpcgroup.com/history. The discovery ended 50 years of unsuccessful oil exploration in the Niger Delta region that predated the birth of Nigeria. See ibid. (list of major events in Nigerian oil and gas beginning with 1908).

[48] "Nigeria Oil," *Worldometer*, https://www.worldometers.info/oil/nigeria-oil/#:~:text=Nigeria%20produces%201%2C938%2C542.73%20barrels%20per,reserves%20(as%20of%202,016.

[49] Founded on September 14, 1960, OPEC is an intergovernmental organization made up of 13 oil exporting countries, including Nigeria. The headquarters of the organization when it was founded was Baghdad, Iraq, but today those headquarters are in Vienna, Austria, where OPEC moved to in 1965. Austria is not an OPEC country. Nigeria joined OPEC in 1971 at the peak of its oil boom. Five founding members of the organization are Iran, Iraq, Kuwait, Saudi Arabia, and Venezuela. Other countries that joined after 1960 are Qatar (1961), Indonesia (1962), Libya (1962), the United Arab Emirates (1967), Algeria (1969), Nigeria (1971), Ecuador (1973), Gabon (1975), Angola (2007), Equatorial Guinea (2017) and Congo (2018). There has been some back and forth in the membership of the organization. Ecuador suspended its membership of OPEC in December 1992, rejoined the organization in October 2007, but decided to withdraw its membership of OPEC effective January 1, 2020. Indonesia suspended its membership in January 2009, rejoined the organization in January 2016, but suspended its membership once more in November 2016. Gabon terminated its membership in January 1995, but rejoined the Organization in July 2016. Qatar terminated its membership on January 1, 2019. "Member Countries," Organization of the Petroleum Exporting Countries, https://www.opec.org/opec_web/en/about_us/25.htm.

industry.[50] Similarly, Nigeria is one of the leading exporters of liquefied natural gas, which accounts for an additional 15.5 percent of exports.[51] Nigeria equally extracts tin ore and coal for domestic use.[52] Its other notable natural resources include iron ore, limestone, niobium, lead, zinc, and arable land.[53]

However, although oil accounts for about 70 percent of government revenue, it contributes only about 9–10 percent of Nigeria's GDP.[54] This is blamed on the inability of the Nigerian national government to refine its crude oil.[55] Whatever the reason, what is clear is that, although important for government revenue, ironically, petroleum remains a small part of the country's overall economy. There are some other downsides. The petroleum industry chronically suffers from oil theft, costing the country potential revenues running into tens of millions in US dollars.[56] Nigeria also endures significant oil losses arising from repeated oil spills, with negative consequences for agriculture and environmental well-being, especially within the site of extraction in the Niger Delta,[57] a point of

---

[50] See Graham Field, "Nigerian National Petroleum Corporation," *Encyclopedia* (Updated November 21, 2020), https://www.encyclopedia.com/social-sciences-and-law/economics-business-and-labor/businesses-and-occupations/nigerian-national-petroleum-corp.

[51] Ibid.

[52] Ibid.

[53] Ibid.

[54] "The Economic Context of Nigeria," note 36, citing the Organization of the Petroleum Exporting Countries (OPEC), referenced in note 49.

[55] See Uyiosa Omoregie, Nigeria's Petroleum and GDP: The Missing Oil Refining Link (unpublished paper available online) (abstract) (pointing out that in 2014, the refining capacity utilization of Nigeria's refineries was a low 14 percent, compared to 90 percent globally). According to this paper, the Gulf States averaged a GDP contribution of more than 30 percent. Ibid. See also Oladehinde Oladipo, "Nigeria's Oil Sector Contribution to GDP among Lowest in OPEC," *Business Day* (Lagos) (November 5, 2019), https://businessday.ng/energy/oilandgas/article/nigerias-oil-sector-contribution-to-gdp-among-lowest-in-opec/.

[56] Ibid.

[57] John Vidal, "Nigeria's Agony Dwarfs the Gulf Oil Spill. The US and Europe Ignore It," *Guardian* (London) (May 29, 2010), https://www.theguardian.com/world/2010/may/30/oil-spills-nigeria-niger-delta-shell.

contention in the protests against foreign oil companies over the years that have roiled drilling in the region.[58]

Back to Agriculture

Despite the oversized shadow crude oil casts over the Nigerian economy, there is still *agriculture*. Oil products have dwarfed but not nullified the sector. Agriculture is a key sector of the Nigerian economy, which, as Table 4.1 shows, constitutes 70 percent of the country's labor force, but, more than oil products, contributes over 21 percent of Nigeria's GDP. Similarly, the industrialization sector comprises 10 percent of the work force and contributes 22.5 percent, several notches more than agriculture. Last but not least is the service sector. As Table 4.1 shows, this sector comprises 20 percent of the labor force, but more than agriculture and industrialization joined together, contributes 56.4 percent to the GDP. The prominence of this sector came to the fore in 2014 when it formed the basis for the Nigerian government's rebasing of the country's economy, an occurrence that made the country the largest economy in Africa, replacing South Africa which used to hold this prize.[59] A common problem impeding the industrialization and service sectors of the Nigerian economy is substandard infrastructure, indicated by erratic power supply, poor road and rail networks, and poor water quality.[60] Chapter 5, which deals with the influence of politics on healthcare reforms in Nigeria, dwells more on the problem of infrastructure.

---

[58] See Jedrzej Georg Frynas, *Oil in Nigeria: Conflict and Litigation Between Oil Companies and Village Communities* (Münster, Germany: Lit Verlag, 2000), 46–56 (discussing community protests against oil companies, government and oil company concessions to protesters, and repressions of protests and security arrangements by different Nigerian regimes). Of the conflict, then President William J. Clinton opined during an address to Nigerian legislators in the course of an official visit to the country from August 25–27 that he "hope[d] government and business will forge a partnership with local people to bring real, lasting social progress, a clean environment, and economic opportunity." William J. Clinton, Remarks to a Joint Session of the Nigerian National Assembly in Abuja (August 26, 2000), https://www.presidency.ucsb.edu/documents/remarks-joint-session-the-nigerian-national-assembly-abuja [hereinafter Clinton's Address to Nigerian Lawmakers].

[59] See Chap. 2, notes 88–90, and accompanying texts.

[60] "The Economic Context of Nigeria," note 36.

Carcasses of Nigeria's Development Programs

List of Eight Programs

Back to the days of independence six decades ago, Nigerian leaders, military and civilian alike, have tried to promote socioeconomic development. The diagram spotlights eight plans unveiled from 1962 to 2009 by these leaders. The carcasses of development plans, encapsulated in Table 4.2, speak to those efforts but also to a failure to achieve development.

The attempt to promote development started with five-year development plans of various degrees of ambitiousness arranged in arithmetic consecutiveness in Arabic numerals. By 1986, under General Ibrahim Babangida, these plans ran their course,[61] soon to be replaced by programs that came under different names, such as "visions." These plans tried to build on lessons learned from prior plans and were concededly underlain by more or less extensive preparations designed to increase their workability. For example, the Third National Development Plan, 1975–1980, is reputed as the largest and most ambitious of all of these plans.[62] "[R]eplete with various projects, output targets, and macroeconomic projections[,]" the plan document ran into two volumes of 1,000 pages.[63] It was driven by five national objectives, some of them carryovers from the Second National Development Plan: to establish Nigeria firmly as "a united, strong, and self-reliant nation; a great and dynamic economy; a just and egalitarian society; a land of bright and full opportunities for all citizens; and a free and democratic society."[64] The plan was preceded

---

[61] The concept of national development plan ended with the Babangida regime that abrogated the Fifth Development Plan after only one year, submerging it into a one-year economic emergency program. In place of the traditional five-year plan, he created two programs: perspective planning to cover 15–20-year period; and three-year rolling plan that replaced the structural adjustment program (SAP) model. See Adekunle Amuwo, "Constructing the Democratic Developmental State in Africa: A Case Study of Nigeria, 1960–2007," Institute for Global Dialogue, Occasional Paper No. 59, (2008), 26, 30, http://www.jstor.com/stable/resrep07753.9.

[62] See generally A. Olufemi Lewis, "Nigeria's Third National Development Plan, 1975–80: An Appraisal of Objectives and Policy Frame," 15(1) *The Developing Economies*, 15(1) (March 1977), 60–79, https://onlinelibrary.wiley.com/doi/abs/10.1111/j.1746-1049.1977.tb00370.x.

[63] Ibid., p. 60.

[64] Ibid.

Table 4.2 Nigeria's economic development programs, 1962–2009

Item no.	Name	Period	Sponsoring administration	Major highlights
1.	First national development plan	1962–1968	Abubakar T. Balewa (1960–1966)	Amalgam of programs from the strong regional governments; emphasized agricultural, industrial, transportation, and manpower development; brainchild of foreign technocrats; created key infrastructure like the Kainji dam, the Port Harcourt refinery, the Niger bridge, and the Nigerian industrial development Bank; plan aimed for improved living standards for Nigerians that make independence meaningful, but was thwarted by the civil war from 1967–1970
2.	Second national development plan	1970–1975	Yakubu Gowon (1966–1975)	First truly national and fully integrated plan that viewed the economy as an organic unit; aimed to create a united, strong, and self-reliant nation, and to promote postwar recovery; and embodied carried-over themes from the previous plan, such as transportation, import-substitution industries, and creation of "a free and democratic society"
3.	Third national development plan	1975–1980	Muhammed-Obasanjo (1975–1979)	Plan built on previous plans, but also stressed research in agriculture on both food and cash crops for domestic consumption and export and raw materials for local industries; research and development on livestock and veterinary; special agricultural development schemes. Plan undermined by various factors that included an overvalued currency and massive food import

4.	Fourth national development plan	1981–1985	Shehu Shagari (1979–1983)	Promoting export-oriented industries; power generation and supply
5.	Fifth national development plan	1986	Ibrahim Babangida (1985–1993)	Development planning in the conventional sense came to an end under the Babangida regime that submerged the fifth National dev. Plan into a one-year economic emergency program, and launched two programs that replaced the five-year plan: perspective planning to cover 15–20-year period; and three-year rolling plan that replaced the structural adjustment program (SAP) model
6.	Vision 2010	1996	Sani Abacha (1993–1998)	An economic blueprint designed to lead Nigeria from poverty and underdevelopment into a democratically stable and economically prosperous nation within a period of about 14 years. The vision statement specifies that by 2010, Nigeria would be transformed into "a united, industrious, caring and God-fearing democratic society, committed to making the basic needs of life affordable for everyone, and creating Africa's leading economy."
7.	National Economic Empowerment and Dev. Strategy (NEEDS)	1999–2007	Olusegun Obasanjo (1999–2007)	Homegrown poverty reduction program

(continued)

Table 4.2 (continued)

Item no.	Name	Period	Sponsoring administration	Major highlights
8.	Vision 2020	2009	Umaru Musa Yar'Adua (2007–2010)	Anchored on a prediction to the effect that by 2020 Nigeria will be able to realize its potential as giant of Africa and emerge as a major player in global international relations by becoming one of the 20 largest economies in the world

Created by the authors from multiple sources, including Aisha Mohammed, "A Case Study of the Pro[b]lematic Nature of Development Plan[ning] in Nigeria," Asabe Shehu Yar'Adua Foundation (February 15, 2020), https://unfccc.int/sites/default/files/resource/The%20Problems%20of%20Development%20Planning%20in%20Nigeria.pdf; L.N. Chete et al., *Industrial Development and Growth in Nigeria: Lessons and Challenges* (Washington, DC: Brookings Institution, 2016–2017), https://www.brookings.edu/wp-content/uploads/2016/07/l2c_wp8_chete-et-al.; Deedam Dorka Godbless et al., "Nigeria Development Plans and Its Challenges: The Way Forward," 5(12) *Int'l Journal of Advanced Academic Research of Social & Management Science* (December 2019), https://www.ijaar.org/articles/Volume5-Number12/Social-Management-Sciences/ijaar-sms-v5n9-sep19-p24.pdf; Emma Ujah and Marvelous Anthony, "From Abacha Comes Vision-2010," *Vanguard* (Lagos) (September 30, 2019), https://www.vanguardngr.com/2019/09/from-abacha-comes-vision-2010/; and E.N. Iheanacho, "National Development Planning in Nigeria: An Endless Search for Appropriate Development Strategy," *Int'l Journal of Economic Development, Research & Investment*, 5(2) (August 2014), 49–60, https://www.academia.edu/36260016/National_Development_Planning_in_Nigeria_An_Endless_Search_for_Appropriate_Development_Strategy by broad consultation with governmental bodies under the auspices of the National Economic Advisory Council (NEAC), which oversaw the plan.[65]

Vision 2020 was equally ambitious.[66] The program was launched during the administration of Umaru Musa Yar'Adua, president from 2009 until 2010, although its foundation goes back to the reign of Olusegun Obasanjo, president from 1999 until 2007, under whose leadership the policy document was signed in 2007. The program declared, "By 2020, Nigeria will be one of the 20 economies in the world, able to consolidate its leadership role in Africa and establish itself as a significant player in the global economic and political arena."[67] Like the Third National Development Plan, Vision 2020 was equally preceded by extensive and meticulous planning. The program took about nine months to produce and its preparation brought together about 1,000 economic and development experts who worked on it.[68] From 2003 to 2007, Nigeria attempted to implement NEEDS, an economic reform program, designed to improve the living standards of Nigerians through means like deregulation and privatization.[69] It aimed to address basic deficiencies like lack of freshwater for household use and irrigation, unreliable power supplies, and decaying infrastructure, while promoting increased agricultural productivity, among other goals.[70]

---

[65] Aisha Mohammed, "A Case Study of the Pro[b]lematic Nature of Development Plan[ning] in Nigeria," Asabe Shehu Yar'Adua Foundation (February 15, 2020), https://unfccc.int/sites/default/files/resources/The%20Problems%20of%20Development%20Planning%20in%20Nigeria.pdf. ("8. The Third National Development Plan (Murtala/Obasanjo 1975–1980)").

[66] See Onyenekenwa Eneh, "Big Dreams and Grand Ambitions: Nigeria's Vision 2020—How Far?" *The Republic*, 4(2) (February/March 2020), https://republic.com.ng/february-march-2020/big-dreams-and-grand-ambitions-nigeria-vision-2020/.

[67] Quoted in Mojeed Alabi, "Months to End of Vision 2020, Nigeria Mulls Another Development Plan," *Premium Times* (Abuja) (November 24, 2019), https://www.premiumtimesng.com/news/top-news/365018-months-to-end-of-vision-2020-nigeria-mulls-another-development-plan.html.

[68] Ibid.

[69] See Isaac O. Abimbola et al., "Assessment of Education Policy Thrust of the National Economic Empowerment and Development Strategy (NEEDS) in Nigeria," *Problems of Education in the 21st Century*, 60 (2014), 23, https://uilspace.unilorin.edu.ng/bitstream/handle/20.500.12484/3590/23-45.Abimbola_Vol.60.pdf?sequence=1&isAllowed=y.

[70] See Ewemade Iyamu, and Joy Ibhade Ojeaga, "National Economic Empowerment Development Strategy (NEEDS) as a Panacea for Employment Creation and Self[-]Employment and Self[-]Relian[ce]," *Journal of Educational and Social Research*, 5(2) (May 2015), 61, 62, https://doi.org/10.5901/jesr.2015.v5n2p61.

Possible Explanation as to Why These Programs Failed to Produce Economic Development

Given these expenditures of putative energies, why did these programs fail to produce economic development? The explanations are legion and include the failure of Nigerian leaders "to properly envision true development and place same on the agenda," misplaced priorities, "poor plan discipline, lack of self-reliance, ineffective executive capacity and public sector inefficiency, technology transfer syndrome," widespread corruption, and ineffective public[-]private partnership."[71] For one thing, many of these plans were little more than slogans. Take Vision 2020, the dream statement that Nigeria will become one of the 20 top economies in the world by the year 2020. The history of the dream dated back to a research by economists at a US investment bank, which sired a prediction that Nigeria would be in the league of 20 top economies by year 2025, a prediction based on assessment of the country's abundant human and material resources, and the unspoken assumption that these resources would be channeled to achieve economic development.[72]

It did not take long for the Nigerian government then headed by Olusegun Obasanjo to corral this prediction into an economic program.[73] However, Nigeria is a country where a majority of the citizenry are still "ill-fed, ill-clothed, ill-housed[,] [...] ill-educated[,]" and "live in [...] rural areas characterized by mass underdevelopment."[74] Given this setting of mass poverty that riles the country, viewed "against the backdrop of [...] policy reversals, summersaults[,] and failures" that mark implementation in Nigeria, Vision 2020 is unrealistically "too ambitious," if not "utopian."[75] The literature on governance in Nigeria rings with the

---

[71] Mohammed, note 65.

[72] Onyenekenwa Cyprian Eneh, "Nigeria's Vision 20:2020-Issues, Challenges and Implications for Development Management," *Asian Journal of Rural Development*, 1 (2011), 21–40, https://doi.org/10.3923/ajrd.2011.21.40 (abstract).

[73] Ibid.

[74] Ibid.

[75] Ibid.

language of "reform" on practically every imaginable topic, including healthcare.[76] Yet "the policies, visions and agenda [of Nigeria's governments] often end up as paper-works rubbished by insincere implementation efforts and corruption."[77]

Finally, the Nigerian government promised a program of postwar reconstruction and rehabilitation of infrastructure damaged during the war, especially in the eastern section of the country that served involuntarily as theater of the war, that it failed to keep.[78] The failure hurt the pace of development in the part of the country that, before the war, was the locus of the fastest growing economy in the world.[79] Perceptive scholars have cited animus toward the Igbo, dominant ethnic group in Eastern Nigeria, as reason for failing to keep the promise.[80] This surely is a factor.[81] Yet the reasons are more complicated in a country rife with endemic corruption and abuse of public office across a succession of military and civilian regimes.[82] In any case, these drawbacks call to mind the argument of Professor Ake years ago to the effect that, like their counterparts in other African countries, Nigerian leaders do not take (socioeconomic) development seriously.[83]

---

[76] Ibid.

[77] Ibid.

[78] Philip C. Aka, "Prospects for Igbo Human Rights in Nigeria in the New Century," *Howard Law Journal*, 48(1) (2004), 165, 209–21 (commenting on Igbo persecutions from the immediate aftermath of the civil war to the periods of Olusegun Obasanjo, first as military ruler from 1976 to 1979 and subsequently as civilian leader from 1999 up until the publication of the piece in 2004).

[79] Ibid., p. 201.

[80] See Philip C. Aka, "Why Nigeria Needs Restructuring Now and How It Can Peacefully Do It," *Denver Journal of International Law & Policy*, 46 (Winter 2017), 132–33.

[81] See Aka, "Prospects for Igbo Human Rights in Nigeria in the New Century," note 78, pp. 209–21.

[82] See, for example, *Corruption in Nigeria: Patterns and Trends: Second Survey on Corruption as Experienced by the Population* (Vienna, Switzerland: United Nations Office on Drugs and Crime, December 2019), https://www.unodc.org/documents/data-and-analysis/statistics/corruption/nigeria/Corruption_in_Nigeria_2019_standard_res_11MB.pdf; and Daniel Jordan Smith, *A Culture of Corruption: Everyday Deception and Popular Discontent in Nigeria* (Princeton, NJ: Princeton University Press, 2007).

[83] Claude Ake, *Democracy and Development in Africa* (Washington, DC: Brookings Institution, 1996).

Impact of the Imminent Shift to Electric Vehicles on Nigeria's Oil-Based Economy

General Motors (GM)

On January 28, 2021, General Motors (GM) made an announcement replete with negative ramifications for countries like Nigeria that build their economies on fossil fuel. Headquartered in Detroit, Michigan, GM is a multinational corporation that designs, manufactures, markets, and distributes vehicles and vehicle parts, as well as sells financial services.[84] GM was founded as a holding company by the industrialist William C. Durant on September 16, 1908.[85] It is the largest US automobile manufacturer and one of the largest in the world.[86] The company assumed its present composition as a result of a restructure in 2009.[87] Key to our purpose here, the company is reputed for producing pickup trucks and SUVs that consume a lot of gasoline.[88]

The Option for Electric Cars

GM announced that it will stop manufacturing gas-powered cars, trucks, and sports utility vehicles (SUVs) by 2035, with the expectation of becoming carbon neutral in all its products and operations by 2040.[89] In

---

[84] See Julia Kollewe, "The History of General Motors," *Vanguard* (London), https://www.theguardian.com/business/2009/apr/30/general-motors-gm-history.

[85] Ibid.; see also "General Motors, American Company," *Encyclopedia Britannica* (last updated January 24, 2021), https://www.theguardian.com/business/2009/apr/30/general-motors-gm-history ("Early History").

[86] See Jerry Hirsch, "GM Is Again the World's Largest Automaker," *Los Angeles Times* (January 20, 2021), https://www.latimes.com/business/la-xpm-2012-jan-20-la-fi-autos-gm-sales-20120120--story.html.

[87] "General Motors, American Company," note 85 ("TARP, Chapter 11, and Recovery").

[88] Elliot Hannon, "General Motors Says It Will Stop Making Gas-Powered Vehicles," *Slate* (January 29, 2021), https://slate.com/news-and-politics/2021/01/general-motors-gm-zero-emission-gas-powered-vehicles.html#:~:text=General%20Motors%20announced%20Thursday%20that,for%20producing%20gas%2Dguzzling%20SUVs.

[89] See "General Motors, the Largest U.S. Automaker, Plans to be Carbon Neutral by 2040," *GM Media* (January 28, 2021), https://media.gm.com/media/us/en/gm/home.detail.html/content/Pages/news/us/en/2021/jan/0128-carbon.html#:~:text=To%20address%20emissions%20

more practical terms, GM plans to introduce 30 all-electric vehicle models world by 2025, by which year the company also projects that 40 percent of its US models will achieve zero-emission.[90] Moreover, GM plans to increase the use of renewable energy, and to eliminate or offset emissions from its factories, buildings, vehicles, and other sources.[91] Earlier, GM has announced that it would invest $27 billion in electric vehicles over the next five years, some of which product, like the electric Hummer pickup truck, it expects to start delivery to customers in 2021.[92]

In unveiling the plan, GM said it "is joining governments and companies around the globe working to establish a safer, greener and better world."[93] GM is working with the Environmental Defense Fund (EDF) to develop a "shared vision" of leaving internal combustion vehicles behind.[94] In the meantime, GM will work "to increase fuel efficiency of its traditional internal combustion vehicles in accordance with regional fuel economy and greenhouse gas regulations."[95] Thus, from its internal combustion past, GM has positioned itself as "a global company focused on advancing an all-electric future that is inclusive and accessible to all,"

---

from%20its,company's%20previously%20announced%20global%20goal [hereinafter "GM Goes Carbon Neutral by 2040"]; and Neal E. Boudette, and Coral Davenport, "G.M. Will Sell Only Zero-Emission Vehicles by 2035," *New York Times* (January 28, 2021), https://www.nytimes.com/2021/01/28/business/gm-zero-emission-vehicles.html.

[90] Jody Freeman, "G.M.'s Bold Move on the Climate: The End of the Gasoline-Powered Car Will Transform the Economy" (Opinion), *New York Times* (February 2, 2021).

[91] See Mary T. Barra, "Leadership Message," General Motors, https://www.gmsustainability.com/leadership-perspective/chief-executive-officer.html ("Accelerating Our Response to Climate Change") (stating that GM "will source 100 percent of [its] facilities' electricity from renewables by 2040 globally, and by 2030 in the U.S."). Ms. Barra is GM's Chief Executive Officer (CEO).

[92] See "GM Goes Carbon Neutral by 2040," note 89. These clean-energy initiatives are bold for a company that, until recently, was noted for its recalcitrancy. See ibid. (indicating, "[w]hen one of the most recalcitrant and iconic American companies so markedly changes its tune and embraces the clean-energy transition, something big is happening.").

[93] "GM Goes Carbon Neutral by 2040," note 91, quoting Mary Barra, CEO of the Company. GM added that it "encourage[s] [other automakers] to follow suit and make a significant impact on our industry and on the economy as a whole." Ibid.

[94] "GM Goes Carbon Neutral by 2040," note 91.

[95] According to the company, these initiatives include "fuel economy improvement technologies, such as Stop/Start, aerodynamic efficiency enhancements, downsized boosted engines, […] mass reduction and lower rolling resistance tires." "GM Goes Carbon Neutral by 2040," note 89.

one committed in the years ahead to offering an electric vehicle "for every customer, from crossovers and SUVs to trucks and sedans."[96]

GM's announcement to cease producing cars that run on gasoline and diesel in favor of electric vehicles spelled a marked progression in the embracement of electric cars that has gone on now for many years in the race to clean energy.[97] Its "repercussions will ripple broadly across the economy, accelerating the transition to a broader electric future powered by renewable energy."[98] Due to "declining initial costs and fuel savings," over time electric vehicles are "more affordable and cost-effective" vis-à-vis gas-powered vehicles.[99] For, as the US Department of Energy predicted in 2014, "[w]hether it's a hybrid, plug-in hybrid or all-electric, the demand for electric drive vehicles will continue to climb as prices drop and consumers look for ways to save money at the pump."[100]

The GM option for electricity in place of the internal combustion engine is likely to pile pressure on automakers around the world, for some companies building up for years, to join the clean-energy band-wagon. These giant automakers include Ford Motor (FM), Daimler, Volkswagen, and Toyota. FM indicated that it was not about "to cede the future to any[]" competitor, but rather would invest in market niches where it is dominant and have economic "scale, like the F-150, the Transit van, our Mustang."[101] Daimler, maker of Mercedes-Benz cars, announced that it will "pursue a three-lane drive system strategy involving electric

---

[96] "GM Goes Carbon Neutral by 2040," note 89. What makes these commitments bold is that, until recently, GM is noted for its recalcitrancy on matters relating to clean energy. See ibid. (indicating, "[w]hen one of the most recalcitrant and iconic American companies so markedly changes its tune and embraces the clean-energy transition, something big is happening.").

[97] See "The History of the Electric Car," US Dept. of Energy (September 15. 2014), https://www.energy.gov/articles/history-electric-car.

[98] Freeman, note 90.

[99] Ibid.

[100] "The History of the Electric Car," note 97. See also "Top Five Reasons to Choose an Electric Car: They're a Really Good Buy," Union of Concerned Scientists (March 12, 2018), https://www.ucsusa.org/resources/top-five-reasons-choose-electric-car?gclid=CjwKCAiA4rGCBhAQEiwAelVti0LzPwwTBNJfjFpfnmJ2xKHK02oV7aQx5p9qh45y0al7D1F8iu4B0RoCaW8QAvD_BwE&utm_campaign=CV&utm_medium=search&utm_source=googlegrants (stating four other benefits to drivers of choosing electric cars, apart from reduced emission: reduced oil use, saving money, convenience, and improved driving experience).

[101] Kevin Stankiewicz, "Ford CEO Confident in Electric-Vehicle Strategy, Says Automaker Won't 'Cede the Future to Anyone,'" CNBC (February 5, 2021), https://www.cnbc.com/2021/02/05/ford-wont-cede-the-future-to-anyone-on-electric-vehicles-ceo-farley.html (quoting Jim Farley, CEO of the company).

vehicles, hybrid models and combustion engines."[102] Specifically, by 2022, the company plans to "bring[] more than ten different All-electric vehicles to market" while making its Mercedes-Benz portfolio electric products in an attempt to give its customers "the choice of at least one electric alternative in every Mercedes-Benz model series[.]"[103] For its part, Volkswagen stated that it is accelerating its plans for all-electric vehicles in a bid to become "the world's most desirable brand for sustainable mobility," adding that by 2030 it expects 70 percent of its sales in European markets to be electric cars and 50 percent in the US and China.[104] Last but not least, Toyota announced back in summer 2019 before GM's announcement that it "aims to get half of its global sales from electrified vehicles by 2025, five years ahead of schedule."[105]

With these commitments, it is safe to say that there is a growing consensus, including among automakers, that, in about one decade from now, electric cars would be the wave of the future. Even diehard oil and gas companies will be pressed to produce their own energy transition plans.[106] As Jody Freeman stated, "[i]n the short term, the oil and gas industry can absorb lower demand for certain petroleum products, but in the long term, it will need to rethink its business model."[107] For one thing, with this announcement and its underlying moves, GM sends a message that "taking action to eliminate pollution from all new light-duty vehicles by 2035 is an essential element of any automaker's business plan."[108]

---

[102] "Plans for More Than Ten Different All-Electric Vehicles by 2022," *Daimler*, https://media.daimler.com/marsMediaSite/en/instance/ko/Plans-for-more-than-ten-different-all-electric-vehicles-by-2022-All-systems-are-go.xhtml?oid=29779739.

[103] Ibid. See also Sören Amelang, "Reluctant Daimler Shifts Gear in Race to Sustainable Mobility," *Clean Energy Wire* (March 3, 2021), https://www.cleanenergywire.org/factsheets/reluctant-daimler-plans-radical-push-new-mobility-world; Jack Ewing, "Auto Dinosaurs Show They're Not Dead Yet," *New York Times* (February 18, 2021), https://www.nytimes.com/2021/02/18/business/daimler-earnings-electric-vehicles.html.

[104] Mike Wayland, "VW Expects Half of U.S. Sales to Be Electric Vehicles by 2030," *CNBC* (March 5, 2021), https://www.cnbc.com/2021/03/05/vw-expects-half-of-us-sales-to-be-electric-vehicles-by-2030.html.

[105] Kevin Brickland and Naomi Tajitsu, *Toyota Speeds Up Electric Vehicle Schedule as Demand Heats Up*, Reuters (June 6, 2019), https://www.reuters.com/article/us-toyota-electric/toyota-speeds-up-electric-vehicle-schedule-as-demand-heats-up-idUSKCN1T806X.

[106] See Freeman, note 90.

[107] Ibid.

[108] "GM Goes Carbon Neutral by 2040," note 89, citing Fred Krupp, President of Environmental Defense Fund (EDF).

Impetus for the GM Announcement

Arguably, the remote factor for GM's option for electric cars is the clean-energy program of the new US administration under President Joe Biden Jr. An immediate factor is the signature of an executive order by President Biden directing the Environmental Protection Agency and the Transportation Department to reinstate tough auto fuel-economy rules put in place during the Obama administration, as well as a follow-up order directing the federal government to purchase all-electric vehicles.[109] President Biden is also pushing for a new economic recovery package to include funding to build 500,000 electric vehicle charging stations, and to create a system of rebates and incentives for purchasing electric vehicles.[110] In August 2021, the Biden administration announced a proposal to introduce rules requiring cars to reach an average of about 51 miles per gallon by 2026.[111] The proposal also included additional provisions aimed at boosting the production and sales of electric vehicles.[112] To reiterate, these measures spell bad news for oil-based economies like Nigeria.

Diversification as Tool for Restructuring Nigeria's Economy

An obvious and relatively painless way to restructure the Nigerian economy is to diversify it. Diversification is a term of art in financial investment. It is "a risk management strategy that mixes a wide variety of

---

[109] See David Shephardson, "Biden to Order Agencies to Revisit Vehicle Tailpipe Emissions Standards," Reuters (January 20, 2021), https://www.reuters.com/article/us-usa-biden-executive-actions-transport/biden-to-order-agencies-to-revisit-vehicle-tailpipe-emissions-standards-idUSK-BN29P12Z.

[110] See Steven Lee and Dean Scott, "Long Road, Tough Choices Ahead for Biden Car-Charging Pledge," *Bloomberg Law* (February 22, 2021), https://news.bloomberglaw.com/environment-and-energy/long-road-tough-choices-ahead-for-biden-car-charging-pledge.

[111] See Coral Davenport, "Biden, in a Push to Phase Out Gas Cars, Tightens Pollution Rules," *New York Times* (August 5, 2021; updated August 9, 2021), https://www.nytimes.com/2021/08/05/climate/biden-tailpipe-emissions-electric-vehicles.html.

[112] Ibid.

investments within a portfolio [...] in an attempt at limiting exposure to any single asset or risk."[113] Diversification "smooth[s] out unsystematic risk events in a portfolio, [such that] the positive performance of some investments neutralizes the negative performance of others."[114] The logic is "that a portfolio constructed of different kinds of assets will, on average, yield higher long-term returns and lower the risk of any individual holding or security."[115] The same logic of inoculation against excessive exposure to risk applies here, the much larger phenomenon of a national economy. Diversification achieves this goal by diversifying rather than limiting exposure to any single source, such that the positive performance of some sources will neutralize or smooth out the negative performance of others.

Handled well, diversification as a tool for restructuring an economy works. Costa Rica in Central America serves as a good example. From an economy once solely dependent on coffee, banana, and other agricultural exports, over time the country built up a diversified economy whose mainstays came to include tourism, export of electronic and medical equipment, and information technology services.[116] Today, manufacturing and services account for more than three-quarters of Costa Rica's GDP.[117] It is probably for this same reason that some commentators recommend this technique as a key to sustainable growth and economic development in Nigeria.[118]

---

[113] Troy Segal and Gordon Scott, "Diversification," *Investopedia* (updated March 6, 2020), https://www.investopedia.com/terms/d/diversification.asp.

[114] Ibid.

[115] Ibid.

[116] See "Costa Rica, 2020," Index of Economic Freedom, https://www.heritage.org/index/country/costarica ("Background").

[117] See "Manufacturing and Production Industries," Costa Rica Information, http://costarica-information.com/about-costa-rica/economy/economic-sectors-industries/manufacturing; Steve Colantuoni, "Seven Reasons Why International Companies Should Consider Manufacturing in Costa Rica," The Central American Group, https://www.thecentralamericangroup.com/companies-should-consider-manufacturing-in-costa-rica/.

[118] See O.J. Suberu et al., "Diversification of the Nigerian Economy Toward a Sustainable Growth and Economic Development," *Int'l Journal of Economics, Finance, & Management Science*, 3(2) (2015), 107–114, http://www.sciencepublishinggroup.com/journal/paperinfo?journalid=173&doi=10.11648/j.ijefm.20150302.15.

Health Services as Diversification Technique

More Than an Extension of the Service Sector

Earlier in this book, we defined healthcare as a more or less integrated system with composite elements designed to promote or maintain good health.[119] This suggests that, rather than a mere appendage of say the economic system, health services can be by itself. In other words, in a proposal like here designed to find money for healthcare for Nigeria, health services by themselves can perform a diversification technique. This technique can be an extension of service, but its place of importance in this book is such that it deserves the separate discussion assigned to it here. The significance of this technique, bearing on the message of economic restructuring for healthcare funding in this book, is the proverbial killing of two birds with one stone: healthcare services generate money that goes into health funding while simultaneously contributing to economic development in a restructured Nigerian economy.

Two Possible Roads to the Health-Services-as-Diversification Technique

Two possible ways exist that Nigeria can use to diversify its economy using this technique. What these two approaches have in common is that each affords Nigeria an opportunity it could seize to contribute its talent to global healthcare. This is consistent with the debate on healthcare reform in Africa anchored on health as an economic driver.[120] It is also in line with an anticipated transformation of the healthcare sector in Africa in the next 50 years into a "job-creating sector," nay "a labor-intensive" machine that can create millions of skilled jobs for Africa's youthful populations.[121]

---

[119] See Chap. 3, note 1, and accompanying text.
[120] "The Great Debate Focuses on How to Fix Africa's Healthcare," ECA (February 12, 2019), https://uneca.org/stories/great-debate-focuses-how-fix-africa%E2%80%99s-healthcare.
[121] Mthuli Ncube et al., "Health in Africa over the Next 50 Years," African Development Bank, Economic Brief (March 2013), 20, https://www.afdb.org/fileadmin/uploads/afdb/Documents/Publications/Economic_Brief_-_Health_in_Africa_Over_the_Next_50_Years.pdf.

The first is to turn medical tourism upside down, copying countries like India where Nigerians now go for medical attention.[122] India currently constitutes about 18 percent of the market in global medical tourism, a number that is projected to grow to about 20 percent by 2020 and worth about US$ 9 billion.[123] In short, this involves turning Nigeria into a healthcare mecca for all of Africa and beyond by becoming itself a local destination of medical tourism.

A country like South Africa appears to be headed in this direction that Nigeria can copy and exceed. So also is Ghana, which one report hailed as "an increasingly popular expat [expatriate] destination in West Africa."[124] As the statement elaborated, there the Ministry of Health introduced "a policy to make Ghana a health tourism destination in Africa by creating specialized health centers of excellence for the treatment of complicated diseases[,]" in partnership with some teaching hospitals and the private sector.[125] The Ghanaian government claimed that the program "has already had a positive effect as fewer Ghanaian medical professionals are leaving and many medical experts returning home to work in such facilities."[126] Anyone who views this technique as far-fetched should keep in mind that, as one Nigerian officialdom points out, Nigeria used to be a site of medical tourism.[127]

Some basis for this role already exists. Activities in the health services contributed 0.61 percent of the GDP in 2010 and 0.65 percent in

---

[122] "India Has Become a Popular Hub of Medical Tourism," FreshersLive (updated July 24, 2018), https://www.fresherslive.com/current-affairs/articles/india-has-become-a-popular-hub-of-medical-tourism-14449. The reasons that make India a popular hub of medical tourism for patients from Nigeria and other countries are the relatively low cost of treatment, skilled doctors, and better medical equipment. Ibid.

[123] Ibid.

[124] "Expat Guide to Health Care in Ghana," AETNA, https://www.aetnainternational.com/en/individuals/destination-guides/expat-guide-to-health-care-in-ghana.html.

[125] Ibid.

[126] Ibid.

[127] "Saudi Arabian Royal Family Used to Visit Nigeria for Treatment—Health Minister," Punch (Lagos) (March 3, 2020), https://punchng.com/saudi-arabian-royal-family-used-to-come-to-nigeria-for-treatment-health-minister/ (citing Olorunnimbe Mamora, Minister of State for Health). According to the minister, Nigeria used to benefit from the proceeds of medical tourism in the sense that said citizens of other nations used to travel to Nigeria for treatment in the past. He reportedly stated, "In the 50s and 60s, [...] the royal family from Saudi Arabia used to come to the University Teaching Hospital, Ibadan, for treatment." Ibid.

2013.[128] From 2010 to 2013, the sector recorded a compound annual growth rate (CAGR) of 16 percent and accounted for over 7 percent of the Nigerian labor force.[129] Gauging from current trends, it is projected that "consumption of healthcare goods in Nigeria will grow by a CAGR of 16.2 percent from US\$ 9 billion in 2013 to US\$ 111 in 2030."[130] Going further, a feasibility study conducted by the Dutch embassy in Nigeria in 2015 concluded that "[there] are enough Nigerians who can afford expensive but quality [health]care."[131] The huge monies invested in medical tourism abroad annually by Nigerians suggest that "there is a big market for hospitals that can provide international level of specialist care within the country, directly or through partnerships."[132]

Consistent with these insights and wisdom, in many countries, the health sector is the top employer of labor. According to data from the US Census Bureau, in 2018, the latest for which information exists, healthcare represented the largest US employer in terms of employment and annual payroll.[133] In that year, the more than 907,000 businesses in the Health Care and Social Assistance sector topped all others with 20 million employees and over \$1.0 trillion in annual payroll.[134] Public health jobs can also stimulate the economy, ultimately creating savings that can be channeled into healthcare funding. The challenge, as we elaborate in Chap. 5 on the politics of healthcare reforms in Nigeria, is for the national government to lead the way in designing such health jobs while ensuring that money allocated for healthcare is actually used for the purpose.

Road number two in the application of health services as a technique of diversification is as part of the still ongoing struggle to harmonize

[128] PharmAccess Foundation, *Nigerian Health Sector: Market Study Report* (Pietersbergweg and Amsterdam, Netherlands, March 2015), 10, https://www.rvo.nl/sites/default/files/Market_Study_Health_Nigeria.pdf.
[129] Ibid.
[130] Ibid.
[131] Ibid., p. 15.
[132] Ibid.
[133] Earlene K.P. Dowell, "Health Care Still Largest U.S. Employer: Census Bureau's 2018 County Business Patterns Provides Data on Over 1200 Industries," United States Census Bureau (October 14, 2020), https://www.census.gov/library/stories/2020/10/health-care-still-largest-united-states-employer.html.
[134] Ibid.

traditional and allopathic medicines where Nigeria can play a leadership role, seizing on its untapped potential as Africa's giant. Even in developed societies like the US, the gaps separating allopathic and nonallopathic medicine are getting blurred as the two medicines converge in terms of training and practice. In the US today, there are doctors of osteopathic medicine (DO) whose training goes beyond the confines of allopathic medicine of medical doctors (MD) in an attempt to provide a broader understanding of modern illnesses and treatment options to tackle these diseases.[135]

Increasing the Contributions of the Industrialization and Service Sectors of Nigeria's Economy without Undermining Agriculture

Nigeria can increase the contribution of oil and gas to its GDP by refining its own crude oil. This is for the short time. In the medium-term, to inoculate itself against the volatility and vulnerabilities of the global oil market, Nigeria must reduce its reliance on oil and find non-oil means to support the government budget and provide revenue for healthcare and other social programs. This is especially so as the engine of the global economy moves away from cars powered by fossil oil to ones powered by electricity, as a targeted response to climate change.[136]

---

[135] See, for example, "Osteopathic Medical Education," American Academy of Osteopathy ("Unique training for osteopathic physicians (DO)"), https://www.academyofosteopathy.org/osteopathic-medical-education#:~:text=Unique%20Training%20for%20Osteopathic%20Physicians,body's%20nerves%2C%20muscles%20and%20bones; "Doctor of Osteopathic Medicine," *Medline Plus*, https://medlineplus.gov/ency/article/002020.htm (stating that in addition to the educational preparation for allopathic doctors, "osteopathic physicians receive an additional 300 to 500 hours in the study of hands-on manual medicine and the body's musculoskeletal system"); and *An Osteopathic Approach to Diagnosis and Treatment*, 3rd ed., eds. Eileen L. DiGiovanni et al. (Philadelphia, PA: Lippincott Williams & Wilkins, 2015), 3–4.

[136] The Biden administration terms it "climate crisis," calling to mind the methodology of the Obama administration, of which Biden was part as vice president, to never let a crisis go to waste. See, for example, Stacey Matthews, "Democrats Embrace 'Never Let a Crisis Go to Waste' Motto in Coronavirus Crisis," *North State Journal* (April 29, 2020), https://nsjonline.com/article/2020/04/matthews-democrats-embracenever-let-a-crisis-go-to-waste-motto-in-coronavirus-crisis/.

Next to the three real sectors, as a threshold issue, Nigeria needs more workers in its labor force. A large economy like Nigeria should boast more than 60 million workers in the workforce.[137] We are aware that the number excludes workers in the informal economy, activities "hidden from monetary, regulatory, and institutional authorities."[138] By some estimates, the informal economy constitutes about 50 percent of Nigeria's GDP, an arrowhead of jobs, technical skills, and nutrient of managerial capabilities for both private and public business that makes this underground economy a "major source of economic growth, productivity, and competitiveness."[139] Still, the informal economy is a codeword for "low productivity, reduced tax revenues, poor governance, excessive regulations, and poverty and income inequality."[140] We live in a world where the informal economy, as a share of the GDP, is declining in many world regions.[141] To build a viable economy in the twenty-first century that adequately funds healthcare, that is not the ideal location for Nigeria.

Agriculture

For agriculture, Nigeria needs to mechanize its method of production. The fertility of its soil,[142] together with the diversity of crops that we

---

[137] See Chap. 2, notes 89–91. In 2020, the rate of labor participation in Nigeria was a little over 53 percent. H. Plecher, "Labor Force Participation Rate in Nigeria 2020," *Statista* (October 27, 2020), https://www.statista.com/statistics/993908/labor-force-participation-rate-in-nigeria/. The labor force participation rate for a country "is the proportion of the population ages 15–64 that is economically active during a specified period." Ibid.

[138] Shu Yu and Franziska Ohnsorge, "The Challenges of Informality," Let's Talk Development (January 18, 2019), https://blogs.worldbank.org/developmenttalk/challenges-informality#:~:text=While%20offering%20the%20advantage%20of,and%20poverty%20and%20income%20inequality.

[139] Judith Monye and Oyintare Abang, "Taxing the Informal Sector—Nigeria's Missing Goldmine," *Bloomberg Tax* (October 15, 2020), https://news.bloombergtax.com/daily-tax-report-international/taxing-the-informal-sector-nigerias-missing-goldmine.

[140] Yu and Ohnsorge, note 138.

[141] Thomas F. Alexander, "The Global Informal Economy: Large but On the Decline," IMF Blog (October 30, 2019), https://blogs.imf.org/2019/10/30/the-global-informal-economy-large-but-on-the-decline/.

[142] See "Countries with the Most Arable Land in the World," Beef2Live (February 28, 2021), https://beef2live.com/story-countries-arable-land-world-0-108929 (placing Nigeria 9th out of 50 countries with the most arable land in the world).

enumerated earlier,[143] provides a canvas that could be the basis for improved production. The goal should be to reduce the percentage of the labor force below the current 70 percent (seven out of every ten workers) to around 50 percent (one out of every two workers) or less, while improving the contribution of the sector to the GDP beyond its current 21 percent (see Table 4.1). Next, to give itself the breathing space it needs to improve agriculture, and increase its ability to feed its teaming population, Nigeria needs to reduce the rate of fertility to bring it into better harmony with the rate of agricultural production.

At independence, agriculture was the primary mainstay of the Nigerian economy and has remained so over the years since independence. The agricultural sector used to play the dual role of foreign exchange earner and source of domestic food production. This changed with the discovery of oil in commercial quantity and the heavy reliance of oil and gas as major source of foreign exchange and government revenue. Before oil, Nigeria was self-sufficient or nearly so in food production. In the years since independence, the country lost that self-sufficiency. The loss coincided with the discovery and production of oil in commercial quantity in the country. In the early 1970s, increases in the price of oil in the world market led to "rapid economic growth in transportation, construction, manufacturing, and government services," which in turn led to a mass migration of Nigerians from the rural areas into urban centers.[144] The mass migration resulted in declines in agricultural production "not only of the major export cash crops, like cocoa, palm kernels, cotton and peanuts, but also of basic foods consumed locally[,] such as yams, bananas, cassava and corn."[145]

From the mid-1970s, Nigeria began to import basic commodities like rice and cassava for domestic consumption.[146] The practice seemed to

---

[143] See notes 33–35 and accompanying texts ("Elements of the Non-Petroleum Sectors: (i) Agriculture").

[144] Reuben Kenrick Udo, "Nigeria: Economy," *Encyclopedia Britannica*, https://www.britannica.com/place/Nigeria/Economy.

[145] John Darnton, "Nigeria Emphasizing Food Production," *New York Times* (June 27, 1976), https://www.nytimes.com/1976/06/27/archives/nigeria-emphasizing-food-production.html.

[146] Udo, note 144.

"work[] well as long as revenues from petroleum remained constant," but became less sustainable, beginning in the late 1970s, because of the fluctuations in the price of oil in the world market, complicated by the rapid growth in population.[147] Agriculture still comprised the bulk of the country's labor force, but now "too little food was produced, requiring increasingly costly imports."[148] Nigeria spends about US$ 5 billion year on food imports, US$ 1.5 billion on milk and other dairy products,[149] and an additional US$ 1.3 billion on cereals.[150] Attempts to resolve the food insecurity through programs like "Operation Feed the Nation," unveiled during the 1970s,[151] amounted to little more than sloganeering, given that production methods remained unmechanized.[152]

Because rapid growth negates self-sufficiency in food production, Nigeria needs to strike more balance between population growth and the rate of food production. In 2006, the population growth rate in Nigeria was 3.2 percent, with the contraceptive prevalence rate, the measure of birth control, at 13 percent.[153] This is a figure far above the pace of food production. Demographers worry that Nigeria risks "a demographic explosion[,]"[154] and that its development in infrastructure is "not

---

[147] Ibid.

[148] Ibid.

[149] "Nigeria Spends [US] $5bn on Food Import, [US] $1.5bn on Milk Annually," *Vanguard* (Lagos) (October 2, 2020), https://www.vanguardngr.com/2020/10/nigeria-spends-5bn-on-food-import-1-5bn-on-milk-annually-2/; see also Aina Ojonugwa, "Nigeria Spends [US]$1.3bn Annually On Importation Of Milk—Bogoro," *The Will* (November 23, 2020), https://thewillnigeria.com/news/nigeria-spends-1-3bn-annually-on-importation-of-milk-bogoro/ (Bogoro in the headline refers to Suleiman E. Bogoro, Executive Secretary, Tertiary Education Trust Fund).

[150] Daniel Workman, "Nigeria's Top [Ten] Imports," *World's Top Exports*, http://www.worldstopexports.com/nigerias-top-10-imports/.

[151] Darnton, note 145.

[152] Ibid. ("Most Nigerian farmers have never seen a tractor. They use a hoe").

[153] Onyenekenwa Cyprian Eneh, "Nigeria's Vision 20:2020-Issues, Challenges and Implications for Development Management," *Asian Journal of Rural Development*, 1 (2011), 21–40, https://doi.org/10.3923/ajrd.2011.21.40.

[154] "Nigeria: Economic and Political Overview," Nordea (updated October 2020), https://www.nordeatrade.com/no/explore-new-market/nigeria/economical-context.

progress[ing] fast enough to advance economic growth."[155] The rate of population growth in Nigeria has not been matched by comparative growth in production of healthcare and other social services, including "delivery of water supply, sewerage and sanitation services."[156] Specifically, the disconnect between the rate of population growth and the rate of economic growth works against pursuit of socioeconomic ventures like expanded healthcare even for more able governments.

To be sure, only humans develop an economy. Arguably, a healthy population is the greatest resource Nigeria has. But too much of a good thing sometimes can be a problem. As one Nigerian demographer warned, "[p]opulation is key[,]" and there is little Nigeria "can do to have economic development," if it does not bring population under control.[157] "If [it does not] take care of population, schools can't cope, hospitals can't cope, there's not enough housing."[158] In a nutshell, not only does rapid population growth undermine efforts "to increase food production," "lower birth rates, along with better management of land and water resources, are necessary to avert chronic food shortages."[159] However, despite this wisdom, Nigerian leaders do not take family planning and population control seriously. Rather, they remained steeped in the difficult proposition of "advanc[ing] economic growth and human development [with]in the context of a large and rapidly growing population."[160]

---

[155] Julia Bello-Schüemann and Alex Porter, *Building the Future: Infrastructure in Nigeria Until 2040,* West Africa Report No. 21 (Pretoria, South Africa: Institute for Security Studies, November 2017), 8, https://issafrica.s3.amazonaws.com/site/uploads/war-21.pdf. The Institute for Security Studies (ISS) "is an African non-profit with offices in South Africa, Kenya, Ethiopia and Senegal[,]" which works to "provide[] timely and credible research, practical training and technical assistance to governments and civil society[,]" with an overall aim "to build knowledge and skills that secure Africa's future." Ibid. back cover of report.

[156] Ibid., p. 18.

[157] Quoted in Elisabeth Rosenthal, "Nigeria Tested by Rapid Rise in Population," *New York Times* (April 14, 2012), http://www.nytimes.com/2012/04/15/world/africa/in-nigeria-a-preview-of-an-overcrowded-planet.html?pagewanted=all&_r=0.

[158] Ibid. See also Bello-Schüemann and Porter, note 155 (pointing out that access to basic infrastructure like electricity, roads, clean water, and improved sanitation facilities lag behind rapid population growth in Nigeria).

[159] Nafis Sadik, "Population Growth and the Food Crisis," FAO Corporate Doc. Repository, http://www.fao.org/docrep/U3550t/u3550t02.htm.

[160] Bello-Schüemann and Porter, note 155, p. 2.

We stake no moral claim on the issue, not that we are immoral or amoral. Population control is a politically sensitive issue in Nigeria that we approach gingerly.[161] Consistent with our decision in this book to stop short of political restructure, our main focus is limited to the ability of Nigeria to regain its self-sufficiency in food production, while meeting the still-unmet needs of its long-suffering citizenry for healthcare and other social programs. Nigeria should not depend on other countries to feed its population, especially when it does not have the wherewithal to import food.[162] We assume that a serious country bidding for a major role in Africa and the world the way Nigeria contemplates itself,[163] should be able to feed its population, rather than depend on other countries to do so for it.

Nothing speaks to the Nigerian state's relative incapacity than the sprawling growth of the Nigerian population within two generations from a manageable 56 million residents at independence to over 208 million people today within the same geographic space. Family planning remains a taboo in Nigeria, especially in the Islamic northern portions of the country.[164] In 1987, under the military regime of Ibrahim Babangida, the Nigerian national government introduced a family planning control program as a cornerstone of its Primary Health Care plan (PHC).[165] Building on the program, by the late 1980s, the official policy was strongly to encourage women to have no more than four children, a sub-

---

[161] See, for example, Anne Look, "Nigerian President's Call for Birth Control Sparks Debate," *VOA News* (June 28, 2012), https://www.voanews.com/africa/nigerian-presidents-call-birth-control--sparks-debate; "Nigerian President Goodluck Jonathan Urges Birth Control," *BBC News* (June 27, 2012), https://www.bbc.com/news/world-africa-18610751.

[162] Here, as in healthcare financing, the lesson from one African adage is that, as a national security issue, a serious traveler does not depend wholly or even largely on the legs of another person for his or her own journey. See Chap. 1, note 17 and accompanying text.

[163] See note 73 and accompanying text (commenting on how General Obasanjo corralled Vision 2020, a prediction that Nigeria would rank among the top 20 economies in the world by 2020, into an economic program).

[164] See "The 77 Percent—The Need to Tackle Nigeria's Population Boom," *DW* (October 1, 2019), https://www.dw.com/en/the-77-percent-the-need-to-tackle-nigerias-population-boom/a-50663036.

[165] "Health," in *Nigeria: A Country Study*, ed. Helen Chapin Metz (Washington, DC: GPO for the Library of Congress, 1991).

stantial reduction from the estimated fertility rate of almost seven children per woman in 1987.[166] However, even though contraceptives and family planning information were made available in many health facilities, the military government attached no official sanctions as part of the implementation of the policy.[167]

The picture changed little under the post-military administrations of the Fourth Republic since 1999.[168] To reinforce the connection between access to healthcare and national economic health at the heart of this book, "[t]he severe economic stresses of the late 1980s had serious impacts throughout the country on medical supplies, drugs, equipment, and personnel."[169] More to the relationship between the rapid population growth and access to social services, à la healthcare at issue here, "[i]n the *rapidly growing cities*, inadequate sanitation and water supply increased the threat of infectious disease, while health care facilities were generally not able to keep pace with the rate of urban population growth."[170]

Industrialization

Like with agriculture, the idea is to increase the share of the labor force of this sector as well as its contribution to the GDP from the current 10 percent and 22.5 percent, respectively (see Table 4.1), to numbers above these figures. There should also be more interfacing between this sector and agriculture to increase the quantity and volume of food items that go into processing, to the benefit of industrialization. To ensure that these raw materials get to the processing points where they are needed, when

---

[166] Ibid.

[167] Ibid.

[168] See A.O. Adekunle and E.O. Otolorin, "Evaluation of the Nigerian Population Policy—Myth or Reality?" *African Journal of Medicine and Medical Sciences*, 29(3–4) (2000), 305–10, PMID: 11714012 (abstract) (pointing out that "no appreciable decline" took place "in the rate of natural increase which was expected to fall by 31.03%" by 2000, and calling the rate of 11% in the use of contraceptives as of the date of publication of the piece, "a far cry from the targeted 80% set in the population policy").

[169] "Health," in *Nigeria: A Country Study*, note 165.

[170] Ibid. Emphasis added.

they are needed, good transport, dependable electricity supply, and storage facilities, all products of good infrastructure, are desiderata.[171] Industrialization in Nigeria is mainly import-substitution, an economic development strategy where the state seeks "to develop self-sufficiency by creating an internal market within" the country, through various means, including subsidization of key national industries, and nationalization, among other tools of economic nationalism.[172] To the extent it has evolved so far, Nigerian industrialization is a sporadic endeavor comprising food, garment, wood and furniture products, all of which engage in some type of exporting activity.[173] The country also witnessed the establishment of motor assembly plants, such as Peugeot Motor Car Assembly Plant in Kaduna and the Volkswagen Plant in Lagos.[174] Manufacturing alone constitutes about 4 percent of the Nigerian economy.[175]

Nigerian manufacturing firms suffer acute shortages of basic infrastructure like good roads, portable water, and, steady power supply.[176] Because of power outages, many Nigerian firms rely on self-supply of electricity by using generators, which immensely increases their costs of production and erodes their competitiveness relative to foreign firms.[177]

---

[171] Compared to residents of other countries, Nigerians endure low levels of access to basic infrastructure like electricity, paved roads, sanitation facilities, clean water, and hospitals at the heart of this book; in 2016, the country ranked 162 out of 186 countries and 32 out of 54 countries in Africa in the provision of these facilities. Bello-Schüemann and Porter, note 155, p. 2.

[172] See Troy Segal and Thomas Brock, "Import Substitution Industrialization—ISI," *Investopedia* (Updated January 2, 2021), https://www.investopedia.com/terms/i/importsubstitutionindustrialization.asp.

[173] L.N. Chete et al., *Industrial Development and Growth in Nigeria: Lessons and Challenges* (Washington, DC: Brookings Institution, 2016–2017), 1, 9, https://www.brookings.edu/wp-content/uploads/2016/07/12c_wp8_chete-et-al.

[174] Mohammed, note 65.

[175] "Nigeria Needs Industrialization Now," *Forbes Africa* (May 1, 2017), https://www.forbesafrica.com/investment-guide/2017/05/01/nigeria-needs-industrialization-now/.

[176] See Femi Adekoya, "How Channelling of Infrastructure to Manufacturers Can Drive Productivity," *Vanguard* (Lagos) (January 8, 2020), https://guardian.ng/business-services/industry/how-channelling-of-infrastructure-to-manufacturers-can-drive-productivity/.

[177] See Anthony Osae-Brown, and Ruth Olurounbi, "Nigeria Runs on Generators and Nine Hours of Power a Day," *Bloomberg* (September 22, 2019), https://www.bloomberg.com/news/articles/2019-09-23/nigeria-runs-on-generators-and-nine-hours-of-power-a-day; Samuel Ayokunle Olówósejéjé, "What Nigeria's Poor Power Supply Really Costs and How a Hybrid System Could Work for Business," *The Conversation* (September 22, 2020), https://theconversation.com/what-nigerias-poor-power-supply-really-costs-and-how-a-hybrid-system-could-work-for-business-144609.

In 2016, under the current Buhari administration, at least 50 manufacturing companies shut down.[178] This is mostly because Nigeria does not have workable refineries within its borders to refine its crude oil. Nigeria has four refineries with a combined refining capacity of 445,000 barrels of crude oil per day.[179] A network of pipelines and depots located throughout the country links these refineries.[180] However, none of these refineries is functional.[181] The Buhari regime has pledged to correct this anomaly,[182] even as, contradictorily, it signs agreements to import refined oil from abroad.[183] This development continues a practice begun during the Sani Abacha regime from 1993 until 1995.[184] Importing refined petroleum from its crude oil speaks to the limited progress in the industrialization leg of Nigeria's economy.

Despite these challenges, some commentators see good prospects for industrialization arising from the market size of the country embedded in its large and growing population.[185] It is an optimism, however, that we

---

[178] "Nigeria Needs Industrialization Now," note 175.

[179] The four are two located in Port Harcourt, one established in 1965 and another in 1989; a third refinery in Warri, Mid-Western Nigeria, established in 1978; and the fourth in Kaduna, northern Nigeria, established in 1983. "Refineries and Petrochemicals," Nigerian National Petroleum Corporation, https://www.nnpcgroup.com/NNPC-Business/Midstream-Ventures/Pages/Refineries-and-Petrochemicals.aspx#:~:text=%E2%80%8B%E2%80%8BRefineries%20and%20Petrochemicals&text=NNPC%20has%20four%20refineries%2C%20two,throughout%20Nigeria%20links%20these%20refineries. In addition, Nigeria has a slew of private refineries, one of the most notable of which is the Niger Delta Petroleum Resources. See "Petroleum Refineries and Petrochemicals," Dept. of Petroleum Resources, https://www.dpr.gov.ng/downstream/refinery/.

[180] "Refineries and Petrochemicals," note 179.

[181] "FG Approves [US] $1.5bn for Rehabilitation of Port Harcourt Refinery," *Huhu Online* (March 18, 2021), https://huhuonline.com/index.php/home-4/huhuonline-more-news/14431-fg-approves-1-5bn-for-rehabilitation-of-port-harcourt-refinery.

[182] Ibid.

[183] See "Nigeria to Resume Petrol Imports from Niger Republic," *Huhu Online* (November 20, 2020), https://huhuonline.com/index.php/home-4/huhuonline-more-news/14070-nigeria-to-resume-petrol-imports-from-niger-republic (news story on the signature of a Memorandum of Understanding between Niger and Niger Republic to the north of the country for Nigeria to *resume* importation of petroleum products from its small neighbor).

[184] See James Rupert, "Corruption Flourished in Abacha's Regime," *Washington Post* (June 9, 1998), https://www.washingtonpost.com/wp-srv/inatl/longterm/nigeria/stories/corrupt060998.htm.

[185] "Nigeria Needs Industrialization Now," note 175.

do not share because of the limited spending power of the Nigerian populace, compared to some Western societies, such as the US,[186] and because of the negative ramifications, analyzed under agriculture above, of a rapid population growth for public services, including access to healthcare at the cynosure of this book. For example, under the Fourth Republic since 1999, Nigeria still imports refined crude oil from its crude that it refines in another country.[187] At the current lethargic pace, Nigeria's leaders are nowhere close to mustering anytime soon, the "willful program" necessary to put the country on the path of industrialization.[188]

Service

As with agriculture and industrialization, in services Nigeria should strive higher in both share of labor force and contribution to the GDP. It can increase the 20 percent of the share in the labor force and 56.4 percent in GDP contribution (see Table 4.1), particularly the labor share. Services were among the reasons for the rebasing of Nigeria's oil-based economy in 2014, leading to the emergence of Nigeria over South Africa as the largest economy in Africa.[189] Nollywood, Nigeria's film industry, could form the starting point for the takeoff. Nigerian governments at all levels can play a more active role as economic regulator.[190] Among the three

---

[186] See Abiola Odutola, "Households in Nigeria Spend ₦22.7 Trillion on Food," *Nairametrics* (May 11, 2020), https://nairametrics.com/2020/05/11/nigerian-households-spend-n22-7-trillion-on-food-items-nbs/. As this piece explained, "[f]or a developing country like Nigeria, the consumption pattern is skewed toward food[,] i.e. food is higher than the non-food items[,]" compared to many developed societies where, in contrast, "the consumption pattern is skewed toward non-food items. The more developed a society becomes, the less it spends on food and the more it spends on non[-]food items." Ibid.

[187] See "Nigeria to Resume Petrol Imports from Niger Republic," note 183. A statement, instructively by the Ministry of Petroleum Resources, indicated that the two countries signed a Memorandum of Understanding for the transportation and storage of petroleum products refined in Niger Republic.

[188] "Nigeria Needs Industrialization Now," note 175.

[189] Chapter 2, notes 89–90, and accompanying texts.

[190] Adetokunbo and Edioye, note 37 (portraying the role of the national government as abdicative). According to the authors, the national government "disregarded the service sector," and displayed a "laissez faire attitude toward regulating the activities of various services providers in the country." Ibid.

sectors of the postindustrial economy surveyed in this book, services appears to be the one that affords the most room for growth for Nigeria's economy. Such is the importance of the sector as Nigeria works to free itself from the vulnerabilities of fossil oil. During his speech to Nigerian lawmakers on August 26, 2000, in the course of an official visit to Nigeria, then President William J. Clinton stated, "[i]n the old economy, a country's economic prospects were limited by its place on the map and its natural resources. Location was everything. In the new economy, information, education, and motivation are everything."[191] For Nigeria, services are the wave of the future, the borderless composite of information, education, and motivation of the new economy that the country should bank on to fund healthcare services. To turn medical tourism on its head, healthcare goods grown in Nigeria, dissected independently in this book, should be a part of this new wave.

Conclusion

This chapter contains the denouement of adequate funding of healthcare services in Nigeria through economic restructuring at the heart of this book. Its highlights include a dissection of the composition of the Nigerian economy, based on contributions to labor force and GDP; application of the concept of the postindustrial economy, together with the technique of diversification the concept embeds, to Nigeria; and the packaging of healthcare services as diversification technique and source of funding beyond the generic services category. As we clearly indicated in Chap. 1, this book is not about political restructuring in Nigeria. Yet, given the reality that in many countries, political considerations shape the setup and maintenance of healthcare delivery, including funding, there is no such thing as an apolitical healthcare system. Nigeria is no exception. Thus, within the context of this book, limited to the efforts of the legislative branch under the Fourth Republic since 1999, Chap. 5 deals with the influence of politics on healthcare in Nigeria.

---

[191] Clinton's Address to Nigerian Lawmakers, note 58.

5

Influence of Politics on Healthcare in Nigeria

Abstract Although political restructuring is outside the scope of this study, the book nonetheless integrates the influence of politics, confined to the legislative branch with its power of oversight over the co-branches of government, particularly the executive branch. The chapter surveys the record of Nigeria's national legislators under the Fourth Republic since 1999 and, based on gaps the survey unearths, makes proposals on what should be done going forward, consistent with the message of this book on restructuring the Nigerian economy to improve funding for healthcare.

Keywords Politics • Legislative oversight • Health information system • Political violence • Research and Development (R&D) • Infrastructure deficit

Introduction

As indicated earlier in this book, political restructuring is outside the scope of this work.[1] Yet, in every political system, Nigeria no exception, healthcare reforms are inescapably embedded in politics.[2] Politics matters

---

[1] See Chap. 1, notes 93–108.
[2] See Chap. 1, notes 111–117.

© The Author(s), under exclusive license to Springer Nature Singapore Pte Ltd. 2022
P. C. Aka, J. A. Balogun, *Healthcare and Economic Restructuring*,
https://doi.org/10.1007/978-981-16-9543-8_5
119

in the origination, design, and implementation of healthcare programs, including funding, and the extent to which healthcare is defined as a human right rather than a privilege that a government can alienate when it sees fit.[3] This truism helps explain the observation of health scholars like Clare Bambra to the effect that "explicit acknowledgement of the political nature of health will lead to more effective health promotion strategy and policy, and to more realistic and evidence-based public health and health promotion practice."[4]

Colloquially speaking, politics is "who gets what, when, and how,"[5] and, in more practical terms, the "authoritative allocation of values in a society."[6] Although office holders in Nigeria's three branches of government collectively constitute the authoritative allocators of values in the Nigerian political community, the cynosure of attention and analysis in this book is the legislative branch, a preeminent branch of the government, which represents the people; makes laws for their good governance; and, through its competence in oversight,[7] checkmates the co-branches, especially the executive arm. This limited focus simultaneously addresses

---

[3] See Hassan Wahab and Philip C. Aka, "The Politics of Healthcare Reforms in Ghana under the Fourth Republic Since 1993: A Critical Analysis," *Canadian Journal of African Studies*, 55(1) (2021), 203 (abstract); and Philip C. Aka, *Genetic Counseling and Preventive Medicine in Post-War Bosnia* (Gateway East, Singapore: Palgrave Macmillan, 2020), 55–9.

[4] Clare Bambra et al., "Toward a Politics of Health," *Health Promotion Int'l*, 20(2) (2005), 187 (abstract), https://doi.org/10.1093/heapro/dah608.

[5] See generally Harold D. Lasswell, *Politics: Who Gets What, When and How* (Manhattan, NY: Peter Smith Pub. Inc., 1990).

[6] David Easton, *A Systems Analysis of Political Life* (Hoboken, NJ: John Wiley & Sons, 1965), 30.

[7] In many systems, the responsibility of the legislature breaks down into "passing laws, establishing the government's budget, confirming executive appointments, ratifying treaties, investigating the executive branch, impeaching and removing from office members of the executive and judiciary, and redressing constituents' grievances." "Legislature," *Encyclopedia Britannica*, https://www.britannica.com/topic/legislature. These functions track the oversight concept. Under the US presidential system, which Nigeria adopted in 1979, oversight by Congress takes place through various means that include review, monitor, and supervision of national agencies, programs, activities and executive branch implementation of public policy. Frederick M. Kaiser, "Congressional Oversight," CRS Report for Congress, 97–936 GOV (updated January 2, 2001), http://156.33.195.33/artandhistory/history/resources/pdf/CRS.Oversight.pdf. Other avenues the US Congress uses to realize oversight are authorization, appropriations, investigative, and legislative hearings by standing committees; specialized investigations by select committees; and reviews and studies by congressional support agencies and staff. Ibid. See also Olanrewaju Tejuoso et al., "Health and the Legislature: The Case of Nigeria," *Health Systems & Reform*, 4(2) (2018), 62–4, https://doi.org/10.1080/23288604.2018.1441622.

the reality of political influence on healthcare reforms and rhymes with the explicit acknowledgment of the inherent influence of politics in health that Professor Bambra and her colleagues advised. In Nigeria, the legislative branch is a bicameral institution that goes by the name National Assembly.[8] Consistent with the concept of oversight, Nigerian legislators have responsibility for passing informed legislation governing the healthcare system, allocating adequate financial resources for healthcare, and ensuring that monies voted for healthcare services are used as intended. To what extent they lived up to expectation in this duty under the Fourth Republic since 1999 is one of the purposes of this chapter.

It is necessary that we pause at this point to enter a caveat, namely, that because of time and space constraints, the focus in this book is limited to the national level in Nigeria's federal system,[9] without suggesting that events at the much more numerous state and local government levels are unimportant, because they are. For although preeminent, due to its coordinating role and the overconcentration of political powers in the center under Nigeria's Fourth Republic since 1999,[10] the national government is one out of 782 units in a federal system of government made up of one national government, one Federal Capital Territory based in Abuja, 36 states, and 774 local governments. Next to the record of Nigerian lawmakers on healthcare reforms.

Record Under the Fourth Republic

Survey of the record of legislative activities going back to 1999 reveals two interrelated phenomena: existence of low-level awareness on human rights among the legislators, including the notion of health as human

---

[8] Nigeria's National Assembly comprises two chambers: a House of Representatives of 306 members (lower house), elected based on a four-year term and based on population; and a Senate of 109 members (upper house), three from each of the 36 states and one from Abuja, the Federal Capital Territory, like the members of the House of Representatives, for four-year terms, signifying the equality of the states. See "National Parliaments: Nigeria," Library of Congress, https://www.loc.gov/law/help/national-parliaments/nigeria.php.

[9] For elaboration on the origin and denouement of federalism in Nigeria, see Chap. 2, notes 45–72 ("The Experience of Federalism in Nigeria").

[10] See Chap. 1, notes 93–8.

rights; and the poor implementation of laws related to healthcare many years after passage. We take these issues in turn.

Low-Level Awareness on Healthcare among the Lawmakers

In July 2017, Nigeria established the Legislative Network for Universal Health Coverage (LNUHC).[11] The Network is made up of the Nigerian Senate Committee on Health, the Health Finance and Governance Project of the United States Agency for International Development (USAID), the World Bank, the Bill and Melinda Gates Foundation, and the UK Aid.[12] The Network aims to mobilize Nigerian legislators, national and state alike, to explore means these lawmakers can use to achieve expanded healthcare, using their legislative mandate.[13] The logic behind that mobilization is that "strengthening [their] ability to make, implement, and monitor good health policy [...] have the potential to strengthen the health system overall by moving legislators from audience to collaborators."[14] This is because in Nigeria, legislators and officials of the Ministry of Health "meet only when there is a budget to defend or disease outbreak to" deal with.[15] It took the formation of this Network to discover the limited engagement of Nigerian lawmakers in healthcare. Whether at the national or state level, many lawmakers "were unfamiliar with the concept of [expanded healthcare], [...] unaware of the extent to which the chronic underfunding of health[care] [in the country] [...] negatively affects their constituents; and [...] had never engaged with the federal and state ministries of health to clearly identify legislators' responsibilities and enable them to perform in a way that would strengthen the health system."[16]

---

[11] Tejuoso et al., note 7.
[12] Ibid.
[13] Ibid.
[14] Ibid.
[15] Ibid.
[16] Ibid.

The Network sought to rectify these deficiencies and lackadaisicalness through a training program.[17] Put together by Nigerian Institute of Legislative Studies, the Federal Ministry of Health, and the LNUHC Steering Committee, the training program aimed to explain the basics of expanded healthcare and health financing, to review the National Health Act, and to apply "an interactive case study approach with examples from several Nigerian states to demonstrate how legislators can use their policy making, appropriation, oversight, and accountability functions to move their states toward" expanded healthcare.[18] The training bore some much-needed fruit. Hitherto, state Health Ministries were not questioned about budget allocations, an occurrence that skewed allocations toward secondary care. In the aftermath of the training, legislators became interested in what monies went to primary healthcare.[19] In Lagos State, southwestern Nigeria, the Appropriation Committee contacted the Ministry of Health requesting update on expanded healthcare, including funding, something the Commissioner for Health in the State indicated had never happened before.[20] Similarly, in Bauchi State, North-Eastern Nigeria, legislators used their power to approve revenue to hold health facilities accountable.[21] Although, hitherto, these lawmakers were aware that oversight was part of their responsibilities, absent any training or tools, they lacked any sense of what to look for or the appropriate questions to ask.[22] Perhaps, due to this new awareness of their responsibilities, Bauchi lawmakers played an instrumental role in getting the governor to sign the state's health insurance bill.[23]

The increased solicitude for healthcare, attributable to the LNUHC training, extends to the national level. Here, the Senate indicated it will not pass the budget sent to it in December 2017 by the executive branch unless it included some extra money in the budget, 1 percent of the Consolidated Revenue Fund, set forth in the National Health Act,

[17] Ibid.
[18] Ibid.
[19] Tejuoso et al., note 7.
[20] Tejuoso et al., note 7.
[21] Ibid.
[22] Ibid.
[23] Ibid.

referred to in the preceding paragraph and elaborated subsequently in this chapter, for primary healthcare.[24] The Act created a Fund, called the Basic Health Care Provision Fund, to be fed by sources that include an "annual grant of not less than one percent of [the national government's] Consolidated Revenue Fund."[25] For the 2018 budget, the LNUHC played an instrumental role in implementing this provision.[26]

While these (re)awakenings are a good start, they do not go far enough to repair the underinvestment in healthcare in Nigeria that goes back a long time. In a federal system of government, the center plays an important coordinative and leadership role, much of a snowball effect, that can stir subnational governments, the acclaimed "laboratories of democracy,"[27] into action. However, several of the activities described above emanated from the states.

To rectify the low-level awareness and consolidate their newfound knowledge on healthcare, the legislators can go a step further by including healthcare in their campaign platforms or increasing the priority they assign to healthcare in those platforms. Barack Obama did the same during his run for the US presidency, with concrete result leading not just to his election two times as president but also to the passage of the landmark Affordable Care Act of 2010,[28] as a signature achievement of his administration. Coming closer home, at the legislative level, under their Fourth Republic since 1993, Ghanaian lawmakers across the political aisle made healthcare reforms the centerpiece of their campaign platforms.[29] In Nigeria, in contrast, healthcare and other social service programs are the first to be defunded each time there is a fall in oil revenue. To ensure that they did their part in solidifying this change, the Nigerian electorate

[24] Ibid.
[25] National Health Act, Act No. 8 of 2014, *Federal Republic of Nigeria Official Gazette*, 145 (101) (October 27, 2014), https://www.ilo.org/dyn/natlex/docs/ELECTRONIC/104157/126947/F-693610255/NGA104157.pdf. See also ibid., §11(1) (creating the Fund).
[26] Tejuoso et al., note 7.
[27] See Chap. 2, note 71, and accompanying text.
[28] Patient Protection and Affordable Care Act, Pub. Law 111–148 (March 2010).
[29] Wahab and Aka, note 3, p. 204 (commenting on a commitment to healthcare in the land that the article likened to "the consensus on healthcare among major political parties in the United Kingdom (UK) after World War I," and contrasted "with the entrenched opposition to healthcare reforms in the United States of America (US) that dates back a long time").

should support only political parties and candidates who give healthcare prime importance in their platforms.

Two Laws on Healthcare as Test Case

Two laws stand out among the lot related to healthcare that the Nigerian National Assembly has enacted since 1999. These are the legislation setting up the National Health Insurance Scheme of 1999 (hereinafter the NHIS Act),[30] and the National Health Act (NHA) of 2014.[31] Along with the program it brought into being, the NHIS Act was designed to provide "accessible, affordable[,] and qualitative healthcare for all Nigerians."[32] More elaborately, the legislation aimed to set up an insurance system "where health care services are paid for from the common pool of funds contributed by the participants of the Scheme."[33] The law comprises four sections. Section "Introduction" enumerates various programs developed by the Scheme to achieve universal coverage for different groups, including federal, state, and local government employees (formal sector); workers in the "organized private sector"; members of the armed forces and police; students in higher education; persons in the informal sector, such as members of Community Based Social Health Insurance Programs, and of the Social Health Insurance Program; as well as economically marginal ("vulnerable") groups, such as children under five, pregnant women, disabled persons, prisoners, and refugees or internally displaced persons. The law defines a beneficiary as a person enrolled in the program who is up-to-date in paying his or her premium.[34] Coverage for beneficiaries is

---

[30] See National Health Insurance Scheme: Operational Guidelines (Revised October 2012) [hereinafter NHIS Operational Guidelines]. The law was originally adopted before May 1999, while the country was still under its second long stretch of military dictatorship from 1984 until 1999. The first leg took place from 1966 until 1979.

[31] National Health Act (2014), note 25.

[32] "Foreword," NHIS Operational Guidelines, note 30.

[33] NHIS Operational Guidelines, note 30, p. 6, ("Definition of Key Terms").

[34] Ibid. ("Beneficiary").

limited to four "live birth,"[35] elaborated as "a maximum of four biological children of the principal under the age of 18 years."[36] The law covers "[p]reventive care," defined to include immunization as well as health and family planning education."[37]

Section "Record Under the Fourth Republic," titled "Standards and Accreditation," explains the requirements for accreditation of healthcare facilities, health maintenance organizations, mutual health organizations, and nongovernmental organizations, among others. It includes licentiate and other professional requirements for healthcare workers. Section "What Needs To Be Done" of the NHIS Act aims to tap the "necessary flow of information and records that will ensure the proper implementation of the Scheme,"[38] such as periodic information to operators of the NHIS regarding registration of new enrollees into the program.[39] Section "Conclusion" highlights various offenses and the penalties attached to each offense. This section is designed to ensure compliance with the provisions of the document and are directed at beneficiaries and healthcare providers.[40]

The NHA governs the "regulation, development[,] and management of" Nigeria's healthcare system, including setting standards for healthcare delivery in the country. The legislation comprises seven parts. Part I deals with establishment of a national health system, responsibility for health, and eligibility for health services. This includes the creation of a Fund for primary healthcare referred to before in the previous section,[41] for this book one of the most innovative provisions of the law. Part II focuses on health establishments and technologies, including classification, certification, and evaluation of health institutions; provision of health services at public health institutions and other locations; referrals; and the relationship between public and private health institutions. Part III deals with the rights and obligations of users and health personnel, including emergency treatment, as well as accessing and protecting health records.

---

[35] Ibid., p. 7.
[36] Ibid., p. 17.
[37] Ibid.
[38] Ibid., p. 128.
[39] Ibid., p. 129.
[40] Ibid., p. 136.
[41] See note 24 and accompanying text.

Part IV deals with national health research and information system, including the establishment and composition of a national health research committee, and research involving experimentation with human subjects. Part V focuses on human resources for health, including regulations relating to the management of human resources in the health system, and prohibition of nonemergency medical treatment abroad by government officials. Part VI deals with the use of blood, blood products, and related matters, including the creation of national blood transfusion services, prohibition of human cloning, allocation and use of human organs, regulation relating to donation of body and tissues, and autopsies. Part VII deals with miscellaneous provisions, including the formation of a National Consultative Health Forum by the Minister of Health.

Until its passage in 2014, the NHA was in the work for ten long years from 2004. It was designed to bring to an end "the era of poor access to health care, stock-out syndrome of essential drugs and vaccines, skewed health manpower distribution, mushroom health facilities, hospitals turned to 'mere consulting clinics,' unregulated and unethical health researches, assault on health workers, [and] total paralyzing strikes that [left] the nation no option than unnecessary death of the citizens."[42] However, this has not turned out to be the case so far, given that many of its provisions remain mostly unimplemented many years after the enactment of the law.[43] These include the all-important clause forbidding healthcare workers from denying any patient "emergency medical treatment for any reason," under the pain of possible fine or imprisonment.[44] Testament to the comparatively low salience Nigerian lawmakers assign to healthcare, discussed in the previous section, nongovernmental

---

[42] D. Adegboye and T.M. Akande, "The Role of National Health Act in Nigeria Health System Strengthening," *Savannah Journal of Medical Research and Practice*, 6(1) (2017) (abstract), https://doi.org/10.4314/sjmrp.v6i1.1.

[43] See Angela Onwuzoo, "Six years after enacting National Health Act, Many Provisions Not Implemented," *Punch* (Lagos) (February 16, 2020), https://healthwise.punchng.com/six-years-after-enacting-national-health-act-many-provisions-not-implemented/; and Ebuka Onyeji et al., "Dissecting National Health Act: What Nigerians need to know (1)," *Premium Times* (Abuja) (November 19, 2018), https://www.premiumtimesng.com/health/health-features/296422-dissecting-national-health-act-what-nigerians-need-to-know-1.html.

[44] National Health Act, note 25, §20(1); see also ibid., §20(2) (stipulating punishment for violation of the law).

organizations, rather than the lawmakers or the Ministry of Health, played an instrumental role in bringing about the passage of this law.[45]

What Needs To Be Done

Chapter 4 on modalities for restructuring Nigeria's oil-based economy, in response to changes in the global economy that include the imminence of electric vehicles, gives a glimpse of what Nigerian lawmakers, as popular representatives of their constituents, should do to provide more money for healthcare delivery. Using their oversight powers, these lawmakers, individually and collectively, should work with the executive branch to diversify the Nigerian economy in the direction of services, consistent with the concept of a postindustrial economy, including the application of healthcare as a technique in that diversification mix. Every country is different, and there is no guarantee that adopting the proposals in this book would turn the Nigerian economy into a postindustrial economic haven in the sense of say the US or Japan.[46] But Costa Rica, a much smaller country than Nigeria, is indicator that diversification works when applied diligently and consistently.[47]

To solidify those proposals, we set forth additional measures in this section, illustrative rather than exhaustive of all possibilities for a large country the size of Nigeria, which we present in no particular order of importance. Some of the ensuing measures overlap the proposals tabled in this book, particularly in Chaps. 3 and 4. A common factor that ties these proposals together is the imperativeness of saving money for the healthcare needs of the masses of the Nigerian people. The proposals are: (1) recommitting the Nigerian government to the Abuja Declaration on optimal budgetary allocation, (2) cutting waste and making sure the monies saved actually go into healthcare, (3) promoting preventive rather than curative medicine, (4) stimulating increased participation in the NHIS, and (5) tackling the shortage of healthcare workers. Other

---

[45] Tejuoso et al., note 7.
[46] See Chap. 2, notes 76–78.
[47] See Chap. 4, notes 118–19.

instructive measures are: (6) strengthening the health information system, (7) addressing the public health consequences of political violence, (8) promoting research and development (R& D) within the healthcare system, and (9) firmly tackling Nigeria's infrastructure deficit. Table 5.1 summarizes the nine proposals.

Commit the Nigerian Government to the Abuja Declaration on Optimal Budgetary Allocation

The first measure is for the lawmakers, in concert with the president and members of the executive branch, to commit the country to the Abuja Declaration of 2001 on the allocation of 15 percent of the budget to healthcare. This is necessary, since some Abuja bureaucrats, denominate the Declaration as little more than an "aspiration,"[48] suggesting loose attachment to the pledge. But as we explained in Chap. 1, this mindset is oblivious to the realities of underinvestment in healthcare in many African countries in the postcolonial era, Nigeria included, that necessitated the Declaration,[49] as well as that even many countries with well-established healthcare systems, allocate at least 10 percent of their budget to healthcare.[50]

Cut Waste and Make Sure That the Monies Saved Actually Go into Healthcare Services

A second measure is for Nigerian lawmakers to help cut waste and make sure that the monies saved are channeled into health services. This is given the fact that, as the World Health Organization observed in a 2010 report, due to inefficiencies, in many countries, Nigeria obviously not an

---

[48] Chukwuma Muanya, "Why 15% Budget Allocation to Health is Tall Order, by FG," *Guardian* (Lagos) (October 26, 2020), https://guardian.ng/features/why-15-budget-allocation-to-health-is-tall-order-by-fg/ (quoting Abdulaziz Abdullahi, Permanent Secretary in the Federal Ministry of Health).

[49] See Chap. 1, notes 14–18.

[50] See Aka, *Genetic Counseling and Preventive Medicine in Post-War Bosnia*, note 3, p. 52 (referring to Austria, Belgium, Denmark, France, Germany, the Netherlands, Sweden, and Switzerland).

Table 5.1 Healthcare funding through legislative oversight: parade of nine proposals

Item No.	Proposal	Means
1.	Recommit the Nigerian government to the Abuja Declaration.	• Implement the 15 percent of GDP target of the Declaration. • Debunk the bureaucratic perception of the target as "an aspiration."
2.	Cut waste and invest saved money into healthcare services.	• Cut legislators' emoluments. • Reduce the size of the National Assembly from 469 to 373 members. • Cut the non-salary benefits of the president and vice president. • Cut the number of ministers from 44 to 20. • Minimize corruption in the health sector.
3.	Promote preventive medicine over curative medicine.	• Promote expanded access to vaccines and essential drugs. • Support the update of the healthcare curriculum in tertiary institutions.
4.	Stimulate increased participation in the NHIS.	• Afford Nigerians more opportunity for access to healthcare insurance through increased participation in the NHIS beyond the current less than 5 percent.
5.	Tackle shortage of healthcare workers.	• Increase the pay and improve the working conditions of doctors and other healthcare workers to reduce brain drain.
6.	Strengthen the health information system.	• Leverage and harness the stock of information and communication technology in the country. • Explore opportunities to promote standardization and intersystem operation in the health sector.
7.	Address public health consequences of political violence.	• Provide better funding for disability issues. • Promote nonmilitary solutions to conflicts.
8.	Promote research and development (R&D).	• Commit the government to the African Union's 1 percent of GDP target on R&D. • Use R&D to promote harmonization of traditional and allopathic medicines.
9.	Firmly tackle infrastructure deficit.	• To reverse the pattern of underinvestment in infrastructure, allocate say 5 percent of the GDP to infrastructural development to include maintenance of existing infrastructure, defined to include government-owned hospitals and related health centers.

exception, "between 20 [percent] and 40 [percent] of all health resources [are] wasted."[51] The challenge for Nigerian lawmakers is to block such leakage anywhere it rears its head, using their oversight authority. Two of numerous possible ways these lawmakers can cut waste is by reducing overheads, the cost of running the government, and by curtailing corruption, and channeling those savings into healthcare. To lead by example, the legislators can start with their emoluments, notorious for being among the highest in the world.[52] Such slashing of emoluments is a patriotic gesture that will also serve to bring their benefits more in tune with the current state of the Nigerian economy.[53]

Debate over the remuneration of Nigerian legislators came to a head June 4, 2021, when a Federal High Court in Lagos ordered the Revenue Mobilization, Allocation, and Fiscal Commission (RMAFC) to fix the salaries and allowances of national legislators to harmonize those remunerations with the country's declining economic condition.[54] RMAFC determines the remunerations of public office holders in Nigeria, not National Assembly Service Commission (NASC) which, until the decision, assumed this power.[55] The Court ruled that the NASC lacked such

---

[51] *Health Systems Financing: The Path to Universal Coverage* (World Health Report 2010) (Geneva, Switzerland: World Health Organization, 2010).

[52] Yomi Kazeem, "Nigeria Has Some of the World's Highest Paid Lawmakers and This Start-Up Wants to Slash Their Pay," *Quartz Africa* (June 4, 2015), https://qz.com/africa/417192/nigeria-has-some-of-the-worlds-highest-paid-lawmakers-and-this-start-up-is-trying-to-slash-their-pay/. This is in a country where the minimum wage is the equivalent of about $90 per month, and where most people live on less than $2.00 per day. The national assembly passed only 106 bills out of the 1063 it reviewed in four years, and yet, in 2018, the legislators earned a whopping $480,000, much of this amount from a guaranteed expense allowance of $35,720 per month. Philip Ojisua, "That Is What Politicians Get Paid Around the World: Nigeria: $480,000 (£361,610)," *Love Money* (March 29, 2019), https://www.lovemoney.com/galleries/65052/this-is-what-politicians-get-paid-around-the-world?page=31. See also Yomi Kazeem, "Nigeria's Legislators Will Get [US]$ 43 Million of Taxpayers' Money for a Wardrobe Allowance," *Quartz Africa* (June 16, 2015), https://qz.com/africa/429470/nigerias-legislators-will-get-43-million-of-taxpayers-money-for-a-wardrobe-allowance/.

[53] See John Kalama et al., "Legislator's Jumbo Pay, Cost of Governance and the State of Education in Nigeria: Issues and Contradictions," *Journal of Educational & Social Research*, 4(2) (January 2012), 73, 74. https://citeseerx.ist.psu.edu/viewdoc/download?doi=10.1.1.665.5079&rep=rep1&type=pdf.

[54] See "Court Asks RMAFC to Fix Salaries for NASS Members in Line with Economic Realities," *Huhu Online* (June 4, 2021), https://huhuonline.com/index.php/home-4/huhuonline-more-news/14654-court-asks-rmafc-to-fix-salaries-for-nass-members-in-line-with-economic-realities.

[55] Ibid.

power.[56] The decision is the result of a consolidated lawsuit by more than 1,500 individuals and nongovernmental organizations.[57]

There may be need also to reduce the size of the federal legislature. Currently, Nigeria has 469 members in its bicameral legislature, made up of 360 in the House of Representatives and 109 in the Senate. The number is out of sync with the current state of the Nigerian economy. For purpose of effective representation, the country can maintain both chambers while cutting down the number of members in each chamber. For example, it can cut down the number of senators from the current three from each state to two. That would trim the size of the Senate from 109 to 73, including one seat from Abuja. Similarly, the size of the House of Representatives could be trimmed down to no more than 300. Altogether, this would reduce the size of the two chambers from the current 469 members to 373.[58]

Like the legislature, the executive branch of the Nigerian government receives emoluments and allowances that the poor state of the Nigerian economy cannot sustain.[59] This is particularly the case with the president and vice president whose salaries and allowances the lawmakers should consider pegging down by as much as 50 percent by some suggestions.[60]

---

[56] Ibid.

[57] Ibid.

[58] For a comparable insight, see Yusuf Akinpelu, "Nigerian Senator Wants Number of Lawmakers Reduced by 70% to Save Cost," *Premium Times* (Abuja) (October 3, 2019), https://www.premiumtimesng.com/news/headlines/355832-nigerian-senator-wants-number-of-lawmakers-reduced-by-70-to-save-cost.html (reporting the proposal of one Senator for a reduction in the number of lawmakers representing each state in the Senate to one and in the House of Representatives to three, bringing the total number of national lawmakers to 146, from the current 469, a 69 per cent reduction).

[59] See Yusuf Akinpelu, "Nigeria to Spend ₦7.8 Billion On Entitlements to Ex-Presidents, Deputies, Others in 2021," *Premium Times* (Abuja) (January 22, 2021), https://www.premiumtimesng.com/news/headlines/437916-nigeria-to-spend-n7-8-billion-on-entitlements-to-ex-presidents-deputies-others-in-2021.html. The amount is equivalent to over US$20 million.

[60] See Tunde Ososanya, "Reduce Salaries Earned by Lawmakers by Half—Sanusi Tell Buhari," *Legit* (February 12, 2018), https://www.legit.ng/1151528-reduce-salaries-earned-by-lawmakers-by-sanusi-tells-buhari.html (reporting on the proposal by Sanusi Lamido Sanusi II, former Emir of Kano for a 50 percent cut in the salaries of legislators and ministers). See also Wale Akinola, "Ex-Emir Sanusi Reveals Bombshell, Says Nigeria Will Go Bankrupt with Current Governance Structure," *Legit* (June 14, 2020), https://www.msn.com/en-xl/africa/nigeria/ex-emir-sanusi-reveals-bombshell-says-nigeria-will-go-bankrupt-with-current-governance-structure/ar-BB15sErb?li=BBJGzsi&srcref=rss&post_id=noID (reporting the view of the former Emir that Nigeria's current structure of governance with its huge overhead is unsustainable).

In 2020, the president and vice president received in salary the equivalent of US$ 39,037 and US$ 33,460, respectively.[61] These basic salaries in their ordinariness few would quarrel with. However, the president also received a non-salary benefit allowance the equivalent of US$ 100,382, coming to a total take-home pay the equivalent of US$ 139,419.[62]

The lawmakers could begin the cut with the allowance. Between 2013 and 2015, the government spent the equivalent of US$ 72.3 million on the maintenance of the presidential jet, including supplies, training, and insurance fees.[63] When he took office, Muhammadu Buhari, who has a certain reputation as an austere person, indicated that he will cut down the running of the government by reducing the number of planes in the presidential fleet.[64] Two terms into his period in office, the promise goes mostly unimplemented.

Still on the executive branch, there may be need to reduce the size of the government. Nigeria currently has 28 national ministries with 44 ministers, main and junior.[65] It could cut the ministries to 20 and peg the number of ministers to 20 (the US has 15 with over 320 million citizens), eliminating the duplication of junior ministers. The ministries already have permanent secretaries that could fill in the role currently served by junior ministers. Permanent secretaries are career civil servants, heads of their various ministries who, in the performance of their day-to-day duties as preeminent policy implementers, are ultimately accountable to

---

[61] See Nurudeen Lawal, "What Nigeria's President, Vice President, State Governors and Their Deputies Earn as Salaries, Allowances," *Legit* (September 21, 2019), https://www.legit.ng/1253507-what-nigerias-president-vice-president-state-governors-deputies-earn-salaries-allowances.html; https://www.legit.ng/1253507-what-nigerias-president-vice-president-state-governors-deputies-earn-salaries-allowances.html.

[62] Ibid.

[63] See Oladeinde Olawoyin, "In Four Years, Budget Proposal for Buhari's Presidential Air Fleet Increased by 191%," *Premium Times* (Abuja) (November 14, 2020), https://www.premiumtimesng.com/news/headlines/426094-in-four-years-budget-proposal-for-buharis-presidential-air-fleet-increased-by-191.html (reporting that the national government proposed to spend money for overhead and capital allocation in the 2018 budget approximately 191 percent higher than the appropriation in the 2017 budget).

[64] See ibid. ("Controversial Fleet") (When he came to office in 2015, Buhari "promised to cut down on the waste of public resources and assured Nigerians his administration would cut down on the number of aircraft [on the presidential fleet] inherited from former President Goodluck Jonathan").

[65] See "Full List: Portfolios of Buhari's 44 Ministers—2019–2023," *Premium Times* (Abuja) (August 21, 2019), https://www.premiumtimesng.com/news/headlines/347816-full-list-portfolios-of-buharis-44-ministers-2019-2023.html.

the politically appointed ministers of their respective ministries. The point is that Nigeria should find more creative ways to satisfy the requirements of "federal character" other than through the use of a bloated ministerial list.[66] The trend toward big government under the Fourth Republic needing to be bucked dates back to Goodluck Jonathan (2010–2015) under whose administration public officers in the country making up just 0.013 percent of the country's population took home ₦1.126 trillion out of a national budget of ₦4.6 trillion a year in salaries and allowances,[67] translated to over 24 percent of the budget. Trimming the size of the government and reducing waste and overheads can save money that the National Assembly should make sure go into healthcare services.

To crown these waste-shedding efforts, Nigerian lawmakers should use their oversight powers to help minimize corrupt practices in the health sector, which occurs when a healthcare worker uses his or her public office for private gains. Recently, a group of healthcare scholars identified 49 corrupt practices impeding the standard of care for patients in Nigeria that these scholars grouped under five categories: absenteeism, under-the-counter payments, as well as corrupt practices related to procurement, to health financing, and to employment.[68] To put the matter in perspective, the healthcare programs in Nigeria and Ghana have several features that both unite and distinguish them. They bear similar name and came into operation about the same time (Nigeria in 1999 but fully effective from 2005; Ghana in 2003), under a current instalment of civilian rule each coincidentally denominated the Fourth Republic (Ghana since 1993 and Nigeria since 1999).

---

[66] The "federal character" principle is a provision in the Nigerian constitution which mandates that the composition of Nigerian governments, their agencies, and how they conduct their affairs reflect the ethnic diversity and pluralism of the country. The provision forbids a "predominance of persons from a few states or from a few ethnic or other sectional groups" in government agencies. See Constitution of the Federal Republic of Nigeria (1999), § 14(3).

[67] Rudolf Ogoo Okonkwo, "If Jonathan Had Wanted to Be a Statesman," *Opinion Nigeria* (April 4, 2015), https://opinionnigeria.com/if-jonathan-had-wanted-to-be-a-statesman-by-rudolf-ogoo-okonkwo/.

[68] See Obinna Onwujekwe et al., "Where Do We Start? Building Consensus on Drivers of Health Sector Corruption in Nigeria and Ways to Address It," *Int'l Journal of Health Policy Management*, 9(7) (2020), 286–296, https://doi.org/10.15171/ijhpm.2019.128.

Though adopted about the same time, and this is where the similarity ends and the distinction kicks in, measured by the percentage of population enrolled, Ghana's program has nearly six times more coverage than Nigeria's, as we elaborate shortly below with actual numbers. For another distinguishing factor, the corrupt practices in the Ghanaian healthcare sector occur in a political system where the incidence of corruption is perceived to be relatively mild,[69] compared to Nigeria, where such practices take place in a political system rife with corruption.[70] Like Nigeria, corrupt practices in Ghana's health sector are large scale and pervasive.[71] Under Ghana's current program, since its inception object of numerous studies, surveys of patients and respondents in opinion polls unearth perception of corrupt practices that include: illegal breaches in medical procurement, diversion of budgeted funds by health administrators, healthcare workers stealing time by not coming to work or doing private practice during office hours, doctors prescribing medications that patients do not need, doctors issuing forged sick leaves and medical reports, and failure by healthcare workers to return to patients unused drugs that they have been billed for.[72] Others include illegal charges for services rendered in accessing healthcare under the program, NHIS, whether related to enrollment in the program, accessing drugs, creating and retrieval medical records, allocation of hospital beds, or ambulance services.[73] Juxtaposition of Nigeria with Ghana places Nigeria in the worst of all

---

[69] In December 2020, Ghana ranked 11th among African countries in a corruption index, compared to Kenya 26, Nigeria 41, and Democratic Republic of the Congo 49. See "Corruption Rank | Africa," *Trading Economics*, https://tradingeconomics.com/country-list/corruption-rank?continent=africa.

[70] See Onwujekwe et al., note 68.

[71] See generally *Cost and Impact of Corruption on Education and Health Sectors in Ghana* (Accra, Ghana: Ghana Integrity Initiative (GII) Consortium, 2018).

[72] *Cost and Impact of Corruption on Education and Health Sectors in Ghana*, note 71, pp. 2, 48 (tbl. 14); see also Sophie Witter, and Bertha Garshong, "Something Old or Something New?: Social Health Insurance in Ghana," *BMC Int'l Health & Human Rights*, 9 (August 2009), 6, http://www.ncbi.nlm.nih.gov/pmc/articles/PMC2739838/ (commenting on the surges in informal payments, such as charges for out-of-hours services and advisement for patients to pay for drugs supposedly out of stock, that take away from the otherwise noticeable decrease in out-of-pocket expenses under the NHIS).

[73] *Cost and Impact of Corruption on Education and Health Sectors in Ghana*, note 71, p. 2, 48 (tbl. 14); see also Witter and Garshong, note 72 (commenting on the surges in informal payments, such as charges for out-of-hours services and advisement for patients to pay for drugs supposedly out of stock, that take away from the otherwise noticeable decrease in out-of-pocket expenses under the NHIS).

worlds: corruption in the political system, corruption in the health sec-tor, and a healthcare program with severely low coverage. It dramatizes for Nigerian lawmakers the scale of the abuses in the health sector that they must stem, using their power of oversight.

Promote Preventive Healthcare, Rather than Curative Medicine

A third proposal for Nigerian lawmakers, as representatives of their con-stituents, is to help enthrone preventive, rather than curative, medicine in Nigerian healthcare system. One way to do this is through support for expanded access to vaccines and essential drugs. Immunization rates in Nigeria are among the lowest in the world, and thousands of children still die annually from diseases that could have been prevented through vac-cination.[74] This is especially the case in the northern parts of Nigeria where barely 10 percent of children receive the quantum of vaccination that they need to stay healthy. Similarly, vaccination against tetanus is equally low among women.[75] Still on preventive medicine, another viable approach will be for the lawmakers to support and promote the update of the healthcare curriculum, beginning, say, with tertiary institutions.[76] Given that an innovative educational system can bring about change that can snowball into the larger society, schools of all level provide a labora-tory to test-drive ideas and policies related to healthcare.[77]

Stimulate Increased Participation in the National Health Insurance Scheme

A fourth measure that Nigerian lawmakers should lead, beyond mere passage of the enabling act, is to stimulate increased participation in the NHIS. Over two decades since it was initially adopted in 1999, and

---

[74] Endurance Ophori et al., "Current Trends of Immunization in Nigeria: Prospect and Challenges," *Tropical Medicine & Health*, 42(2) (June 2014), 67–75, https://doi.org/10.2149/tmh.2013-13.
[75] Ibid.
[76] See generally Joseph A. Balogun, *Healthcare Education in Nigeria: Evolution and Emerging Paradigms* (England, UK: Routledge, 2020).
[77] Ibid.

sixteen years since its effective operation from 2005, the program still covers less than 5 percent of Nigeria's population, most of them federal workers.[78] By contrast, Ghana's similarly named program, unveiled in 2003, enrolled little over 35 percent of the country's population as of 2017.[79] The low coverage is an unflattering achievement for a program avowedly designed to provide "accessible, affordable[,] and qualitative healthcare for *all* Nigerians."[80]

Tackle the Shortage of Healthcare Workers

In addition to the four highlighted above, Nigerian lawmakers should also, using the instrumentality of their oversight power, work in concert with the executive branch, to tackle the shortage of healthcare workers. The shortage was among the multiple problems afflicting Nigeria's healthcare system that we documented in Chap. 3, commenting on the huge burden of diseases relative to resources that ranks among the features of Nigeria's healthcare system. To recapitulate, the doctor–patient ratio in the country is about 1 doctor per 5,000 patients, well below the WHO recommendation of 1 doctor per 600 patients,[81] and it is a shortage compounded by the equally low ratio of paramedical personnel like psychologists and social workers in the country.[82]

---

[78] See Arin Dutta, and Charles Hongoro. *Scaling Up National Health Insurance in Nigeria: Learning from Case Studies of India, Colombia, and Thailand* (Washington, DC: Futures Group, Health Policy Project, 2013), iv, 1, https://www.healthpolicyproject.com/pubs/96_NigeriaInsuranceFinal.pdf. (the estimated enrolment as of the publication of this report was 3 percent or about 5 million persons).

[79] Doris Dokua Sasu, "Share of Population with National Health Insurance Scheme (NHIS) Membership in Ghana from 2014 to 2017," *Statista* (February 9, 2021), https://www.statista.com/statistics/1172722/share-of-people-with-active-national-health-insurance-membership-in-ghana/.

[80] Note 32 and accompanying text. Emphasis added.

[81] See Chukwuma Muanya, and Adaku Onyenucheya, "Bridging Doctor-Patient Ratio Gap to Boost Access to Healthcare Delivery in Nigeria," *Guardian* (Lagos) (February 4, 2021), https://guardian.ng/features/health/bridging-doctor-patient-ratio-gap-to-boost-access-to-healthcare-delivery-in-nigeria/.

[82] Akindare Okunola, "[Five] Facts Every Nigerian Should Know About Our Health Care," *Global Citizen* (September 9, 2020), https://www.globalcitizen.org/en/content/health-care-facts-nigeria-covid-19/?utm_source=paidsearch&utm_medium=usgrant&utm_campaign=verizon&gclid=Cj0KCQiAtqL-BRC0ARIsAF4K3WGZxHt-Yz41A7plT75mK9ftJcCI-GjctLUo_rcIqLU_7fEgaOJGkZgaAry7EALw_wcB.

Although well-maintained hospitals are important, the utility of a hospital or health center lies in the competence and commitment of its workers. Therefore, a conceivable way to minimize the shortage of health-care workers is to improve the conditions of these workers, right now considered among the worst in the world, measured in terms of benefits and equipment.[83] These deplorable working conditions account for the migration of many of these workers to other countries,[84] resulting in a brain drain that many analysts and policymakers lament.[85] Using their oversight powers, the lawmakers, as grassroots representatives of the people, should lead the search for creative ways through various means, including better pay and improved working conditions, to stem the brain drain.

Strengthen the Health Information System

An effective health information system is critical for providing care, preventing diseases, and promoting wellness in hospitals and other health-care centers. Thus, the National Health Act of 2014 requires healthcare providers to "establish and maintain a health information system as part of the national health information system."[86] Despite this mandate, collection and maintenance of patient records in many hospitals and other healthcare centers in Nigeria are still mostly undigitized, sometimes

---

[83] "Nigeria Ranked [Seventh] among Countries Facing Shortage of Health Workers, *HealthFacts.Ng* (May 11, 2017), https://www.physicianleaders.org/news/how-many-patients-can-primary-care-physician-treat (last visited February 10, 2021).

[84] See Mercy Abang, "Nigeria's Medical Brain Drain: Healthcare Woes As Doctors Flee," *Al Jazeera News* (April 8, 2019), https://www.aljazeera.com/features/2019/4/8/nigerias-medical-brain-drain-healthcare-woes-as-doctors-flee; and Molly Fosco, "Doctor Drain: An Exodus from Nigeria Threatens Its Healthcare System. *Ozy* (2018), https://www.ozy.com/around-the-world/doctor-drain-an-exodus-from-nigeria-threatens-its-health-care-system/87072/.

[85] See Sola Ogundipe et al., "Shortage of Medical Personnel: Tougher Times Ahead for Nigerians (1)," *Vanguard* (Lagos) (January 27, 2015), https://www.vanguardngr.com/2015/01/shortage-medical-personnel-tougher-times-ahead-nigerians-1/ (quoting Ruiz Gama Vaz, then WHO's representative in the country).

[86] National Health Act (2014), note 25, §38(1(a)).

resulting in lost patient data, duplicate record keeping, and, in some cases, misdiagnosis.[87] Moreover, the country lacks a unified database of health indicators, an occurrence that impedes intersystem tracking.[88] Given this void, much data compilation on Nigeria's healthcare system is done by nongovernmental organizations. This problem is among the issues we discussed in Chap. 3 on characteristic features of Nigeria's healthcare system, specifically the huge burden of diseases relative to resources. Using its oversight power, the Nigerian National Assembly should ensure that the government leverages and harnesses the stock of information and communication technology in the country while exploring opportunities to promote standardization and intersystem operation in the country's health sector.

Address the Public Health Consequences of Political Violence

Civilian rule is supposed to produce "democratic dividends" for the masses of Nigerian people, top among which is peace and basic security necessary for productive economic activities. Instead, under the Fourth Republic since 1999, much like during the military era preceding it, Nigeria has gyrated from one conflict to the other,[89] with negative ramifications for socioeconomic development,[90] including access to healthcare. In addition to the Boko Haram terrorism that has engulfed the country since 2009, these conflicts, with their mayhem of maims and deaths, include banditry and kidnappings in the North-West region of the country; clashes between farming communities and Fulani herdsmen over access to rural farm lands for cattle grazing; agitation for resource control

---

[87] Okunola, note 82.

[88] Ibid.

[89] See Philip C. Aka, "Understanding the Paradox of Civil Rule and Human Rights Violations under President Olusegun Obasanjo," *San Diego Int'l Law Journal*, 4(2003), 209.

[90] Philip C. Aka, "Bridging the Gap Between Theory and Practice in Humanitarian Action: Eight Steps to Humanitarian Wellness in Nigeria," *Willamette Journal of Int'l Law & Dispute Resolution*, 24 (Fall 2016), 1–50.

in the Niger Delta, fountainhead of the country's oil wealth; labor disputes of all types, resulting in closure of higher educational institutions for extended periods of time; and agitation for separate statehood outside Nigeria.[91] We classify these conflicts as acts of *political violence*, given that they embed some degree of force to achieve a political end, such as the replacement of a current regime with a supposedly better government that will subjectively improve the lives of the parties perpetrating the violence.[92] Because of these conflicts, compounded by effects of global warming like flooding, as of December 2020, the number of internally displaced persons (IDPs) in Nigeria stood at 2.7 million.[93] This number is one of the largest in Africa and hard-hit states include Adamawa, Bauchi, Benue, Borno, Gombe, Kaduna, Kano, Nasarawa, Plateau, Taraba, Yobe, and Zamfara.[94]

Living with violence or in fear of violence is a public health issue of utmost importance.[95] The health consequences of violence include increased incidences of posttraumatic stress disorder, anxiety, depression, suicide, cardiovascular disease risk, and premature mortality.[96] Besides the individuals directly affected, victims of political violence, some of whom become physically or mentally disabled, include witnesses of the acts of violence, family members, and the Nigerian society at large. In concert with members of the executive branch, Nigeria's National Assembly should use its oversight authority to help address the public health consequences of political violence through various means, including more funding for disability issues, and support for nonmilitary solutions for conflicts.

---

[91] Ibid.

[92] We define political violence as "hostile or aggressive acts motivated by a desire to affect change in the government." "Political Violence," *Your Dictionary*, https://www.yourdictionary.com/political-violence.

[93] "Nigeria," IDMC: Internal Displacement Monitoring Center, https://www.internal-displacement.org/countries/nigeria.

[94] "Nigeria IDP Figures Analysis," IDMC (September 13, 2016), http://www.internal-displacement.org/sub-saharan-africa/nigeria/figures-analysis (as of February 2016, the Office of the UN High Commissioner for Refugees put the number of IDPs at 2,241,484).

[95] Frederick Rivara, "The Effects of Violence on Health," *Health Affairs* (Millwood), 38(10) (October 2019), 1622–29, https://doi.org/10.1377/hlthaff.2019.00480.

[96] Ibid.

Promote Research and Development (R&D) Within the Healthcare System

Research and development (R&D) stands for the translation of an idea or discovery "into a product that addresses a health need," the ultimate aim being "a safe and effective product that is appropriate, affordable, acceptable, and accessible to those who need it most."[97] The logic underlying R&D is that "[i]n order for devices and tools to improve the lives of those who need them most, they must be affordable, accessible, and appropriate for the communities and settings in which they will be used."[98] Production and timely dissemination of R&D are the tools for measuring the level of innovation within a healthcare system. To meet the healthcare needs of the future, including ensuring that "the most effective health solutions" remain available when they are needed, a healthcare system worth its salt must "invest in [R & D]."[99]

Little wonder then that the African Union (AU), the OAU successor, recommends that African countries devote at least 1 percent of their GDP to R&D, a target only three countries, excluding Nigeria, so far have met.[100] Using its oversight mandate, the National Assembly should work in concert with the executive branch to meet this target. One of the avenues of this effort should be harmonization of traditional and allopathic medicines in the country, in an effort, at least initially, to eliminate or minimize some of the negative (side)effects of traditional medicine.

Tackle the Broader Issue of Infrastructure Deficit that Negatively Impacts the Healthcare System

Infrastructure are physical and organizational facilities necessary for the effective operation of a society and its economy that necessarily includes

---

[97] "Why Research and Development," GHTC: Global Health Technologies Coalition, https://www.ghtcoalition.org/why-research-and-development.

[98] Ibid.

[99] Ibid.

[100] See "New UIS Data for SDG 9.5 on Research and Development (R & D)," UNESCO (June 29, 2020), http://uis.unesco.org/en/news/new-uis-data-sdg-9-5-research-and-development-rd. For more on the AU, see "Profile: African Union," *BBC News* (August 24, 2017), https://www.bbc.com/news/world-africa-16910745.

hospitals, clinics, and related healthcare centers.[101] They are the touch-stone of a properly developed economy, necessary for improved health-care delivery.[102] Good infrastructure facilitates healthcare and well-equipped medical centers form part of the stock of a country's infra-structure. Such is the nature of the interlocking relationship between the two variables that today, proper equipment and supplies are a necessary part of every hospital or healthcare center. Given this interconnection, Nigeria has an infrastructure deficit dating back several decades,[103] that, if not fixed, its government will not get healthcare delivery right.

A proposal the national government published back in 2017 pointed to "deplorable infrastructure" as a main factor undermining economic performance in the country.[104] Nigeria's infrastructure problem is so encompassing it covers many aspects of life in the country all the way down to prison-correction facilities.[105] Nigeria needs about US$ 100 bil-

---

[101] See "Infrastructure," *Merriam-Webster*, https://www.merriam-webster.com/dictionary/infra-structure (portraying infrastructure as the "underlying structure" of a country's economy and the "fixed installations" necessary for its effective function). There is no universal element to these fixed installations but, broadly speaking, these facilities include streets, roads, highways, and railways; bridges; mass transit, airports, and airways, water supply and resources, waste management and waste water management, power generation and transmission, and information and communica-tion technologies (ICT) or telecommunications, and healthcare centers. See Julia Bello-Schüemann and Alex Porter, *Building the Future: Infrastructure in Nigeria Until 2040*, West Africa Report No. 21 (Pretoria, South Africa: Institute for Security Studies, November 2017), 3 ("Methodology") (dividing the term into four main categories: transportation, energy, water and sanitation, and information and communication technologies); Vivien Foster, and Nataliya Pushak, *Nigeria's Infrastructure: A Continental Perspective* (Washington, DC: World Bank Group, June 2011), 5, tbl. 1, https://doi.org/10.1596/1813-9450-5686 (identifying eight categories: air transport, informa-tion and communications technology (ICT), ports, power, railways, roads, water resources, as well as water and sanitation).

[102] See William Ascher, and Corinne Krupp, "Distributional Implications of Alternative Financing of Physical Infrastructure Development," in *Physical Infrastructure Development: Balancing the Growth, Equity, and Environmental Imperatives*, eds. William Ascher and Corinne Krupp (New York: Springer, 2010), 35–68 (portraying physical infrastructure as "the backbone of any developed economy and a pillar of quality of life").

[103] See generally Bello-Schüemann and Porter, note 101; and Foster and Pushak, note 101.

[104] Federal Republic of Nigeria, Economic Recovery and Growth Plan (Abuja, Nigeria: Ministry of Budget and Planning, February 2017–2020), 11, https://estateintel.com/wp-content/uploads/2017/03/Nigeria-Economic-Refom-Plan-2.pdf.

[105] See "Nigeria 2020 Human Rights Report," *U.S. Dept. of State* (March 30, 2021), 7, https://www.state.gov/wp-content/uploads/2021/03/NIGERIA-2020-HUMAN-RIGHTS-REPORT.pdf ("Prison and Detention Center Conditions") (pointing out that "[m]any of the 240 prisons [in the country] were 70 to 80 years old and lacked basic facilities," like "potable water, inadequate

lion every year to address its deficit in infrastructure.[106] "Addressing Nigeria's infrastructure challenges will require sustained expenditure of almost [US]$ 14.2 billion per year over [ten years] or about 12 percent of GDP," over and above the estimated US$ 5.9 billion [as of 2011] the country [...] spends."[107] In 2016, the country ranked 32 out of 54 countries in infrastructure development.[108] To put the matter in broader perspective, that year

> only 16 [percent] of Nigeria's roads [were] paved, compared on average to half the roads in the world's lower middle-income countries. Similarly, in 2016, only about 30 [percent] of Nigeria's population had access to improved sanitation facilities compared to, on average, more than half of the population in the country's global income peers. The situation for access to clean water and electricity is similar.[109]

Nigeria needs to pursue "access to basic physical infrastructure as a fundamental component of future economic and human development strategies in [the country]."[110] Fixing Nigeria's infrastructure problem will "catalyze progress across multiple other systems, in particular the economy, *health* and education."[111] Left to fester, the problem could get worse

---

sewage facilities," and were so overcrowded that one cell in Ikoyi Prison in Lagos State "held approximately 140 inmates despite a maximum capacity of 35").

[106] See "Nigeria Needs $100bn Annually to Address Infrastructural Deficit–Emefiele," *The Will* (September 25, 2021), https://thewillnigeria.com/news/nigeria-needs-100bn-annually-to-address-infrastructural-deficit-emefiele/ (quoting Godwin Emefiele, the country's Central Bank governor).

[107] Foster and Pushak, note 101, p. 1 ("Synopsis").

[108] Bello-Schüemann and Porter note 101, p. 7.

[109] Ibid., p. 2. Nigeria's African income peers were Cameroon, Cape Verde, Republic of the Congo, Ivory Coast, Djibouti, Egypt, Ghana, Kenya, Lesotho, Mauritania, Morocco, São Tomé and Príncipe, Sudan, Swaziland, Tunisia and Zambia. Ibid., p. 4 (tbl. 1). Its global income peers were Armenia, Bangladesh, Bhutan, Bolivia, Cambodia, El Salvador, Guatemala, Honduras, India, Indonesia, Kosovo, Kyrgyz, Laos, Federal States of Micronesia, Moldova, Mongolia, Myanmar, Nicaragua, Pakistan, Palestine, Papua New Guinea, Philippines, Samoa, Solomon Islands, Sri Lanka, Syria, Tajikistan, Timor-Leste, Tonga, Ukraine, Uzbekistan, Vanuatu, Vietnam, and Yemen. Ibid.

[110] Bello-Schüemann and Porter note 101, p. 3.

[111] Ibid. Emphasis added. See also Foster and Pushak, note 101, p. 1 ("Synopsis") (positing that "[r]aising [Nigeria's] infrastructure endowment to that of the region's middle-income countries could boost annual growth by around 4 percentage points").

by 2040.[112] The Nigerian government continues to lament the infrastructure deficit while doing little in practical terms to rectify it.[113]

A complicating factor is rapid population growth commented upon in Chap. 4.[114] Needless to say, Nigeria has not matched its rapid growth in population with a simultaneous increase in the delivery of social services, such as water supply, sewerage, and sanitation services,[115] much less healthcare products at the cynosure of this book. "Without drastic improvements in Nigeria's basic physical infrastructure, [rapid growth in population] will compound the existing deficit" in infrastructure.[116] Despite some progress over the past decades, levels of access to basic physical infrastructure such as clean water and improved sanitation, electricity and (paved) roads in Nigeria are inadequate, given its income levels, faced with rapid population growth, compared to peer middle-income countries in Africa and globally, who, on average, boast "more extensive and better road networks, and better access to electricity, clean water[,] and improved sanitation."[117]

Ultimately, if Nigeria is able to overcome its problem of deficit in infrastructure, and is more able to punch within its economic weight, it could improve healthcare and other social services and move closer to realizing its ambition of a major role in global affairs.[118] For, though the

---

[112] Bello-Schüemann and Porter note 101, p. 7 (predicting that on the current developmental trajectory, by 2040 Nigeria is expected to rank second to last among its peers of global lower middle-income countries).

[113] See Abdullahi Maikudi, "Nigeria Needs [US]$ 2.3trn To Bridge Infrastructural Deficit–Osinbajo," *The Will* (March 18, 2021), https://thewillnigeria.com/news/nigeria-needs-2-3trn-to--bridge-infrastructural-deficit-osinbajo/ (quoting Nigerian Vice President Yemi Osinbajo's statement to the effect that Nigeria requires the equivalent of US$ 2.3 trillion over the next 30 years to address its infrastructural deficit). According to this news story, the government held out partnership between the public and private sectors as the only viable way to close the gap because the government cannot do it alone. Ibid.

[114] See Chap. 4, notes 154–71, and accompanying texts.

[115] See Bello-Schüemann and Porter note 101, p. 2 ("Levels of access to basic infrastructure such as electricity, roads, clean water and improved sanitation facilities have not kept pace with rapid population growth in Nigeria").

[116] Ibid., p. 3.

[117] Ibid., p. 1. For the identity of these peer countries in Africa and globally, see note 109.

[118] Jakke Cilliers et al., *Power and Influence in Africa: Algeria, Egypt, Ethiopia, Nigeria, and South Africa*, Africa Futures Paper No. 14 (Pretoria, South Africa: Institute for Security Studies, March 2015), 1, https://issafrica.s3.amazonaws.com/site/uploads/AfricanFuturesNo14-V2.pdf. ("Summary") ("If Nigeria were able to take the necessary steps that would see far-reaching changes

challenges are, without question, substantial, they are not insurmountable, given the material and human capabilities of the country and possible payoff in economic growth.[119] In his address to the US Congress on April 28, 2021, President Biden included updated infrastructure among progressive programs that "propel us [Americans] into the future."[120] The same wisdom holds even more true for Nigeria.

In a nutshell, Nigeria is afflicted with a long pattern of underinvestment in many social welfare sectors even as the population grows by leaps and bounds that has been going on since the end of the destructive civil war in 1970. As representatives of their local communities, the legislators should lead on these matters, using their oversight responsibilities, beginning with sufficient outlay of budgetary allocations. To reverse the historical pattern of underinvestment in infrastructure, it does not hurt, if, like with the Abuja Declaration and R&D, the National Assembly sets for the country a target of say 5 percent of the GDP for infrastructural development. The money should cover maintenance of existing infrastructure, broadly defined to include government-owned hospitals and related healthcare centers.

Conclusion

This chapter explores the influence of politics in Nigeria's healthcare system in the measured manner, tied to legislative oversight, that influence is defined in this book. Its scrutiny of the period under the Fourth Republic since 1999 uncovered low-level awareness of healthcare issues among lawmakers, marked by passage of few, mostly unimplemented,

---

to the governance issues and social challenges that currently beset the country, it could become Africa's lone superpower").

[119] Foster and Pushak, note 101, p. 2 ("Synopsis").

[120] See "Analysis: Biden Pitches Big Government as Antidote to Crises," Associated Press (April 29, 2021), https://www.usnews.com/news/politics/articles/2021-04-28/analysis-biden-pitches-big-government-as-antidote-to-crises. The other items on Biden's list of programs, also instructive for Nigeria, were education, child care, and science. Ibid. See also Alicia Parlapiano, "Biden's $4 Trillion Economic Plan, In One Chart," *New York Times* (April 29, 2021), https://www.nytimes.com/2021/04/28/upshot/biden-families-plan-american-rescue-infrastructure.html.

laws. However, the situation appears to be changing for good and the chapter marshalled nine proposals designed to improve legislative oversight over healthcare. Highlights of the recommendations include attentiveness to the public health consequences of political violence, progress on research and development (R&D), and the need to tackle the country's infrastructure deficit in a more determined bid to reverse the culture of disinvestment in the health sector that predates the Fourth Republic.

6

Conclusion

Abstract This chapter recapitulates the central message of the book, revolved around the restructure of Nigeria's oil-based economy to generate better funding for healthcare delivery. It includes an introspective statement on the contributions of the book to comparative analysis, including comparative health studies, and comparative human rights studies.

Keywords Comparative analysis • Comparative healthcare studies • Comparative human rights studies

Healthcare and Economic Restructuring in Nigeria

Healthcare services in Nigeria are at a nadir. Few sectors of Nigeria's national life have been marked by neglect and underinvestment like healthcare. Over 60 years since independence from the UK, Nigeria is nowhere close to the evolution of a comprehensive national healthcare

© The Author(s), under exclusive license to Springer Nature Singapore Pte Ltd. 2022
P. C. Aka, J. A. Balogun, *Healthcare and Economic Restructuring*,
https://doi.org/10.1007/978-981-16-9543-8_6

system enjoined in 1978 by the international health community,[1] nor to its subsequent self-promise in 2014 of "ensur[ing] the most possible catchments for the health insurance scheme throughout the" country,[2] including provision of "emergency medical treatment for any reason" for the masses of Nigerian citizens.[3] As the business scholar Oren Harari once stated, "[t]he electric light did not come from the continuous improvement of candles."[4] Accordingly, to optimize healthcare services for its long-suffering citizens in the current installation of civilian rule known as the Fourth Republic, cosmetic changes around the margins will not do. Instead, Nigeria must embrace more thoroughgoing measures, such as restructuring its oil-based economy to generate better funding for healthcare, along the lines of the formulation in this book.

Healthcare delivery is an onerous but not impossible task. A well-functioning healthcare system is predicated on multiple, converging and complementary factors.[5] These factors include adequate funding built on a strong economy, able to address the underinvestment in healthcare that goes back a long time in Nigeria.[6] After over two decades of the Fourth Republic bestriding two centuries and 60 years of independent nationhood, Nigeria needs to take healthcare delivery to its teeming population more seriously, including adopting policies that ensure that population growth does not outpace healthcare services. The route to improve healthcare, as this book demonstrates, is through improvement of the economic sector, which is the main generator of funding for the healthcare system.

---

[1] Chapter 1, notes 67–68, and accompanying texts.

[2] National Health Act, Act No. 8, of 2014, Federal Republic of Nigeria Official Gazette, 145(101) (October 27, 2014), §40, https://www.ilo.org/dyn/natlex/docs/ELECTRONIC/104157/12694 7/F-693610255/NGA104157.pdf.

[3] Ibid., §20(1).

[4] Quoted in Alastair Masson, "Candles and Light: A 12-Month Retrospective in Technology Services Management," NTT Data, https://uk.nttdata.com/Insights/Blog/ Candles-and-Light-A-12-Month-Retrospective-in-Technology-Service-Management.

[5] Philip C. Aka, *Genetic Counseling and Preventing Medicine in Post-War Bosnia* (Gateway East, Singapore: Palgrave Macmillan, 2020), 46–8 (discussing four hallmarks of a good healthcare system indicated as good laws, good funding, healthcare as a human right rather than a privilege, and good politics).

[6] Olanrewaju Tejuoso et al., "Health and the Legislature: The Case of Nigeria," *Health Systems & Reform*, 4(2) (2018), 62–4, doi: 10.1080/23288604.2018.1441622 ("Next Steps: Growing the Economy to Strengthen Health Care").

Politics can play a supporting—and complementary—role via legislative oversight, comporting with democratic practices, that reduces wastes and ensures that saved monies are punctiliously applied to healthcare services. To accomplish the task of analysis marked out for them, concepts need to be robustly defined. Accordingly, Chap. 5 on the appropriate influence of politics in Nigerian healthcare reform elaborated a list of nine proposals to facilitate increased funding for healthcare through legislative oversight.

Introspection on the Theoretical Contributions of this Book

The comparative terminology in the subtitle of this book justifies these introspections.

Comparison is a tool of methodology[7] that researchers use "to relate the particularities of individual countries to broader trends and processes[,]"[8] in an ultimate attempt designed to learn best-practices from other cultures.[9] The technique of comparative analysis involves "studying and comparing which solutions [...] work best for certain types of problems, as well as observing patterns of failure across multiple

---

[7] For some scholars, the response to argument on methodology in comparative analysis is to let fools contest in that what gets the job of analysis done should suffice. See John Ohnesorge, "Administrative Law in East Asia: A Comparative-Historical Analysis," in *Comparative Administrative Law*, eds. Susan Rose-Ackerman and Peter L. Lindseth (Northampton, MA: Edward Elgar, 2010), 78 (stating that the goal of a research is served if the purpose of the project in question is made so clear that the readers can judge "for themselves what is gained from the comparison," specifically "whether the materials and the argument support the final conclusions," and if, for the researcher, the method used generates useful insights). But such nondeliberate(d) approach would not do for us here.

[8] Michael J. Sodaro, *Comparative Politics: A Global Introduction,* 3rd ed. (Boston, MA: McGraw-Hill, 2008), 27.

[9] See Karen Evans, "Comparative Successes or Failures? Some Methodological Issues in Conducting International Comparative Research Inpost—Secondary Education," *Education-Line.* Paper Presented at the British Educational Research Association Annual Conference, University of Sussex at Brighton (September 2–5 1999), http://www.leeds.ac.uk/educol/documents/00001309.htm (stating that "comparative studies are motivated by the need to borrow, advise, evaluate and the curiosity-motivated need to find out and describe practices from other cultures").

systems."[10] Comparative analysis enables a user of the tool to "identify and interrogate [the user's] own often unarticulated assumptions of the way" things really are.[11] This is because, as the English writer Rudyard Kipling (1865–1936) once famously stated, a person who knows only England knows not England well.[12] Similarly, studying other people's healthcare arrangements and experiences affords the examiner "multiple vantage points from which to gain a fresh perspective on strengths and weaknesses" of one's own healthcare system. Through the comparative method, the researcher "reaches conclusions about cause and effect through structured and systematic comparing and contrasting of cases" that would be hard to achieve otherwise.[13] Unlike physical and biological scientists, who "use laboratories to reproduce experiments in their search for scientific laws and factors," social scientists "cannot conduct such laboratory experiments in their search for generalizations about politics."[14] The closest to lab experiments these social scientists settle for is the comparative method.[15] "Through comparative studies, [these non-physical scientists] can compensate for the lack of laboratory experiments by comparing political experiences and phenomena in one setting with those in other settings."[16] In a nutshell, comparative analysis is some mind-travel abroad that "awakens us to the varieties of human experience and shows us that there are different ways of doing things than what we are used to in our own country[,]" such that "[i]n the end we come home with a greater sensitivity to both the positive and negative features of our

[10] Mary Ko Zimmerman, "Comparative Health-Care Systems," *Encyclopedia of Sociology* (updated February 10, 2020), https://www.encyclopedia.com/social-sciences/encyclopedias-almanacs-transcripts-and-maps/comparative-health-care-systems.

[11] Kate O'Regan, and Nick Friedman, "Equality," in *Comparative Constitutional Law*, eds. Tom Ginsburg and Rosalind Dixon (Northampton, MA: Edward Elgar Publishing, 2011), 473, 496 (analyzing the concept and practice of equality in comparative constitutional law, focusing on Canada, the UK, the Council of Europe, and South Africa).

[12] Rudyard Kipling, "The English Flag," *Bartleby* (1891), bartleby.com/364/122.html ("And what should they know of England who only England know?").

[13] Sodaro, note 8, p. 13.

[14] Frank L. Wilson, *Concepts and Issues in Comparative Politics: An Introduction to Comparative Analysis* (Upper Saddle River, NJ: Prentice Hall, 1996), 4.

[15] Ibid.

[16] Ibid.

homeland as well as an enhanced appreciation of why other people do things differently."[17]

Although social science research focuses on "what is and why," it may also legitimately delve into what should be in instances when agreed-upon criteria exist "for deciding what makes one thing better than another."[18] By its nature, this research combines the best of what is and what should be, *describing* healthcare reforms in Nigeria as it is now, focusing on the need to restructure the country's economy to better fund healthcare and remove the pattern of underinvestment in social programs in the country that goes back more than 60 years, while *prescriptively* incorporating suggestions on the ideal way forward. Two subfields of comparative analysis that, more or less, inform this study and to which subject areas, in turn, it contributes its findings on Nigeria are comparative healthcare studies, and comparative human rights studies.

Healthcare studies is inherently comparative. Primarily, healthcare is a socioeconomic and political issue in many countries across the world and the object of international concern.[19] Thus, as a (sub)field, comparative healthcare studies fosters full understanding of the dynamics of healthcare systems, including cross-country learning and cooperation capable of generating evidence-based information that will help policymakers to rationalize the structure and funding of their healthcare systems.[20] Studying other people's healthcare arrangements and experiences affords

[17] Sodaro, note 8, p. 28. Given these multiple benefits, as Amartya Sen most aptly observed, "[o]ne of the oddities in the contemporary world is [an] astonishing failure to make adequate use of policy lessons that can be drawn from the diversity of experiences that the heterogeneous world already provides." See Amartya Sen, "Universal Healthcare: The Affordable Dream," *Vanguard* (London) (January 6, 2015), https://www.theguardian.com/society/2015/jan/06/-sp-universal-healthcare-the-affordable-dream-amartya-sen.

[18] See Michael G. Maxfield and Earl R. Babbie, *Research Methods for Criminal Justice and Criminology, 7th Ed.* (Stamford, CT: Cengage Learning, 2015), 32–3 (commenting on social scientific theory). See also Jonathan E. Adler and Catherine Z. Elgin, eds., *Philosophical Inquiry: Classic and Contemporary Readings* (Indianapolis, IN: Hackett Publishing Co., Inc., 2007), 449 (contrasting empirical judgments based on description and moral judgments embedded in prescription); and James N. Danziger, *Understanding the Political World: A Comparative Introduction to Political Science,* 11th ed. (New York: Pearson, 2013), 5–7 (including description and prescription, along with an explanation of three types of political knowledge).

[19] See Marie L. Lassey et al., *Health Care Systems Around the World: Characteristics, Issues, Reforms* (New York: Pearson, 1996) (book's back cover).

[20] Aka, note 5, p. 109.

the examiner "multiple vantage points from which to gain a fresh perspective on strengths and weaknesses" of one's own healthcare system.[21]
Because many of the problems countries confront in delivering quality
healthcare to their citizens are similar, "[t]here are lessons to be learned
from comparing health-care systems internationally that can only aid in
addressing these problems."[22] Again, as the adage goes, truly knowing
England means knowing more than just England.[23] In the contemporary
period "[h]eightened interest in comparative healthcare studies—the
health reform experiences of other countries—coincided with the
national debates in the United States on healthcare in the early 1990s
under William J. Clinton."[24]

The WHO, a global health czar, appears to believe in the comparative
method and puts premium on comparative healthcare studies. In a statement on sustainable health financing that it adopted on May 25, 2005,
the World Health Assembly, a WHO agency, urged member states "to
share experiences on different methods of health financing, including the
development of social health-insurance schemes, and private, public, and
mixed schemes."[25] The same document also advised the WHO director-
general "to create sustainable and continuing mechanisms, including
regular international conferences [...], in order to facilitate the continuous *sharing of experiences and lessons* learnt on social health insurance."[26]
The World Bank believes similarly. Hence, then World Bank President
Kim advised that, in shooting for the "brighter future" of universal
healthcare, states should "not forget the lessons of the past[,]"[27] including
best practices from other countries.

---

[21] Zimmerman, note 10.

[22] Ibid. ("Review of Selected Health-Care Systems").

[23] Kipling, note 12.

[24] Aka, note 5, p. 110.

[25] WHA58.33, "Sustainable Health Financing, Universal Coverage, and Social Health Insurance," Doc. A58/20, 58th World Health Assembly (May 25, 2005),1(7), https://cdn.who.int/media/docs/default-source/health-financing/sustainable-health-financing-universal-coverage-and-social-health-insurance.pdf?sfvrsn=f8358323_3.

[26] Ibid., 2(3).

[27] Jim Yong Kim, Speech at Conference on Universal Health Coverage in Emerging Economies, Center for Strategic and International Studies, Washington, DC (January 14, 2014).

The comparative human rights subfield involves the study of human rights ideas and practices, including health as human right, in countries across the globe and intergovernmental organizations, such as the UN system,[28] in an attempt to minimize atrocities and impunities, including those bearing on health as human right. Contributions to the field are evident in the call for the adoption of a preventive approach to human rights by then UN Secretary-General Ban Ki-moon.[29] Such contributions also reached a high point in the appeal by Samantha Power and her colleagues for scholars and policymakers to move from inspiration to impact in the attempt to realize human rights in a world where human rights atrocities are galore, despite a flurry of domestic and international activities aimed at protecting and promoting these rights.[30] This work focused on Nigeria draws on these ideas of human rights, while making its own contribution to the field, including heeding the advice to "realiz[e] human rights" by "moving from inspiration to impact."[31]

---

[28] See generally Charles R. Beitz, *The Idea of Human Rights* (New York: Oxford University Press, 2009).

[29] See Rebecca M.M. Wallace and Olga Martin-Ortega, *International Law*, 7th ed. (London: Sweet & Maxwell, 2013), 319.

[30] See generally Samantha Power and Graham Allison, eds., *Realizing Human Rights: Moving from Inspiration to Impact* (New York: St. Martin's Press, 2000).

[31] Ibid.

References

Abang, Mercy. 2019. Nigeria's Medical Brain Drain: Healthcare Woes as Doctors Flee. *Al Jazeera News*, April 8. https://www.aljazeera.com/features/2019/4/8/nigerias-medical-brain-drain-healthcare-woes-as-doctors-flee.

Abdullah, Ali Arazeem. 2011. Trends and Challenges of Traditional Medicine in Africa. *African Journal of Traditional Complementary and Alternative Medicines* 8 (5 Suppl): 115–123.

Abimbola, Isaac O., Esther Ore Omosewo, and Johnson Enero Upahi. 2014. Assessment of Education Policy Thrust of the National Economic Empowerment and Development Strategy (NEEDS) in Nigeria. *Problems of Education in the 21st Century* 60: 23–45. https://uilspace.unilorin.edu.ng/bitstream/handle/20.500.12484/3590/23-45.Abimbola_Vol.60.pdf?sequence=1&isAllowed=y.

Adegboye, D., and T.M. Akande. 2017. The Role of National Health Act in Nigeria Health System Strengthening. *Savannah Journal of Medical Research and Practice* 6 (1). https://doi.org/10.4314/sjmrp.v6i1.1.

Adekile, Oluwakemi Mary. 2013. Compensating Victims of Personal Injuries in Tort: The Nigerian Experience in Fifty Years. *SSRN*. https://doi.org/10.2139/ssrn.3111539.

Adekoya, Femi. 2020. How Channelling of Infrastructure to Manufacturers Can Drive Productivity. *Vanguard* (Lagos), January 8. https://guardian.ng/

© The Author(s), under exclusive license to Springer Nature Singapore Pte Ltd. 2022
P. C. Aka, J. A. Balogun, *Healthcare and Economic Restructuring*,
https://doi.org/10.1007/978-981-16-9543-8

business-services/industry/how-channelling-of-infrastructure-to-manufacturers-can-drive-productivity/.

Adekunle, A.O., and E.O. Otolorin. 2000. Evaluation of the Nigerian Population Policy – Myth Or Reality? *African Journal of Medicine and Medical Sciences* 29 (3–4): 305–310.

Adetokunbo, Abiodun Moses, and Ochuwa Priscillia Edioye. 2020. Response of Economic Growth to the Dynamics of Service Sector in Nigeria. *Future Business Journal* 6 (27) https://fbj.springeropen.com/articles/10.1186/s43093-020-00018-9.

Adler, Jonathan E., and Catherine Z. Elgin, eds. 2007. *Philosophical Inquiry: Classic and Contemporary Readings*. Indianapolis, IN: Hackett Publishing Co., Inc.

Africa: The Struggle for Development. 1999. Pp. 1–10. In *Global Studies: Africa*, 8th ed., eds. R. C. Grote, E. L. Harvey, Jeffress H. Ramsay, F. Jeffress Ramsay, E. Jeffress Ramsay, and Wayne Edge. New York: McGraw-Hill.

Africa's New Number One. 2014. *Economist*, April 12. https://www.economist.com/leaders/2014/04/12/africas-new-number-one.

African Charter on the Rights and Welfare of the Child (ACRWC). 1999. OAU Doc. CAB/LEG/24.9/49. Entered into Force 1999. https://www.achpr.org/public/Document/file/English/achpr_instr_charterchild_eng.pdf.

African Charter on the Rights and Welfare of the Child. Health and Human Rights. https://www.who.int/hhr/African%20Child%20Charter.pdf.

Agbakoba Writes Senate, Proposes "Simple Way to Restructure Nigeria". 2020. *Elombah News*. Last Updated November 4. https://elombah.com/agbakoba-writes-senate-proposes-simple-way-to-restructure-nigeria/.

Agbakwuru, Johnbosco. 2020. Only [Six] States Viable, as Katsina Made N8bn but Got N136bn Federal Allocation. *Vanguard* (Lagos), July 27. https://www.vanguardngr.com/2020/07/only-6-states-viable-as-katsina-made-n8bn-but-got-n136bn-federal-allocation/.

Aka, Philip C. 2002a. The "Dividend of Democracy": Analyzing U.S. Support for Nigerian Democratization. *Boston College Third World Law Journal* 22 (2): 225–279.

———. 2002b. The Military, Globalization, and Human Rights in Africa. *New York Law School Journal of Human Rights* 18 (3): 362–438.

———. 2003. Nigeria Since 1999: Understanding the Paradox of Civil Rule and Human Rights Violations under President Olusegun Obasanjo. *San Diego Int'l Law Journal* 4 (1): 209–276.

———. 2004. Prospects for Igbo Human Rights in Nigeria in the New Century. *Howard Law Journal* 48 (1): 165–269.

———. 2016. Bridging the Gap Between Theory and Practice in Humanitarian Action: Eight Steps to Humanitarian Wellness in Nigeria. *Willamette Journal of International Law & Dispute Resolution* 24 (1): 1–51.

———. 2017a. Why Nigeria Needs Restructuring Now and How It Can Peacefully Do It. *Denver Journal of International Law & Policy* 46 (Winter): 123–157.

———. 2017b. *Human Rights in Nigeria's External Relations: Building the Record of a Moral Superpower.* Lanham, MD: Lexington Books.

———. 2018. The Senegambia Confederation in Historical Perspective. In *African Intellectuals and the State of the Continent: Essays in Honor of Professor Sulayman S. Nyang,* ed. Olayiwola Abegunrin and Sabella Abidde, 37–66. Newcastle upon Tyne, UK: Cambridge Scholars Publishing.

———. 2020. *Genetic Counseling and Preventive Medicine in Post-War Bosnia.* Gateway East, Singapore: Palgrave Macmillan.

Aka, Philip C., Ibrahim J. Gassama, A.B. Assensoh, and Hassan Wahab. 2017. Ghana's National Health Insurance Scheme (NHIS) and the Evolution of a Human Right to Healthcare in Africa. *Chicago-Kent Journal of International & Comparative Law* 17 (2): 1–65.

Ake, Claude. 1996. *Democracy and Development in Africa.* Washington, DC: Brookings Institution Press.

Akinola, Wale. 2020. Ex-Emir Sanusi Reveals Bombshell, Says Nigeria Will Go Bankrupt with Current Governance Structure. *Legit,* June 14. https://www.msn.com/en-xl/africa/nigeria/ex-emir-sanusi-reveals-bombshell-says-nigeria-will-go-bankrupt-with-current-governance-structure/ar-BB15sErb?li=BBJGzsi&srcref=rss&post_id=noID.

Akinpelu, Yusuf. 2019. Nigerian Senator Wants Number of Lawmakers Reduced by 70% to Save Cost. *Premium Times* (Abuja), October 3. https://www.premiumtimesng.com/news/headlines/355832-nigerian-senator-wants-number-of-lawmakers-reduced-by-70-to-save-cost.html.

———. 2021. Nigeria to Spend ₦7.8 Billion On Entitlements to Ex-Presidents, Deputies, Others in 2021. *Premium Times* (Abuja), January 22. https://www.premiumtimesng.com/news/headlines/437916-nigeria-to-spend-n7-8-billion-on-entitlements-to-ex-presidents-deputies-others-in-2021.html.

Akwagyiram, Alexis. 2019. Muhammadu Buhari: Nigeria's Converted Democrat Comes Back from the Brink. *Reuters,* February 26. https://www.reuters.com/article/us-nigeria-election-buhari-newsmaker/muhammadu-buhari-nigerias-converted-democrat-comes-back-from-the-brink-idUSKCN1QF2SN.

Alabi, Mojeed. 2019. Months to End of Vision 2020, Nigeria Mulls Another Development Plan. *Premium Times* (Abuja), November 24. https://www.premiumtimesng.com/news/top-news/365018-months-to-end-of-vision-2020-nigeria-mulls-another-development- plan.html.

Alexander, Thomas F. 2019. The Global Informal Economy: Large but On the Decline. *IMF Blog*, October 30. https://blogs.imf.org/2019/10/30/the-global-informal-economy-large-but-on-the-decline/.

Amelang, Sören. 2021. Reluctant Daimler Shifts Gear in Race to Sustainable Mobility. *Clean Energy Wire*, March 3. https://www.cleanenergywire.org/factsheets/reluctant-daimler-plans-radical-push-new-mobility-world.

American Academy of Osteopathy. Osteopathic Medical Education. https://www.academyofosteopathy.org/osteopathic-medical-education#:~:text=Unique%20Training%20for%20Osteopathic%20Physicians,body's%20nerves%2C%20muscles%20and%20bones.

Amuwo, Adekunle. 2008. Constructing the Democratic Developmental State in Africa: A Case Study of Nigeria, 1960–2007. Institute for Global Dialogue, Occasional Paper No. 59, http://www.jstor.com/stable/resrep07753.9.

Anna, Cara. 2020. As US Struggles, Africa's COVID-19 Response Is Praised. AP. September 22. https://apnews.com/article/virus-outbreak-ghana-africa-pandemics-donald-trump-0a31db50d816a463a6a29bf86463aaa9?campaign_id=9&emc=edit_nn_20210307&instance_id=27836&nl=the-morning&regi_id=124708682&segment_id=52986&te=1&user_id=3018d6faed4962db07930c7110d6aad4.

Aregbeshola, Bolaji. 2019. Health Care in Nigeria: Challenges and Recommendations. *Social Protection*, February 7. https://socialprotection.org/discover/blog/health-care-nigeria-challenges-and-recommendations.

Asakitikpi, Alex E. 2019. Healthcare Coverage and Affordability in Nigeria: An Alternative Model to Equitable Healthcare Delivery, June 3. Open-Access Peer-Reviewed Chapter. https://www.intechopen.com/books/universal-health-coverage/healthcare-coverage-and-affordability-in-nigeria-an-alternative-model-to-equitable-healthcare-delive. From *Universal Health Coverage*, ed. Aida Isabel Tavares. London, UK: IntechOpen. https://doi.org/10.5772/intechopen.85978.

Ascher, William, and Corinne Krupp. 2010. Distributional Implications of Alternative Financing of Physical Infrastructure Development. In *Physical Infrastructure Development: Balancing the Growth, Equity, and Environmental Imperatives*, ed. William Ascher and Corinne Krupp, 35–68. New York: Springer.

Aso Rock Clinic Gulps ₦9.17bn in Four Years. 2019. *Sahara Reporters*, January 7. http://saharareporters.com/2019/01/07/aso-rock-clinic-gulps-n917bn-four-years%E2%80%8B.

Assim, Usang Maria. 2020. Why the Child's Rights Act Still Doesn't Apply Throughout Nigeria. *The Conversation*, September 24. https://theconversation.com/why-the-childs-rights-act-still-doesnt-apply-throughout-nigeria-145345.

Associated Press. 2021. Analysis: Biden Pitches Big Government as Antidote to Crises, April 29. https://www.usnews.com/news/politics/articles/2021-04-28/analysis-biden-pitches-big-government-as-antidote-to-crises.

Ating, Nelly. 2020. Nigeria's Next-Generation Protest Movement. *Foreign Policy*, October 28. https://foreignpolicy.com/2020/10/28/nigerias-youth-protest-movement-end-sars/.

Ayoade, J.A.A. 2010. Nigeria: Positive Pessimism and Negative Optimism: A Valedictory Lecture. *Nigerian Voice*, September 17. http://www.thenigerianvoice.com/print/34992/1/nigeria-positive-pessimism-and-negative-optimism-a.html.

Azeez, Yusuf Abdul. 2015. Alternative Medicine in Nigeria: The Legal Framework, International Conference on Language, Literature, Culture, and Education, April 25–26. https://icsai.org/procarch/2icllce/2icllce-90.pdf.

Azikiwe, Nnamdi, 1904–1996. 2018. *Encyclopedia*. Updated June 11. https://www.encyclopedia.com/people/history/historians-miscellaneous-biographies/nnamdi-azikiwe.

Babalola, Dele. 2019. *The Political Economy of Federalism in Nigeria*. London: Palgrave Macmillan.

Balogun, Joseph A. 2020. *Healthcare Education in Nigeria: Evolution and Emerging Paradigms*. Abingdon, UK: Routledge.

Balogun, Joseph A., and Philip C. Aka. 2022, forthcoming. Strategic Reforms to Resuscitate the Nigerian Healthcare System. In *Nigeria in the Fourth Republic: Confronting the Contemporary Political, Economic and Social Dilemmas*, ed. E. Ike Udogu. Lanham, Boulder, New York, and London: Lexington Books.

Bambas, Alexandra, Juan Antonio Casas, Harold A. Drayton, and América Valdés, eds. 2000. *Health and Human Development in the New Global Economy: The Contributions and Perspectives of Civil Society in the Americas*. Geneva, Switzerland: World Health Organization.

Bambra, Clare, Debbie Fox, and Alex Scott-Samuel. 2005. Toward a Politics of Health. *Health Promotion Int'l* 20 (2): 187–193. https://doi.org/10.1093/heapro/dah608.

Barra, Mary T. Leadership Message. General Motors. https://www.gmsustainability.com/leadership-perspective/chief-executive-officer.html.

Beitz, Charles R. 2009. *The Idea of Human Rights.* New York: Oxford University Press.

Bello-Schüemann, Julia, and Alex Porter. 2017. *Building the Future: Infrastructure in Nigeria Until 2040.* West Africa Report No. 21. Pretoria, South Africa: Institute for Security Studies, November. https://issafrica.s3.amazonaws.com/site/uploads/war-21.pdf.

Biden Seeks to Make Half of the New U.S. Auto Fleet Electric by 2030. 2021. *Reuters*, August 5. https://www.reuters.com/business/autos-transportation/biden-set-target-50-evs-by-2030-industry-backs-goal-2021-08-05/.

Blakeman, Bradley A. 2020. States Are the Laboratories of Democracy. *The Hill*, May 7. https://thehill.com/opinion/judiciary/496524-states-are-the-laboratories-of-democracy.

Boudette, Neal E., and Coral Davenport. 2021. G.M. Will Sell Only Zero-Emission Vehicles by 2035. *New York Times*, January 28. https://www.nytimes.com/2021/01/28/business/gm-zero-emission-vehicles.html.

Brickland, Kevin, and Naomi Tajitsu. 2019. Toyota Speeds Up Electric Vehicle Schedule as Demand Heats Up. *Reuters*, June 6. https://www.reuters.com/article/us-toyota-electric/toyota-speeds-up-electric-vehicle-schedule-as-demand-heats-up-idUSKCN1T806X.

Brown, Ola. *Fixing Healthcare in Nigeria: A Guide to Some of the Key Policy Decisions That Will Provide Better Healthcare to All Nigerians.* 2018. Self-published. https://www.dropbox.com/s/g8a2m2n49wlavui/Fixing%20Nigeria%20(2).pdf?dl=0.

Bruno, Greg. 2008. Religion and Politics in Iran. Council on Foreign Relations, June 19. https://www.cfr.org/backgrounder/religion-and-politics-iran.

Buhari Sets Up Health Sector Reform Committee, Names Osinbajo Chairman. 2021. *Vanguard* (Lagos), September 6. https://www.vanguardngr.com/2021/09/buhari-sets-up-health-sector-reform-committee-names-osinbajo-chairman/.

Buhari's Medical Tourism in London. 2021. *Huhu Online*, March 31. Editorial. https://huhuonline.com/index.php/home-4/opinions/14460-editorial-buhari-s-medical-tourism-in-london.

Bunche, Ralph J. 1936. French and British Imperialism in West Africa. *The Journal of Negro History* 21 (1): 31–46.

Campbell, John. 2020a. Nigeria and the Nation-State. Council on Foreign Relations, November 16. https://www.cfr.org/teaching-notes/nigeria-and-nation-state.

———. 2020b. *Nigeria and the Nation-State: Rethinking Diplomacy with the Postcolonial World*. Lanham, MD: Roman & Littlefield.

Campbell, John, and Matthew T. Page. 2018. *Nigeria: What Everyone Needs to Know*. New York: Oxford University Press.

Campbell, John, and Robert I. Rotberg. 2021. The Giant of Africa Is Failing. *Foreign Affairs*, May 31.

Cennimo, David J. 2021. What Is COVID-19? *Medscape*. Updated January 4. https://www.medscape.com/answers/2500114-197401/what-is-covid-19.

Centers for Disease Control and Prevention [USA]. COVID-19: Frequently Asked Questions: Basics. https://www.cdc.gov/coronavirus/2019-ncov/faq.html.

Chambers, Whittaker. 1952. *Witness*. New York: Random House.

Chete, L.N., J.O. Adeoti, F.M. Adeyinka, and O. Ogundele. 2016–17. *Industrial Development and Growth in Nigeria: Lessons and Challenges*. Working Paper No. 8. Washington, DC: Brookings Institution.

Chidiebe, Runice C.W. 2017. Cancer Patients Paying with Their Blood in Nigeria. *The Cable*, August 22. https://www.thecable.ng/cancer-patients-paying-blood-nigeriathecountry'scancer.

Child's Rights Act, Act No. 26. 2003. https://www.refworld.org/pdfid/5568201f.4.pdf

Cilliers, Jakkie, Julia Schünemann, and Jonathan D. Moyer. 2015, March. *Power and Influence in Africa: Algeria, Egypt, Ethiopia, Nigeria, and South Africa*. Africa Futures Paper No. 14. Denver, CO: Institute for Security Studies. https://issafrica.s3.amazonaws.com/site/uploads/AfricanFutures No14-V2.pdf.

Clausen, Lily B. 2015. Taking on the Challenges of Health Care in Africa. *Stanford Business*, June 16. https://www.gsb.stanford.edu/insights/taking-challenges-health-care-africa.

Clinton, William J. 2000. Remarks to a Joint Session of the Nigerian National Assembly in Abuja, August 26. https://www.presidency.ucsb.edu/documents/remarks-joint-session-the-nigerian-national-assembly-abuja.

Coffey, Frank. 1998. *America on Wheels: The First 100 Years: 1896–1996*. Los Angeles, CA: General Publishing Group.

Colantuoni, Steve. Seven Reasons Why International Companies Should Consider Manufacturing in Costa Rica. The Central American Group. https://www.thecentralamericangroup.com/companies-should-consider-manufacturing-in-costa-rica/.

Constitution of the Federal Republic of Nigeria. 1999. http://www.nigeria-law.org/ConstitutionOfTheFederalRepublicOfNigeria.htm#StatesOfTheFederation.

Corruption in Nigeria: Patterns and Trends: Second Survey on Corruption as Experienced by the Population. 2019. Vienna, Switzerland: United Nations Office on Drugs and Crime. December. https://www.unodc.org/documents/data-and-analysis/statistics/corruption/nigeria/Corruption_in_Nigeria_2019_standard_res_11MB.pdf.

Corruption Rank | Africa. *Trading Economics.* https://tradingeconomics.com/country-list/corruption-rank?continent=Africa.

Cost and Impact of Corruption on Education and Health Sectors in Ghana. 2018. Accra, Ghana: Ghana Integrity Initiative (GII) Consortium.

Costa Rica. 2020. Index of Economic Freedom. https://www.heritage.org/index/country/costarica.

Could COVID Reduce Medical Travel from Nigeria? 2020. *International Medical Travel Journal,* October 2. https://www.imtj.com/news/could-covid-reduce-medical-travel-nigeria/.

Countries in the World by Population. 2020. *Worldometer.* https://www.worldometers.info/world-population/population-by-country/.

Countries with the Most Arable Land in the World. 2021. Beef2Live, February 28. https://beef2live.com/story-countries-arable-land-world-0-108929.

Country Background Note: Nigeria. 2019. London: UK Home Office. Updated December 5. https://assets.publishing.service.gov.uk/government/uploads/system/uploads/attachment_data/file/856368/Nigeria_-_Background_-_CPIN_-_v2.0__January_2020__gov.uk.pdf.

Country Comparison – Area. C.I.A. *World Factbook.* https://www.cia.gov/library/publications/the-world-factbook/rankorder/2147rank.html.

Country Policy and Information Note: Nigeria: Medical and Healthcare Issues. Version 2.0. 2018. London: UK Home Office. Updated August 28. https://www.justice.gov/eoir/page/file/1094261/download.

Country Policy and Information Note: Nigeria: Medical and Healthcare Issues. Version 3.0. 2020. London, UK: Home Office. January. https://assets.publishing.service.gov.uk/government/uploads/system/uploads/attachment_data/file/857358/NGA_-_Medicalissues_-_CPIN_-_v3.0.finalG.pdf.

Court Asks RMAFC to Fix Salaries for NASS Members in Line with Economic Realities. 2021. *Huhu Online*, June 4. https://huhuonline.com/index.php/home-4/huhuonline-more-news/14654-court-asks-rmafc-to-fix-salaries-for-nass-members-in-line-with-economic-realities.

Crossman, Ashley. 2019. Post-Industrial Society in Sociology. *Thoughtco*. Updated May 30. https://www.thoughtco.com/post-industrial-society-3026457.

Crowder, Michael. 1964. Indirect Rule: French and British Style in Africa. *Journal of the International African Institute* 34 (3): 197–205.

Crowe, Sybil E. 1981. *The Berlin West African Conference, 1884–1885*. New York: Longmans, Green. Originally Published in 1942.

Dangote Seeks 1 [Percent] Tax on Business Profits for Health Sector Funding. 2020. *The Will*, November 19. https://thewillnigeria.com/news/dangote-seeks-1-tax-on-business-profits-for-health-sector-funding/.

Danziger, John N. 2013. *Understanding the Political World: A Comparative Introduction to Political Science*. 11th ed. New York: Pearson.

Darnton, John. 1976. Nigeria Emphasizing Food Production. *New York Times*, June 27. https://www.nytimes.com/1976/06/27/archives/nigeria-emphasizing-food-production.html.

Darwin, John. 2011. Britain, the Commonwealth[,] and the End of Empire. *BBC*. Last Updated March 3. http://www.bbc.co.uk/history/british/modern/endofempire_overview_01.shtml.for-biden-car-charging-pledge.

Davenport, Coral. 2021. Biden, in a Push to Phase Out Gas Cars, Tightens Pollution Rules. *New York Times*, August 5, Updated August 9. https://www.nytimes.com/2021/08/05/climate/biden-tailpipe-emissions-electric-vehicles.html.

Deaton, Angus S., and Robert Tortora. 2015. People in Sub-Saharan Africa Rate Their Health and Healthcare Among the Lowest in the World. *Health Affairs* 34 (3): 3519–3527.

Department of Petroleum Resources. Petroleum Refineries and Petrochemicals. https://www.dpr.gov.ng/downstream/refinery/.

Detterman, Brook J. 2021, February 27. Biden Administration Rapidly Advances Climate Change Agenda. *National Law Review* XI (58). https://www.natlawreview.com/article/biden-administration-rapidly-advances-climate-change-agenda.

DiGiovanni, Eileen L., S. Schiowitz, and D.J. Dowling, eds. 2015. *An Osteopathic Approach to Diagnosis and Treatment*. 3rd ed. Philadelphia, PA: Lippincott Williams & Wilkins.

Disease Control and Prevention (Establishment) Act. 2018, November 12. Act No. 18. *Federal Republic of Nigeria Official Gazette* 145(105). http://extwprlegs1.fao.org/docs/pdf/nig195227.pdf.

Do We Need Unviable [Thirty-Two] States? Editorial Commentary. 2019. *Guardian* (Lagos), November 19. https://guardian.ng/opinion/do-we-need-unviable-32-states/.

Doctor of Osteopathic Medicine. *Medline Plus.* https://medlineplus.gov/ency/article/002020.htm.

Dowell, Earlene K.P. 2020. Health Care Still Largest U.S. Employer: Census Bureau's 2018 County Business Patterns Provides Data on Over 1,200 Industries. United States Census Bureau, October 14. https://www.census.gov/library/stories/2020/10/health-care-still-largest-united-states-employer.html.

Dutta, Arin, and Charles Hongoro. 2013. *Scaling Up National Health Insurance in Nigeria: Learning from Case Studies of India, Colombia, and Thailand.* Washington, DC: Futures Group, Health Policy Project. https://www.healthpolicyproject.com/pubs/96_NigeriaInsuranceFinal.pdf.

Dwyer, Katie. 2018. [Six] Critical Risks Facing the Pharmaceutical Industry. *Risk & Insurance*, June 29. https://riskandinsurance.com/6-critical-risks-facing-pharmaceuticals/.

Easton, David. 1965. *A Systems Analysis of Political Life.* Hoboken, NJ: John Wiley & Sons.

Ebatamehi, Sebastiane. Top 10 Countries with Improved Healthcare System in Africa 2020. 2020. *African Exponent*, February 26. https://www.africanexponent.com/post/7167-top-10-african-countries-with-best-healthcare-system-2020.

Ebi, Dave. 2019. Why Is Nigeria Called Giant of Africa. *Quora.* Updated March 20. https://www.quora.com/Why-is-Nigeria-called-giant-of-Africa.

ECA. 2019. The Great Debate Focuses on How to Fix Africa's Healthcare, February 12. https://uneca.org/stories/great-debate-focuses-how-fix-africa%E2%80%99s-healthcare.

Egunyomi, Ayobami. 2017. Fifty-Seven Years After: The Case for Restructuring Nigeria. Council on Foreign Relations. Posted November 8. https://www.cfr.org/blog/fifty-seven-years-after-case-restructuring-nigeria.

Ekwe-Ekwe, Herbert. 2012. The Igbo Genocide and Its Aftermath. *Pambazuka News*, February 21. https://www.pambazuka.org/human-security/igbo-genocide-and-its-aftermath.

Elders, M. Joycelyn. 2009. Health Care vs. Sick Care: A Significant Difference. United Methodist News Service, June 25. https://pnhp.org/news/health-care-vs-sick-care/.

Eneh, Onyenekenwa Cyprian. 2011. Nigeria's Vision 20:2020 – Issues, Challenges and Implications for Development Management. *Asian Journal of Rural Development* 1: 21–40. https://doi.org/10.3923/ajrd.2011.21.40.

Eneh, Onyenekenwa. 2020. Big Dreams and Grand Ambitions: Nigeria's Vision 2020 – How Far? *The Republic*, February/March. https://republic.com.ng/february-march-2020/big-dreams-and-grand-ambitions-nigeria-vision-2020/.

Evans, Karen. 1999. Comparative Successes Or Failures? Some Methodological Issues in Conducting International Comparative Research Inpost – Secondary Education. Education-Line. Paper Presented at the British Educational Research Association Annual Conference, University of Sussex at Brighton, September 2–5. http://www.leeds.ac.uk/educol/documents/00001309.htm.

Ewepu, Gabriel. 2019. Nigeria: 2020 Budget – Only [Four] States Are Viable in Nigeria – Report. *Guardian* (Lagos), October 23. https://allafrica.com/stories/201910240037.html.

Ewing, Jack. 2021. Auto Dinosaurs Show They're Not Dead Yet. *New York Times*, February 18. https://www.nytimes.com/2021/02/18/business/daimler-earnings-electric-vehicles.html.

Expat Guide to Health Care in Ghana. AETNA. https://www.aetnainternational.com/en/individuals/destination-guides/expat-guide-to-health-care-in-ghana.html.

Falola, Toyin. 2021. *Understanding Modern Nigeria: Ethnicity, Democracy, and Development*. New York: Cambridge University Press.

Farley, Alan. 2020. What Does "Guns and Butter" Refer To? *Investopedia*. Updated February 11. https://www.investopedia.com/ask/answers/08/guns-butter.asp.

Fayehun, Funke, and Uche Charlie Isiugo-Abanihe. 2020. EndSARS: How Nigeria Can Tap Into Its Youthful Population. *The Conversation*, October 25. https://theconversation.com/endsars-how-nigeria-can-tap-into-its-youthful-population-148319.

Federal Republic of Nigeria. 2017–2020. *Economic Recovery and Growth Plan*. Abuja, Nigeria: Ministry of Budget and Planning. February. https://estateintel.com/wp-content/uploads/2017/03/Nigeria-Economic-Refom-Plan-2.pdf.

Felter, Claire. 2021. How Dangerous Are New COVID-19 Strains? Council on Foreign Relations, January 7. https://www.cfr.org/in-brief/how-dangerous-are-new-covid-19-strains?gclid=Cj0KCQiA1KiBBhCcARIsAPWqoSqLu ooY_obXNC_aRxXuELh5kVnMYG8xr-NpA1rHgIvtD8sP0qVZ HqwaAnzjEALw_wcB.

FG Approves [US] $1.5bn for Rehabilitation of Port Harcourt Refinery. 2021. *Huhu Online*, March 18. https://huhuonline.com/index.php/home-4/ huhuonline-more-news/14431-fg-approves-1-5bn-for-rehabilitation-of-port-harcourt-refinery.

Field, Graham. 2020. Nigerian National Petroleum Corporation. *Encyclopedia.* Updated November 21. https://www.encyclopedia.com/social-sciences-and-law/economics-business-and-labor/businesses-and-occupations/ nigerian-national-petroleum-corp.

Findlay, Justin. 2019. Presidents and Military Leaders of Nigeria Since Independence. *World Atlas*, August 1. https://www.worldatlas.com/articles/ nigerian-presidents-and-military-leaders-since-independence.html.

Five Things About Nigeria: The Superpower with No Power. 2019. *BBC News*, February 4. https://www.bbc.com/news/world-africa-47217557.

Forbes Africa. 2017. Nigeria Needs Industrialization Now, May 1. https://www. forbesafrica.com/investment-guide/2017/05/01/nigeria-needs-industrialization-now/.

Fosco, Molly. 2018. Doctor Drain: An Exodus from Nigeria Threatens Its Healthcare System. *Ozy*. https://www.ozy.com/around-the-world/doctor-drain-an-exodus-from-nigeria-threatens-its-health-care-system/87072/.

Foster, Vivien, and Nataliya Pushak. 2011. *Nigeria's Infrastructure: A Continental Perspective*. Washington, DC: World Bank Group. https://doi.org/10.159 6/1813-9450-5686.

Frank, Etim O., and Wilfred I. Ukpere. 2012. The Impact of Military Rule on Democracy in Nigeria. *Journal of Social Sciences* 33 (3): 285–292. https:// www.researchgate.net/publication/261672856_The_Impact_of_Military_ Rule_on_Democracy_in_Nigeria.

Freeman, Jody. 2021. G.M.'s Bold Move on the Climate: The End of the Gasoline-Powered Car Will Transform the Economy. Opinion. *New York Times*, February 2.

Frynas, Jedrzej Georg. 2000. *Oil in Nigeria: Conflict and Litigation Between Oil Companies and Village Communities*. Münster-Hamburg-Berlin-Wi, Germany: Lit Verlag.

Full List: Portfolios of Buhari's 44 Ministers—2019–2023. 2019. *Premium Times* (Abuja), August 21. https://www.premiumtimesng.com/news/headlines/347816-full-list-portfolios-of-buharis-44-ministers-2019-2023.html.

Gaffey, Conor. 2017. Nigeria's President Buhari Didn't Get the Memo About Health Tourism. *Newsweek*, August 25. http://www.newsweek.com/nigeria-president-muhammadu-buhari-health-tourism-655006.

Gathara, Patrick. 2021. Charity Alone Will Not End the Calamity of COVID-19 in Africa. *Al Jazeera*, July 31. https://www.aljazeera.com/opinions/2021/7/31/accountability-is-africas-best-route-out-of-the-pandemic.

Gavin, Michelle. 2019. The Post-Presidential Legacy of Nigeria's Goodluck Jonathan. Council on Foreign Relations, July 16. https://www.cfr.org/blog/post-presidential-legacy-nigerias-goodluck-jonathan.

GDP—Composition, by Sector of Origin—Agriculture (%) 2020 Country Ranks, by Rank. *Countries of the World*. https://photius.com/rankings/2020/economy/gdp_composition_by_sector_of_origin_agriculture_2020_0.html.

GDP—Composition, by Sector of Origin—Industry (%) 2020 Country Ranks, by Rank. *Countries of the World*. https://photius.com/rankings/2020/economy/gdp_composition_by_sector_of_origin_industry_2020_0.html.

GDP—Composition, by Sector of Origin—Services (%) 2020 Country Ranks, by Rank. *Countries of the World*. https://photius.com/rankings/2020/economy/gdp_composition_by_sector_of_origin_services_2020_0.html.

GDP—Per Capita (PPP). 2020 Country Ranks, by Rank. *Countries of the World*. https://photius.com/rankings/2020/economy/gdp_per_capita_2020_0.html.

GDP—Purchasing Power Parity. 2020. Country Ranks, by Rank. *Countries of the World*. https://photius.com/rankings/2020/economy/gdp_purchasing_power_parity_2020_0.html.

General Motors, American Company. 2021. *Encyclopedia Britannica*. Last Updated January 24. https://www.theguardian.com/business/2009/apr/30/general-motors-gm-history.

General Motors, the Largest U.S. Automaker, Plans to be Carbon Neutral by 2040. 2021. GM Media, January 28. https://media.gm.com/media/us/en/gm/home.detail.html/content/Pages/news/us/en/2021/jan/0128-carbon.html#:~:text=To%20address%20emissions%20from%20its,company's%20previously%20announced%20global%20goal.

Gibraltar Population (Live). *Worldometer*. https://www.worldometers.info/world-population/gibraltar-population/.

Gimba, Haruna. 2016. Nigeria Lost $[US]1 b[illion] to Medical Tourism. *Health Reporter*, April 27. http://healthreporters.info/2016/04/27/nigeria-lost-1b-to-medical-tourism-buhari/.

Global Action Plan for the Prevention and Control of Noncommunicable Diseases 2013–2020. 2013. Geneva, Switzerland: World Health Organization.

Global Conflict Tracker. 2021. Council on Foreign Relations. Last Updated September 1. https://www.cfr.org/global-conflict-tracker/conflict/boko-haram-nigeria.

Global Health Workforce Alliance. Nigeria. https://www.who.int/workforcealliance/countries/nga/en/.

Global Health—Nigeria. Centers for Disease Control and Prevention. https://www.cdc.gov/globalhealth/countries/nigeria/default.htm.

Godbless, Deedam Dorka, Akpe Churchill Ikechukwu, and Juliana Ozimonu Emeto, Nigeria Development Plans and Its Challenges: The Way Forward. 2019. *Int'l Journal of Advanced Academic Research of Social & Management Science* 5(12), 1–12. December. https://www.ijaar.org/articles/Volume5-Number12/Social-Management-Sciences/ijaar-sms-v5n9-sep19-p24.pdf.

Gregory, Derek. 2009. Grand Theory. In *The Dictionary of Human Geography*, ed. Derek Gregory, Ron Johnston, Geraldine Pratt, Michael J. Watts, and Sarah Whatmore, 5th ed., 315–316. London: Wiley-Blackwell Publishing.

Hannon, Elliot. 2021. General Motors Says It Will Stop Making Gas-Powered Vehicles. *Slate*, January 29. https://slate.com/news-and-politics/2021/01/general-motors-gm-zero-emission-gas-powered-vehicles.html#:~:text=General%20Motors%20announced%20Thursday%20that,for%20producing%20gas%2Dguzzling%20SUVs.

Harry, S. Truman. 2009. *Independent* (London), January 20. https://www.independent.co.uk/news/presidents/harry-s-truman-1451147.html.

Hayes, Adam, and Michael Boyle. 2021. Adam Smith and "The Wealth of Nations." *Investopedia*. Updated April 28. https://www.investopedia.com/updates/adam-smith-wealth-of-nations/.

Health. 1991. In *Nigeria: A Country Study*, ed. Helen Chapin Metz. Washington, DC: GPO for the Library of Congress.

Helium Health. About Us. https://heliumhealth.com/about.html.

Hirsch, Jerry. 2021. GM Is Again the World's Largest Automaker. *Los Angeles Times*, January 20. https://www.latimes.com/business/la-xpm-2012-jan-20-la-fi-autos-gm-sales-20120120-story.html.

History. 1991. In *Nigeria: A Country Study*, ed. Helen Chapin Metz. Washington, DC: GPO for the Library of Congress.

History of Health Insurance in Nigeria. Health Insurance. https://www.ehealth-insurance.com.ng/history-of-health-insurance-in-nigeria/#:~:text=Health%20insurance%20in%20Nigeria%20has,NHIS)%20Act%2035%20of%201999.&text=The%20Nigerian%20healthcare%20system%20is,and%20public%20managed%20medical%20facilities.

HIV/AIDS: The Basics. 2020. National Institutes of Health. Last Viewed September 24. https://hivinfo.nih.gov/understanding-hiv/fact-sheets/hivaids-basics#:~:text=HIV%20stands%20for%20human%20immuno deficiency,stands%20for%20acquired%20immunodeficiency%20syndrome.

Hoffman, Jan. 2019. Johnson & Johnson Ordered to Pay $572 Million in Landmark Opioid Trial. *New York Times*, August 26, Updated August 30. https://www.nytimes.com/2019/08/26/health/oklahoma-opioids-johnson-and-johnson.html.

Holy Bible, New International Version.

Nigeria Maternal Mortality Rate 2000–2020. *Macro Trends*. https://www.macrotrends.net/countries/NGA/nigeria/maternal-mortality-rate.

Huber, B. Rose. 2015. Sub-Saharan Africans Rate Their Health and Health Care Among the Lowest in the World. Woodrow Wilson School of Public & Int'l Affairs, Princeton University, February 25.

Human Rights Day 10 December. United Nations. https://www.un.org/en/observances/human-rights-day#:~:text=2020%20Theme%3A%20Recover%20Better%20%2D%20Stand,are%20central%20to%20recovery%20efforts.

Husted, Thomas F., and Lauren Ploch Blanchard. 2020. *Nigeria: Current Issues and U.S. Policy.* Congressional Research Service, RL 33964, September 18. https://fas.org/sgp/crs/row/RL33964.pdf.

IDMC: Internal Displacement Monitoring Center. Nigeria. https://www.internal-displacement.org/countries/nigeria.

Igwe, Charles. 2015. How Nollywood Became the Second[-]Largest Film Industry. British Council, November 6. https://www.britishcouncil.org/voices-magazine/nollywood-second-largest-film-industry#:~:text=The%20term%20'Nollywood'%20was%20coined,and%20Bollywood%20in%20India's%20Bombay.

Iheanacho, E.N. 2014. National Development Planning in Nigeria: An Endless Search for Appropriate Development Strategy. *International Journal of Economic Development, Research & Investment* 5 (2): 49–60. https://www.academia.edu/36260016/National_Development_Planning_in_Nigeria_An_Endless_Search_for_Appropriate_Development_Strategy.

India Has Become a Popular Hub of Medical Tourism. 2018. FreshersLive. Updated July 24. https://www.fresherslive.com/current-affairs/articles/india-has-become-a-popular-hub-of-medical-tourism-14449.

Infrastructure. *Merriam-Webster*. https://www.merriam-webster.com/dictionary/infrastructure.

International Covenant on Economic, Social and Cultural Rights. 1966. General Assembly Resolution 2200A (XXI). Adopted and Opened for Signature, Ratification, and Accession December 16. Entry into Force January 3, 1976.

Iraq Profile—Timeline. 2018. *BBC News*, October 3. https://www.bbc.com/news/world-middle-east-14546763.

Is There a Role for Trado-Medicine in the Nigerian Health Sector? 2018. *Nigeria Health Watch*, October 4. https://nigeriahealthwatch.medium.com/is-there-a-role-for-trado-medicine-in-the-nigerian-health-sector-d824d13a47e8.

Ityavyar, Dennis A. 1987. The State, Class[,] and Health Services in Nigeria. *Africa Spectrum* 22 (3): 285–314. https://www.jstor.org/stable/40174297.

Iyamu, Ewemade, and Joy Ibhade Ojeaga. 2015. National Economic Empowerment Development Strategy (NEEDS) as a Panacea for Employment Creation and Self[-] Employment and Self[-]Relian[ce]. *Journal of Educational and Social Research* 5 (2): 61–68. https://doi.org/10.5901/jesr.2015.v5n2p61.

Jackson, Robert H., and Carl G. Rosberg. 1982. Why Africa's Weak States Persist: The Empirical and the Juridical in Statehood. *World Politics* 35 (1): 1–24. http://www.jstor.org/stable/2010277.

Joseph, Richard A. 1983. Class, State, and Prebendal Politics in Nigeria. *The Journal of Commonwealth & Comparative Politics* 21 (3): 21–38. https://doi.org/10.1080/14662048308447434.

Kaiser, Frederick M. 2001. *Congressional Oversight*. CRS Report for Congress, 97-936 GOV. Updated January 2. http://156.33.195.33/artandhistory/history/resources/pdf/CRS.Oversight.pdf.

Kalama, John, Charity E. Etebu, Charles A. Martha, and Sophia M. John. 2012. Legislator's Jumbo Pay, Cost of Governance and the State of Education in Nigeria: Issues and Contradictions. *Journal of Educational & Social Research* 4 (2): 73–77. https://citeseerx.ist.psu.edu/viewdoc/download?doi=10.1.1.665.5079&rep=rep1&type=pdf.

Kangoye, Thierry. 2013. Does Aid Unpredictability Weaken Governance?: Evidence from Developing Countries. *Developing Economies* 51 (2): 121–144.

Kazeem, Yomi. 2015a. Nigeria's Legislators Will Get [US] $43 Million of Taxpayers' Money for a Wardrobe Allowance. *Quartz Africa*, June 16. https://qz.com/africa/429470/nigerias-legislators-will-get-43-million-of-taxpayers-money-for-a-wardrobe-allowance/.

———. 2015b. Nigeria Has Some of the World's Highest Paid Lawmakers and This Start-Up Wants to Slash Their Pay. *Quartz Africa*, June 4. https://qz.com/africa/417192/nigeria-has-some-of-the-worlds-highest-paid-lawmakers-and-this-start-up-is-trying-to-slash-their-pay.

Kenton, Will. 2019. Political Economy. *Investopedia*. Updated August 4. https://www.investopedia.com/terms/p/political-economy.asp.

Kerry, Marie-Paule, and Matshidiso Moeti. 2016. Foreword. In *Public Financing for Heath in Africa: From Abuja to the SDGs*, 5. Geneva, Switzerland: World Health Organization. https://www.afro.who.int/sites/default/files/2017-06/WHO-HIS-HGF-Tech.Report-16.2-eng.pdf.

Kim, Jim Yong. 2014. Speech at Conference on Universal Health Coverage in Emerging Economies, Center for Strategic and International Studies. Washington, DC, January 14.

Kipling, Rudyard. 1891. The English Flag. *Bartleby*. http://www.bartleby.com/364/122.html.

Kirk-Greene, A.H.M. 1971. *Crisis and Conflict in Nigeria: A Documentary Sourcebook, Vol, 1*. London: Oxford University Press.

Klieman, Kairn A. 2012. U.S. Oil Companies, the Nigerian Civil War, and the Origins of Opacity in the Nigerian Oil Industry. *Journal of American History* 99 (1): 155–158. https://doi.org/10.1093/jahist/jas072.

Koce, Francis, Gurch Randhawal, and Bertha Ochieng. 2019. Understanding Healthcare Self-Referral in Nigeria from the Service Users' Perspective: A Qualitative Study of Niger State. *BMC Health Services Research* 19 (209): 1–14. https://doi.org/10.1186/s12913-019-4046-9.

Kollewe, Julia. The History of General Motors. *Vanguard* (London). https://www.theguardian.com/business/2009/apr/30/general-motors-gm-history.

Labor Force—By Occupation—Agriculture (%). 2020. Country Ranks, by Rank. *Countries of the World*. https://photius.com/rankings/2020/economy/labor_force_by_occupation_agriculture_2020_0.html.

Labor Force—By Occupation—Industry (%). 2020 Country Ranks, by Rank. *Countries of the World*. https://photius.com/rankings/2020/economy/labor_force_by_occupation_industry_2020_0.html.

Labor Force—By Occupation—Service (%). 2020 Country Ranks, by Rank. *Countries of the World*. https://photius.com/rankings/2020/economy/labor_force_by_occupation_services_2020_0.html.

Lassey, Marie L., William R. Lassey, and Mark J. Jinks. 1996. *Health Care Systems Around the World: Characteristics, Issues, Reforms.* New York: Pearson.

Lasswell, Harold D. 1990. *Politics: Who Gets What, When and How.* Manhattan, NY: Peter Smith Pub. Inc.

Lawal, Nurudeen. 2019. What Nigeria's President, Vice President, State Governors and Their Deputies Earn as Salaries, Allowances. *Legit.* September 21. https://www.legit.ng/1253507-what-nigerias-president-vice-president-state-governors-deputies-earn-salaries-allowances.htmlhttps://www.legit.ng/1253507-what-nigerias-president-vice-president-state-governors-deputies-earn-salaries-allowances.html.

Lee, Steven, and Dean Scott. 2021. Long Road, Tough Choices Ahead for Biden Car-Charging Pledge. *Bloomberg Law,* February 22. https://news.bloomberglaw.com/environment-and-energy/long-road-tough-choices-ahead-for-biden-car-charging-pledge.

Legislature. *Encyclopedia Britannica.* https://www.britannica.com/topic/legislature.

Leonhardt, David. 2020. The Morning: The Transition Begins. *New York Times,* November 24.

Lessons from COVID-19: Building a Stronger Global Health System. 2020. *Foreign Policy,* May 26. https://foreignpolicy.com/events/fp-virtual-dialogue-lessons-from-covid-19/.

Lewis, A. Olufemi. 1977. Nigeria's Third National Development Plan, 1975–80: An Appraisal of Objectives and Policy Frame. *The Developing Economies* 15 (1): 60–79. https://onlinelibrary.wiley.com/doi/abs/10.1111/j.1746-1049.1977.tb00370.x.

Liechtenstein Population (Live). *Worldometer.* https://www.worldometers.info/world-population/liechtenstein-population/.

Longley, Robert. 2020. What Is Federalism? Definition and How It Works in the US. *Thoughtco.* Updated August 2. https://www.thoughtco.com/federalism-powers-national-and-state-governments-3321841#:~:text=In%20the%20case%20of%20the,and%20the%20individual%20state%20governments.

Look, Anne. 2012. Nigerian President's Call for Birth Control Sparks Debate. *VOA News,* June 28. https://www.voanews.com/africa/nigerian-presidents-call-birth-control-sparks-debate.

Machung, Saminu. 2016. How LifeBank is Solving the Problem of Blood Scarcity – One Hospital at a Time. The Cable Lifestyle, November 9. https://lifestyle.thecable.ng/lifebank-solving-problem-blood-scarcity-one-hospital-time/.

Maikudi, Abdullahi. 2021. Nigeria Needs [US] $2.3trn To Bridge Infrastructural Deficit–Osinbajo. *The Will*, March 18. https://thewillnigeria.com/news/ nigeria-needs-2-3trn-to-bridge-infrastructural-deficit-osinbajo/.

Main Causes of Death and Disability in Nigeria in 2017. *Statista*. https://www. statista.com/statistics/1122916/main-causes-of-death-and-disability-in-nigeria/.

Maio, Alyssa. 2019. What Is Nollywood and How Did It Become the [Second]-Largest Film Industry. *Studio Binder*, December 5. https://www.studiobinder. com/blog/what-is-nollywood/.

Manufacturing and Production Industries. Costa Rica Information. http:// costarica-information.com/about-costa-rica/economy/economic-sectors-industries/manufacturing.

Marvasti, Farshad Fani, and Randall S. Stafford. 2012. From "Sick Care" to Health Care: Reengineering Prevention into the U.S. System. *New England Journal of Medicine* 367 (10): 889–891. https://doi.org/10.1056/ NEJMp1206230.

Marx, Karl, and Friedrich Engels. 1998. *The German Ideology, Including Theses on Feuerbach*. Amherst, NY: Prometheus.

Masson, Alastair. Candles and Light: A 12-Month Retrospective in Technology Services Management. NTT Data. https://uk.nttdata.com/Insights/Blog/ Candles-and-Light-A-12-Month-Retrospective-in-Technology-Service-Management.

Maxfield, Michael G., and Earl R. Babbie. 2015. *Research Methods for Criminal Justice and Criminology*. 7th ed. Stamford, CT: Cengage Learning.

Mbamalu, Socrates. 2019. Nigeria Has a Mental Health Problem. *Al Jazeera*, October 2. https://www.aljazeera.com/economy/2019/10/2/nigeria-has-a-mental-health-problem.

Merelli, Annalisa. 2019. No Benevolent Dictators: 150 Years of Data Proves It: Strongmen are Bad for the Economy. *Quartz*, August 19. https://qz. com/1688397/data-proves-it-authoritarian-leaders-are-bad-for-the-economy/.

Milakovich, Michael E., and George Gordon. 2009. *Public Administration in America*. 10th ed. Belmont, CA: Wadsworth Publishing.

Miller, Stuart Creighton. 1982. *Benevolent Assimilation: The American Conquest of the Philippines, 1899–1903*. New Haven, CT: Yale University Press.

Mills, C. Wright. 1959. *The Sociological Imagination*. New York: Oxford University Press.

Mobarak, Ahmed Mushfiq, and Rifaiyat Mahbub. 2020. What the US Can Learn from How African Countries Handled COVID. *CNN*, November 3. https://www.cnn.com/2020/11/03/africa/africa-coronavirus-lessons-opinion-intl/index.html.

Mohammed, Aisha. 2020. A Case Study of the Pro[b]lematic Nature of Development Plan[ning] in Nigeria. Asabe Shehu Yar'Adua Foundation, February 15. https://unfccc.int/sites/default/files/resource/The%20Problems%20of%20Development%20Planning%20in%20Nigeria.pdf.

Monye, Judith, and Oyintare Abang. 2020. Taxing the Informal Sector – Nigeria's Missing Goldmine. Bloomberg Tax, October 15. https://news.bloombergtax.com/daily-tax-report-international/taxing-the-informal-sector-nigerias-missing-goldmine.

Moore, Travis. Dillon Rule and Home Rule: Principles of Local Governance. LRO Snapshot (Nebraska Legislature). https://nebraskalegislature.gov/pdf/reports/research/snapshot_localgov_2020.pdf.

More About Sacred Heart Hospital[,] Lantoro. Sacred Heart Hospital, Lantoro, Abeokuta. https://www.sacredhearthospitallantoro.org/about.php.

Mothibe, Mmamosheledi E., and Mncengeli Sibanda. 2019. *African Traditional Medicine: South African Perspective*. London: IntechOpen. https://www.intechopen.com/books/traditional-and-complementary-medicine/african-traditional-medicine-south-african-perspective.

Muanya, Chukwuma. 2020. Why 15 [Percent] Budget Allocation to Health Is Tall Order, by FG. *Guardian* (Lagos), October 26. https://guardian.ng/features/why-15-budget-allocation-to-health-is-tall-order-by-fg.

Muanya, Chukwuma, and Adaku Onyenucheya. 2021. Bridging Doctor-Patient Ratio Gap to Boost Access to Healthcare Delivery in Nigeria. *Guardian* (Lagos), February 4. https://guardian.ng/features/health/bridging-doctor-patient-ratio-gap-to-boost-access-to-healthcare-delivery-in-nigeria/.

Naidoo, Prinesha. 2020. Nigeria Tops South Africa as the Continent's Biggest Economy. *Bloomberg*, March 3. Updated March 4. https://www.bloomberg.com/news/articles/2020-03-03/nigeria-now-tops-south-africa-as-the-continent-s-biggest-economy.

National Health Act. 2014. Act No. 8. Federal Republic of Nigeria Official Gazette. 145(101), October 27. https://www.ilo.org/dyn/natlex/docs/ELECTRONIC/104157/126947/F-693610255/NGA104157.pdf.

National Health Insurance Scheme No. 35. 1999. http://www.nigeria-law.org/National%20Health%20Insurance%20Scheme%20Decr....

National Health Insurance Scheme: Operational Guidelines. 2012. Revised October.

National Parliaments: Nigeria. Library of Congress. https://www.loc.gov/law/help/national-parliaments/nigeria.php.

Ncube, Mthuli, Aly Abou-Sabaa, Charles L. Lufumpa, and Agnes Soucat. 2013. Health in Africa over the Next 50 Years. African Development Bank. Economic Brief. March. https://www.afdb.org/fileadmin/uploads/afdb/Documents/Publications/Economic_Brief_-_Health_in_Africa_Over_the_Next_50_Years.pdf.

Neustadt, Richard E. 1960. *Presidential Power: The Politics of Leadership.* Hoboken, NJ: Wiley.

New State Ice Co. v. Liebmann, 285 U.S. 262 (1932).

New UIS Data for SDG 9.5 on Research and Development (R & D). 2020. UNESCO, June 29. http://uis.unesco.org/en/news/new-uis-data-sdg-9-5-research-and-development-rd.

Niger River. *New World Encyclopedia.* https://www.newworldencyclopedia.org/entry/Niger_River.

Nigeria [Wi]ll Lose Ten Years of Economic Gain Under Buhari's Administration— World Bank. 2021. *Economic Confidential*, June 24. https://economicconfidential.com/2021/06/nigeria-economic-gain-buhari-administration/.

Nigeria Demographics. *Worldometer.* https://www.worldometers.info/demographics/nigeria-demographics.

Nigeria GDP Per Capita. *Trading Economics.* https://tradingeconomics.com/nigeria/gdp-per-capita#:~:text=GDP%20per%20capita%20in%20Nigeria%20is%20expected%20to%20reach%202300.00,according%20to%20our%20econometric%20models.

Nigeria IDP Figures Analysis. 2016. IDMC, September 13. http://www.internal-displacement.org/sub-saharan-africa/nigeria/figures-analysis.

Nigeria Independence Act 1960. 1960. 1960 CH. 55 8 & 9 ELIZ. 2. July 29. https://www.legislation.gov.uk/ukpga/1960/55/pdfs/ukpga_19600055_en.pdf.

Nigeria Life Expectancy 1950–2020. Macro Trends. https://www.macrotrends.net/countries/NGA/nigeria/life-expectancy#:~:text=The%20current%20life%20expectancy%20for,a%200.58%25%20increase%20from%202018.

Nigeria Looks Back on [Twenty] Years of Sharia Law in the North. 2019. *DW*, October 27. https://www.dw.com/en/nigeria-looks-back-on-20-years-of-sharia-law-in-the-north/a-51010292.

Nigeria Needs $100bn Annually to Address Infrastructural Deficit–Emefiele. 2021. *The Will*, September 25. https://thewillnigeria.com/news/nigeria-needs-100bn-annually-to-address-infrastructural-deficit-emefiele/.

Nigeria Oil. *Worldometer*. https://www.worldometers.info/oil/nigeria-oil/#:~:text=Nigeria%20produces%201%2C938%2C542.73%20barrels%20per,reserves%20(as%20of%202016.

Nigeria Population (Live). *Worldometer*. https://www.worldometers.info/world-population/nigeria-population/.

Nigeria Population 2020 (Live). *World Population Review*. https://worldpopulationreview.com/countries/nigeria-population.

Nigeria Ranked [Seventh] Among Countries Facing Shortage of Health Workers. 2017. *HealthFacts.Ng*, May 11. https://www.physicianleaders.org/news/how-many-patients-can-primary-care-physician-treat.

Nigeria Religious Records. FamilySearch. https://www.familysearch.org/wiki/en/Nigeria_Religious_Records#:~:text=In%20terms%20of%20Nigeria's%20major,Ijaw%20(south)%20were%2098%25.

Nigeria Report 2013. Centers for Disease Control and Prevention. https://www.cdc.gov/globalhealth/countries/nigeria/why/default.htm.

Nigeria Republic Act 1963. 1963. 1963 CH. 57. December 18. https://www.legislation.gov.uk/ukpga/1963/57/enacted.

Nigeria Sharia Architect Defends Law. *BBC News*. http://news.bbc.co.uk/2/hi/africa/1885052.stm.

Nigeria Spends [US] $5bn on Food Import, [US] $1.5bn on Milk Annually. 2020. *Vanguard* (Lagos), October 2. https://www.vanguardngr.com/2020/10/nigeria-spends-5bn-on-food-import-1-5bn-on-milk-annually-2/.

Nigeria to Resume Petrol Imports from Niger Republic. 2020. *Huhu Online*, November 20. https://huhuonline.com/index.php/home-4/huhuonline-more-news/14070-nigeria-to-resume-petrol-imports-from-niger-republic.

Nigeria: Age Structure from 2010 to 2020. *Statista*. https://www.statista.com/statistics/382296/age-structure-in-nigeria.

Nigeria: Economic and Political Overview. 2020. Nordea. Updated October. https://www.nordeatrade.com/no/explore-new-market/nigeria/economical-context.

Nigeria: History of Modern Medical Services. 1991. *Photius Courtsoukis*, June 1991. https://photius.com/countries/nigeria/society/nigeria_society_history_of_modern_me~10005.html.

Nigeria: Only [Ten] States Economically Viable, [Seventeen] Insolvent—Viability Index Report. 2019. *PM News*, May 13. https://www.pmnewsnigeria.com/2019/05/13/nigeria-only-10-states-economically-viable-17-insolvent-viability-index-report/.

Nigeria: Sanitation, Drinking-Water and Hygiene Status Overview. UN-Water Global Analysis and Drinking Water (GLAAS). https://www.who.int/water_sanitation_health/monitoring/investments/nigeria-10-nov.pdf?ua=1.

Nigeria's Buhari "Broke Promise to End Medical Tourism". 2016. *BBC News,* June 7. https://www.bbc.com/news/business-36468154.

Nigeria's Economy Can't Afford Another Lockdown—Buhari. 2020. *Huhu Online,* October 29. https://huhuonline.com/index.php/home-4/huhuonline-more-news/13976-nigeria-s-economy-can-t-afford-another-lockdown-buhari.

Nigeria—Agriculture. *Nations Encyclopedia.* https://www.nationsencyclopedia.com/economies/Africa/Nigeria-AGRICULTURE.html.

Nigeria—Location, Size, and Extent. *Nations Encyclopedia.* https://www.nationsencyclopedia.com/Africa/Nigeria-LOCATION-SIZE-AND-EXTENT.html.

Nigerian Economy 2020. *Countries of the World.* https://theodora.com/wfbcurrent/nigeria/nigeria_economy.html.

Nigerian Employment in Services (% of Total Employment). 2021. *Trading Economics,* February. https://tradingeconomics.com/nigeria/employment-in-services-percent-of-total-employment-wb-data.html#:~:text=Employment%20in%20services%20(%25%20of%20total%20employment)%20(modeled%20ILO%20estimate,compiled%20from%20officially%20recognized%20sources.

Nigerian National Petroleum Corporation. History of the Nigerian Petroleum Industry. http://www.nnpcgroup.com/history.

Nigerian National Petroleum Corporation. Refineries and Petrochemicals. https://www.nnpcgroup.com/NNPC-Business/Midstream-Ventures/Pages/Refineries-and-Petrochemicals.aspx#:~:text=%E2%80%8B%E2%80%8BRefineries%20and%20Petrochemicals&text=NNPC%20has%20four%20refineries%2C%20two,throughout%20Nigeria%20links%20these%20refineries.

Nigerian President Goodluck Jonathan Urges Birth Control. 2012. *BBC News,* June 27. https://www.bbc.com/news/world-africa-18610751.

Nigeria—Religions. *Nations Encyclopedia.* https://www.nationsencyclopedia.com/Africa/Nigeria-RELIGIONS.html.

Nwakanma, Obi. 2017. The President's Power Is Tyrannical Power in Nigeria. *Vanguard* (Lagos), March 26. https://www.vanguardngr.com/2017/03/presidents-power-tyrannical- power-nigeria/.

O'Regan, Kate, and Nick Friedman. 2011. Equality. In *Comparative Constitutional Law*, ed. Tom Ginsburg and Rosalind Dixon, 473–503. Northampton, MA: Edward Elgar Publishing.

Obunadike, Kenneth. 2020. [Seven] Most Common Jobs in Nigeria. LA-Job Portal, August 17. https://latestjobsinnigeria.com.ng/7-most-common-jobs-in-nigeria/.

Odutola, Abiola. 2020. Households in Nigeria Spend ₦22.7 Trillion on Food. *Nairametrics*, May 11. https://nairametrics.com/2020/05/11/Nigerian-house holds-spend-n22-7-trillion-on-food-items-nbs/.

OECD. 2012. Nigeria. Last Updated September. https://www.oecd.org/swac/publications/Nigeria_e-version_en_light.pdf.

OECD. Official Development Assistance (ODA). Paris, France: OECD. https://www.oecd.org/dac/financing-sustainable-development/development-finance-standards/official-development-assistance.htm.

Office of the UN High Commissioner for Human Rights. Ratification Status for Nigeria. https://tbinternet.ohchr.org/_layouts/15/TreatyBodyExternal/Treaty.aspx?CountryID=127&Lang=EN.

Ogbuoji, Osondi, Ipchita Bharali, Natalie Emery, and Kaci Kennedy McDade. 2019. Closing Africa's Health Financing Gap. Brookings, March 1. https://www.brookings.edu/blog/future-development/2019/03/01/closing-africas-health-financing-gap/.

Ogundipe, Sola, Chioma Obinna, and Gabriel Olawale. 2015. Shortage of Medical Personnel: Tougher Times Ahead for Nigerians (1). *Vanguard* (Lagos), January 27. https://www.vanguardngr.com/2015/01/shortage-medical-personnel-tougher-times-ahead-nigerians-1/.

Oh, Erick. 2014. Nigeria's Film Industry: Nollywood Looks to Expand Globally. U.S. International Trade Commission (USITC). Executive Briefing on Trade. October. https://www.usitc.gov/publications/332/erick_oh_nigerias_film_industry.pdf.

———. 2017a. Nigeria's Services Economy: The Engine for Future Growth. U.S. International Trade Commission (USITC). Executive Briefings on Trade. March. https://www.usitc.gov/publications/332/executive_briefings/nigeria_srv_ebot_oh-final.pdf.

———. 2017b. Nigeria's Services Economy: The Engine for Future Growth. U.S. International Trade Commission (USITC). Executive Briefings on Trade. March. https://www.usitc.gov/publications/332/executive_briefings/nigeria_srv_ebot_oh-final.pdf.

Ohnesorge, John. 2010. Administrative Law in East Asia: A Comparative-Historical Analysis. In *Comparative Administrative Law*, ed. Susan Rose-Ackerman and Peter L. Lindseth, 78–91. Northampton, MA: Edward Elgar.

Ojisua, Philip. 2019. That Is What Politicians Get Paid Around the World: Nigeria: $480,000 (£361,610). *Love Money*, March 29. https://www.love-money.com/galleries/65052/this-is-what-politicians-get-paid-around-the-world?page=31.

Ojonugwa, Aina. 2021. Rtd. Col. Umar Dangiwa Says IPOB Threat Exaggerated and Buhari Has Mismanaged Nigeria's Diversity. *The Will*, July 7. https://thewillnigeria.com/news/rtd-col-umar-dangiwa-says-ipob-threat-exaggerated-and-buhari-has-mismanaged-nigerias-diversity/.

Ojonugwa, Aina. Go Home, Protesting Nigerians Boo Buhari in UK. *The Will*, April 2. https://thewillnigeria.com/news/go-home-protesting-nigerians-boo-buhari-in-uk/.

Okonkwo, Rudolf Ogoo. 2015. If Jonathan Had Wanted to Be a Statesman. *Opinion Nigeria*, April 4. https://opinionnigeria.com/if-jonathan-had-wanted-to-be-a-statesman-by-rudolf-ogoo-okonkwo/.

Okotie, Sylvester. 2017. The Nigerian Economy Before the Discovery of Crude Oil. In *The Political Economy of Oil and Gas Activities in the Nigerian Aquatic Ecosystem*, ed. Prince E. Ndimele, 71–81. Cambridge, MA: Academic Press.

Okunola, Akindare. 2020. [Five] Facts Every Nigerian Should Know About Our Health Care. *Global Citizen*, September 9. https://www.globalcitizen.org/en/content/health-care-facts-nigeria-covid-19/?utm_source=paisearch&utm_medium=usgrant&utm_campaign=verizon&gclid=Cj0KCQiA tqL-BRC0ARIsAF4K3WGZxHt-Yz41A7pIT75mK9ftJcCI-GjctLUo_rcIqLU_7fEgaOJGkZgaAry7EALw_wcB.

Ola-David, Tolulope. 2018. The Need for Restructuring Nigeria's Political System. Oxford University Politics Blog, November 2. https://blog.politics.ox.ac.uk/the-need-for-restructuring-nigerias-political-system/.

Oladipo, Oladehinde. 2019. Nigeria's Oil Sector Contribution to GDP among Lowest in OPEC. *Business Day* (Lagos), November 5. https://businessday.ng/energy/oilandgas/article/nigerias-oil-sector-contribution-to-gdp-among-lowest-in-opec/.

Olawoyin, Oladeinde. 2020. In Four Years, Budget Proposal for Buhari's Presidential Air Fleet Increased by 191 [Percent]. *Premium Times* (Abuja), November 14. https://www.premiumtimesng.com/news/headlines/426094-in-four-years-budget-proposal-for-buharis-presidential-air-fleet-increased-by-191.html.

Olówósejéjé, Samuel Ayokunle. 2020. What Nigeria's Poor Power Supply Really Costs and How a Hybrid System Could Work for Business. *The Conversation*, September 22. https://theconversation.com/what-nigerias-poor-power-supply-really-costs-and-how-a-hybrid-system-could-work-for-business-144609.

Omoregie, Uyiosa. Nigeria's Petroleum and GDP: The Missing Oil Refining Link. Unpublished Paper Available Online.

Onogu, Sanni. 2016. The Burden of Cancer in Nigeria. *Vanguard* (Lagos), August 27. https://www.vanguardngr.com/2016/08/burden-cancer-nigeria/.

Onoh, J.K. 2018. *The Nigerian Oil Economy: From Prosperity to Glut*. New York: Routledge. First Published 1983 by Croom Helm Ltd.

Onoka, Chima, Obinna Onwujekwe, Benjamin Uzochukwu, and Nkoli Ezumah. 2012. Why Are States Not Adopting the Formal Sector Program of the NHIS and What Strategies Can Encourage Adoption? Alliance for Health Policy and Systems Research, Policy Brief October. https://www.who.int/alliance-psr/projects/alliancehpsr_nigeriapolicybriefstates.pdf?ua=1.

Onwujekwe, Obinna, Charles T. Orjiakor, Eleanor Hutchinson, Martin McKee, Prince Agwu, Chinyere Mbachu, Pamela Ogbozor, Uche Obi, Aloysius Odii, Hyacinth Ichoku, and Dina Balabanova. 2020. Where Do We Start? Building Consensus on Drivers of Health Sector Corruption in Nigeria and Ways to Address It. *International Journal of Health Policy Management* 9 (7): 286–296. https://doi.org/10.15171/ijhpm.2019.128.

Onwuzoo, Angela. 2020. Six Years After Enacting National Health Act, Many Provisions Not Implemented. *Punch* (Lagos), February 16. https://healthwise.punchng.com/six-years-after-enacting-national-health-act-many-provisions-not-implemented/.

Onyeji, Ebuka, Ayodom Owoseyi, and Mike Adebowale. 2018. Nigeria: Dissecting National Health Act—What Nigerians Need to Know (1). *Premium Times* (Abuja). https://www.premiumtimesng.com/health/health-features/296422-dissecting-national-health-act-what-nigerians-need-to-know-1.html.

Ophori, Endurance, Musa Y. Tula, Azuka V. Azih, Rachel Okojie, and Precious E. Ikpo. 2014. Current Trends of Immunization in Nigeria: Prospect and Challenges. *Tropical Medicine & Health* 42 (2): 67–75. https://doi.org/10.2149/tmh.2013-13.

Opportunities for Private Companies in Nigeria's Health Care Sector, and Efforts to Improve Provision. Oxford Business Group. https://oxfordbusinessgroup.com/overview/opportunities-private-companies-nigerias-health-care-sector-and-efforts-improve-provision.

Orchard, Chris. The Business Benefits of a Healthy Workforce. Harvard School Public Health. https://www.hsph.harvard.edu/ecpe/the-business-benefits-of-a-healthy-workforce/#:~:text=That's%20in%20part%20because%20the,reflected%20in%20health%20care%20costs

Organization of the Petroleum Exporting Countries. Member Countries. https://www.opec.org/opec_web/en/about_us/25.htm.

Ortiz-Ospina, Esteban. 2017. "Life Expectancy" – What Does This Actually Mean? *Our World in Data*, August 28. https://ourworldindata.org/life-expectancy-how-is-it-calculated-and-how-should-it-be-interpreted.

Osae-Brown, Anthony. 2021. Nigeria's Buhari Takes Medical Trip Abroad Before Doctor Strike. *Bloomberg*, March 30. https://www.bloomberg.com/news/articles/2021-03-30/nigeria-s-buhari-takes-medical-trip-abroad-before-doctor-strike.

Osae-Brown, Anthony, and Ruth Olurounbi. 2019. Nigeria Runs on Generators and Nine Hours of Power a Day. *Bloomberg*, September 22. https://www.bloomberg.com/news/articles/2019-09-23/nigeria-runs-on-generators-and-nine-hours-of-power-a-day.

Osaghae, Eghosa E. 1998. *The Crippled Giant: Nigeria since Independence*. Bloomington and Indianapolis: Indiana University Press.

Osamuyi, Osarumen. 2016. LifeBank Will Hold the Largest-Ever Blood Drive in Lagos, on February 13, 2016. Tech Cabal, February 4. https://techcabal.com/2016/02/04/lifebank-will-hold-the-largest-ever-blood-drive-in-lagos-on-february-13-2016/.

Ososanya, Tunde. 2018. Reduce Salaries Earned by Lawmakers by Half – Sanusi Tell Buhari. *Legit*, February 12. https://www.legit.ng/1151528-reduce-salaries-earned-by-lawmakers-by-sanusi-tells-buhari.html.

Ostien, Philip, and Albert Dekker. 2010. Sharia and National Law in Nigeria. In *Sharia Incorporated: A Comparative Overview of the Legal Systems of Twelve Muslim Countries in Past and Present*, ed. Jan Michiel Otto, 555–612. Leiden, Netherlands: Leiden University Press.

Paden, John. 2015. Religion and Conflict in Nigeria. United States Institute of Peace. Special Report No. 359. February. https://www.usip.org/sites/default/files/SR359-Religion-and-Conflict-in-Nigeria.pdf.

Parlapiano, Alicia. 2021. Biden's $4 Trillion Economic Plan, In One Chart. *New York Times*, April 29. https://www.nytimes.com/2021/04/28/upshot/biden-families-plan-american-rescue-infrastructure.html.

Patient Protection and Affordable Care Act, Pub. Law 111–148. March 2010.

PharmaAccess Foundation. 2015. Nigerian Health Sector: Market Study Report. Pietersbergweg and Amsterdam, Netherlands. March. https://www.rvo.nl/sites/default/files/Market_Study_Health_Nigeria.pdf.

Plans for More Than Ten Different All-Electric Vehicles by 2022. Daimler. https://media.daimler.com/marsMediaSite/en/instance/ko/Plans-for-more-than-ten-different-all-electric-vehicles-by-2022-All-systems-are-go.xhtml?oid=29779739.

Plecher, H. 2020. Labor Force Participation Rate in Nigeria 2020. *Statista*, October 27. https://www.statista.com/statistics/993908/labor-force-participation-rate-in-nigeria/.

Political Violence. *Your Dictionary.* https://www.yourdictionary.com/political-violence.

Powell, Anita. South Africa Debates Bill for National Health Care. Learning English. https://learningenglish.voanews.com/a/south-africa-debates-bill-for-national-heath-care/5127964.html.

Power, Samantha, and Graham Allison, eds. 2000. *Realizing Human Rights: Moving from Inspiration to Impact.* New York: St. Martin's Press.

Preemption. Legal Information Institute. Cornell Law School. https://www.law.cornell.edu/wex/preemption#.

Presidential Plane Parked in London Since May. 2017. Vanguard (Lagos), July 10. Editorial. https://www.vanguardngr.com/2017/07/presidential-plane-parked-london-since-may/.

Profile: African Union. 2017. *BBC News*, August 24. https://www.bbc.com/news/world-africa-16910745.

PwC. Restoring Trust to Nigeria's Healthcare System. https://www.pwc.com/ng/en/assets/pdf/restoring-trust-to-nigeria-healthcare-system.pdf.

Quinn, John James. 2017. *Global Geopolitical Power and African Political and Economic Institutions: When Elephants Fight.* Lanham, MD: Lexington Books.

Raymond, Nate. 2021. McKinsey to Pay $573 Million to Settle Claims Over Opioid Crisis Role: Source. Reuters, February 3. https://www.reuters.com/article/us-usa-mckinsey/mckinsey-to-pay-573-million-to-settle-claims-over-opioid-crisis-role-source-idUSKBN2A405Q.

Ritchie, Hannah, and Max Roser. 2018. Mental Health. *Our World in Data.* April. https://ourworldindata.org/mental-health.

Rivara, Frederick. 2019. The Effects of Violence on Health. *Health Affairs (Millwood)*38(10):1622–1629.https://doi.org/10.1377/hlthaff.2019.00480.

Rosenthal, Elisabeth. 2012. Nigeria Tested by Rapid Rise in Population. *New York Times*, April 14. http://www.nytimes.com/2012/04/15/world/africa/in-nigeria-a-preview-of-an-overcrowded-planet.html?pagewanted=all&_r=0.

Roser, Max, Esteban Ortiz-Ospina, and Hannah Ritchie. 2013. Life Expectancy. *Our World in Data*. Last Revised October 2019. https://ourworldindata.org/life-expectancy#twice-as-long-life-expectancy-around-the-world.

Rupert, James. 1998. Corruption Flourished in Abacha's Regime. *Washington Post*, June 9. https://www.washingtonpost.com/wp-srv/inatl/longterm/nigeria/stories/corrupt060998.htm.

Rwandan Government Proposes to Prioritize Health, Agriculture in Budget for Next Fiscal Year. 2020. *Xinhuanet*, May 21. http://www.xinhuanet.com/english/2020-05/21/c_139075836.htm#:~:text=%22Key%20priorities%20for%20the%202020,by%20COVID%2D19%2C%22%20said.

Sadik, Nafis. Population Growth and the Food Crisis. FAO Corporate Doc. Repository. http://www.fao.org/docrep/U3550t/u3550t02.htm.

Sasu, Doris Dokua. 2021. Share of Population with National Health Insurance Scheme (NHIS) Membership in Ghana from 2014 to 2017. *Statista*, February 9. https://www.statista.com/statistics/1172722/share-of-people-with-active-national-health-insurance-membership-in-ghana/.

Saudi Arabian Royal Family Used to Visit Nigeria for Treatment—Health Minister. 2020. *Punch* (Lagos), March 3. https://punchng.com/saudi-arabian-royal-family-used-to-come-to-nigeria-for-treatment-health-minister/.

Sawe, Benjamin Elisha. 2019. The Economy of Japan. *World Atlas*, August 21. https://www.worldatlas.com/articles/the-economy-of-japan.html.

Scott-Emuakpor, Ajayi. 2010. The Evolution of Health Care Systems in Nigeria: Which Way Forward in the Twenty-First Century. *Nigeria Medical Journal* 51 (2): 53–65.

Segal, Troy, and Thomas Brock. 2021. Import Substitution Industrialization – ISI. *Investopedia*. Updated January 2. https://www.investopedia.com/terms/i/importsubstitutionindustrialization.asp.

Segal, Troy, and Gordon Scott. 2020. Diversification. *Investopedia*. Updated March 6. https://www.investopedia.com/terms/d/diversification.asp.

Sen, Amartya. 2015. Universal Healthcare: The Affordable Dream. *Vanguard* (London), January 6. https://www.theguardian.com/society/2015/jan/06/-sp-universal-healthcare-the-affordable-dream-amartya-sen.

Sharma, Anju. 2004. African States Confirm Support for Traditional Medicine. *Science and Development Network*, September 3. https://www.scidev.net/global/news/african-states-confirm-support-for-traditional-med/.

Sheetz, Kathleen. Slave Coast. *Encyclopedia Britannica*. https://www.britannica.com/place/Slave-Coast.

Shephardson, David. 2021. Biden to Order Agencies to Revisit Vehicle Tailpipe Emissions Standards. *Reuters*, January 20. https://www.reuters.com/article/us-usa-biden-executive-actions-transport/biden-to-order-agencies-to-revisit-vehicle-tailpipe-emissions-standards-idUSKBN29P12Z.

Smith, Daniel Jordan. 2007. *A Culture of Corruption: Everyday Deception and Popular Discontent in Nigeria*. Princeton, NJ: Princeton University Press.

Sodaro, Michael J. 2008. *Comparative Politics: A Global Introduction*. 3rd ed. Boston, MA: McGraw-Hill.

Soyinka, Wole. 2019. Lessons from Nigeria's Militarized Democratic Experiment. *New York Times*, Op-Ed. October 19.

———. 2020a. Lessons for Nigeria's Militarized Democratic Experiment. *New York Times*, October 9. https://www.nytimes.com/2019/10/09/opinion/nigeria-militarized-democratic-experiment.html.

———. 2020b. Between Dividers-In-Chief and Dividers-In-Law. *Premium Times* (Abuja), September 15. https://opinion.premiumtimesng.com/2020/09/15/between-dividers-in-chief-and-dividers-in-law-by-wole-soyinka/.

Special Committee on Health, Productivity, and Disability Management. 2009. Healthy Workforce/Healthy Economy: The Role of Health, Productivity, and Disability Management in Addressing the Nation's Health Care Crisis: Why an Emphasis on the Health of the Workforce is Vital to the Health of the Economy. *Journal of Occupational and Environmental Medicine* 51 (1): 114–119. https://doi.org/10.1097/JOM.0b013e318195dad2.

Speech of Sir Abubakar Tafawa Balewa, October 1, 1960. 2009. Reprinted in *Blackpast*, August 20. https://www.blackpast.org/global-african-history/1960-sir-abubakar-tafawa-balewa-independence-day/.

Stankiewicz, Kevin. 2021. Ford CEO Confident in Electric-Vehicle Strategy, Says Automaker Won't "Cede the Future to Anyone." 2021. *CNBC*, February 5. https://www.cnbc.com/2021/02/05/ford-wont-cede-the-future-to-anyone-on-electric-vehicles-ceo-farley.html.

Suberu, O.J., O.A. Ajala, M.O. Akande, and Adeyinka Olure-Bank. 2015. Diversification of the Nigerian Economy Toward a Sustainable Growth and Economic Development. *Int'l Journal of Economics, Finance, & Management Science* 3 (2): 107–114. http://www.sciencepublishinggroup.com/journal/paperinfo?journalid=173&doi=10.11648/j.ijefm.20150302.15.

Suleiman, Dauda Eneyamire. 2016. Mental Health Disorders in Nigeria: A Highly Neglected Disease. *Annals of Nigerian Medicine* 10 (2): 47–48. Editorial. https://www.anmjournal.com/article.asp?issn=0331-3131;year=2016;volume=10;issue=2;spage=47;epage=48;aulast=Suleiman#ref1.

Sustainable Development Goals Fund. From MDGs to SDGs. https://www.sdgfund.org/mdgs-Sdgs.

Tejuoso, Olanrewaju, Gafar Alawade, and Elaine Baruwa. 2018. Health and the Legislature: The Case of Nigeria. *Health Systems & Reform* 4 (2): 62–64. https://doi.org/10.1080/23288604.2018.1441622.

The 77 Percent—The Need to Tackle Nigeria's Population Boom. 2019. *DW*, October 1. https://www.dw.com/en/the-77-percent-the-need-to-tackle-nigerias-population-boom/a-50663036.

The American State and Local Government. *The USA Online*. https://www.the-usaonline.com/government/state-local-government.htm.

The Economic Context of Nigeria. 2020. Nordea, October.

The Future of Healthcare in Africa. 2014. Economist Intelligence Unit. London. http://www.economistinsights.com/sites/default/files/downloads/EIU-Janssen_HealthcareAfrica_Report_Web.pdf.

The Nigerian Diaspora in the United States. 2015. MPI. Revised June. https://www.migrationpolicy.org/sites/default/files/publications/RAD-Nigeria.pdf.

The Nigerian Diaspora. *Pilot Guides*. https://www.pilotguides.com/study-guides/the-nigerian-diaspora/#:~:text=The%20Nigerian%20diaspora%20is%20one,is%20very%20difficult%20to%20estimate.&text=Nigerian%20Americans%20are%20notably%20distinct,recent%20immigrants%20from%20the%20country.

The Structure of Power in Iran. Frontline (PBS). https://www.pbs.org/wgbh/pages/frontline/shows/tehran/inside/govt.html.

The Transition to Electric Vehicles. 2021. *New York Times* The Morning, August 6. https://outlook.live.com/mail/0/inbox/id/AQMkADAwATE2MTAwAC04NDcxLTY0YzEtMDACLTAwCgBGAAADmoSvjna2Kkmn8zqi9wi6ewcAnCBhZglRtU2kkOJpbeS6MQAAAgEMAAAAnCBhZglRtU2kkOJpbeS6MQAEku8U%2BAAAAA%3D%3D.

The World Population and the Top Ten Countries with the Highest Populations. *Internet World Stats*. https://www.internetworldstats.com/stats8.htm.

Theses on Feuerback, Thesis 11 (1845). 1950. *Selected Works, Vol. 1, Marx Engels*, 13–15. Moscow: Foreign Languages Publishing House.

Tonga Population (Live). Worldometer. https://www.worldometers.info/world-population/tonga-population/#:~:text=Tonga%202020%20population%20is%20estimated,of%20the%20total%20world%20population.

Top Four Priorities of the 2020 Budget. 2019. Channels Television. Updated October 8. https://www.channelstv.com/2019/10/08/top-four-priorities-of-the-2020-budget/.

Tran, Mark. 2010. President Umaru Yar'Adua Returns to Nigeria. *Guardian* (London), February 23. https://www.theguardian.com/world/2010/feb/24/president-yaradua-back-in-nigeria.

Tripp, Charles R.H. 2002. *A History of Iraq.* New York: Cambridge University Press.

Twin, Alexandra. 2019. World's Top 10 Oil Exporters. *Investopedia.* Updated October 23. https://www.investopedia.com/articles/company-insights/082316/worlds-top-10-oil-exporters.asp.

Twin, Alexandra, and Margaret James. 2020. Outsourcing. *Investopedia.* Updated July 5. https://www.investopedia.com/terms/o/outsourcing.asp.

Udo, Reuben Kenrick. Nigeria: Economy. *Encyclopedia Britannica.* https://www.britannica.com/place/Nigeria/Economy.

Ujah, Emma, and Marvelous Anthony. 2019. From Abacha Comes Vision-2010. *Vanguard* (Lagos), September 30. https://www.vanguardngr.com/2019/09/from-abacha-comes-vision-2010/

UN General Assembly. United Nations Millennium Declaration. 2000. Doc. A/RES/55/2, September 18. https://www.un.org/en/development/desa/population/migration/generalassembly/docs/globalcompact/A_RES_55_2.pdf.

Unemployment Crisis: More Nigerians Dump White[-]Collar Jobs for Blue[-]Collar Jobs. 2018. *The Nation*, July 29. https://thenationonlineng.net/unemployment-crisis-more-nigerians-dump-white-collar-jobs-for-blue-collar-jobs/.

Union of Concerned Scientists. 2018. Top Five Reasons to Choose an Electric Car: They're a Really Good Buy, March 12. https://www.ucsusa.org/resources/top-five-reasons-choose-electric-car?gclid=CjwKCAiA4rGCBhAQEiwAelVti0LzPwwTBNJfjFpfnmJ2xKHK02oV7aQx5p9qh45y0al7D1F8iu4B0Ro-CaW8QAvD_BwE&utm_campaign=CV&utm_medium=search&utm_source=googlegrants.

United Nations Economic Commission for Africa. 2020. Policy Brief: Impact of COVID-19 in Africa, May 28. https://www.uneca.org/sites/default/files/PublicationFiles/sg_policy_brief_on_covid-19_impact_on_africa_may_2020.pdf.

United States Embassy in Nigeria. 2012. Nigeria Fact Sheet. January. https://photos.state.gov/libraries/nigeria/487468/pdfs/Nigeria%20overview%20Fact%20Sheet.pdf.

Universal Declaration of Human Rights. 1948. G.A. Res. 217A, December 10.

US Dept. of Defense. 2013. *The Dictionary of Military Terms.* New York: Skyhorse Publishing.

US Dept. of Energy. 2014. The History of the Electric Car, September 15. https://www.energy.gov/articles/history-electric-car.

US Dept. of State. 2021. Nigeria 2020 Human Rights Report, March 30. https://www.state.gov/wp-content/uploads/2021/03/NIGERIA-2020-HUMAN-RIGHTS-REPORT.pdf.

US Embassy and Consulate in Nigeria. Medical Assistance. https://ng.usembassy.gov/u-s-citizen-services/local-resources-of-u-s-citizens/doctors/.

US States: Population, Land Area, and Population Density. States101. https://www.states101.com/populations.

Uwakwe, Richard. 2018. Mental Health Service and Access in Nigeria: A Short Overview. *International Journal of Global Social Work* 2 (103): 1–5. https://doi.org/10.15344/ijgsw/2018/103.

Varrella, Simona. 2020. Oil Industry in Nigeria – Statistics and Facts. *Statista*, November 6.

Vidal, John. 2010. Nigeria's Agony Dwarfs the Gulf Oil Spill. The US and Europe Ignore It. *Guardian* (London), May 29. https://www.theguardian.com/world/2010/may/30/oil-spills-nigeria-niger-delta-shell.

Virginia Premier. What Is Health Insurance and Why Is It Important?. https://www.virginiapremier.com/what-is-health-insurance-and-why-is-it-important/.

Wahab, Hassan, and Philip C. Aka. 2021. The Politics of Healthcare Reforms in Ghana under the Fourth Republic Since 1993: A Critical Analysis. *Canadian Journal of African Studies* 55 (1): 203–221. https://doi.org/10.1080/00083968.2020.1801476.

Wallace, Rebecca M.M., and Olga Martin-Ortega. 2013. *International Law.* 7th ed. London: Sweet & Maxwell.

Wallerstein, Immanuel. 1974. *The Modern-World System.* Cambridge, MA: Academic Press.

Wayland, Mike. 2021. VW Expects Half of U.S. Sales to Be Electric Vehicles by 2030. *CNBC*, March 5. https://www.cnbc.com/2021/03/05/vw-expects-half-of-us-sales-to-be-electric-vehicles-by-2030.html.

Weber, Lauren. 2017. Healthier Workers Are More Productive, Study Finds. *Wall Street Journal*, August 8. https://www.wsj.com/articles/healthy-workers-are-more-productive-study-finds-1502219651.

What Does the Acronym UNICEF Stand For: Frequently Asked Questions. UNICEF. https://www.unicef.org/about-unicef/frequently-asked-questions#1.

What Is Purchasing Power Parity (PPP)? 2020. *Investopedia.* Updated August 19. https://www.investopedia.com/updates/purchasing-power-parity-ppp/.

White House. 2021. Fact Sheet: President Biden Takes Executive Actions to Tackle the Climate Crisis at Home and Abroad, Create Jobs, and Restore Scientific Integrity Across Federal Government, January 27. https://www. whitehouse.gov/briefing-room/statements-releases/2021/01/27/ fact-sheet-president-biden-takes-executive-actions-to-tackle-the-climate-crisis-at-home-and-abroad-create-jobs-and-restore-scientific-integrity-across-federal-government/.

Whiting, Kate. 2019. [Five] Facts to Know About Africa's Powerhouse – Nigeria. World Economic Forum. August 9. https://www.weforum.org/ agenda/2019/08/nigeria-africa-economy/#:~:text=Last%20year%2C%20 Nigeria's%20economy%20was,2%20million%20barrels%20each%20day.

Why Research and Development. GHTC: Global Health Technologies Coalition. https://www.ghtcoalition.org/why-research-and-development.

Wilson, Frank L. 1996. *Concepts and Issues in Comparative Politics: An Introduction to Comparative Analysis.* Upper Saddle River, NJ: Prentice Hall.

Witter, Sophie, and Bertha Garshong. 2009. Something Old or Something New? Social Health Insurance in Ghana. *BMC Int'l Health & Human Rights.* August. http://www.ncbi.nlm.nih.gov/pmc/articles/PMC2739838.

Workman, Daniel. Nigeria's Top [Ten] Imports. World's Top Exports. http:// www.worldstopexports.com/nigerias-top-10-imports/.

World Health Assembly, 58th. 2005. Sustainable Health Financing, Universal Coverage, and Social Health Insurance. Doc. A58/20. May 25. https://cdn. who.int/media/docs/default-source/health-financing/sustainable-health-financing-universal-coverage-and-social-health-insurance.pdf?sfvrsn= f8358323_3.

World Health Organization. 1978. Declaration of Alma-Ata. International Conference on Primary Health Care, Alma-Ata, USSR. September 6-12. https://www.who.int/publications/almaata_declaration_en.pdf.

———. 2010. *The World Health Report: Health Systems Financing: The Path to Universal Coverage.* Geneva, Switzerland: World Health Organization.

———. 2011. The Abuja Declaration: Ten Years On. https://www.who.int/ healthsystems/publications/abuja_declaration/en/.

———. 2016. *Public Financing for Heath in Africa: From Abuja to the SDGs.* Geneva, Switzerland: World Health Organization.

———. 2019. *Global Report on Traditional and Complementary Medicine.* Geneva, Switzerland: World Health Organization.

World Health Organization and Federal Ministry of Health, Nigeria. 2006. *WHO-AIMS Report on Mental Health System in Nigeria: A Report of the*

Assessment of the Mental Health System in Nigeria Using the World Health Organization Assessment Instrument for Mental Health Systems (WHO-AIMS). Geneva, Switzerland; Abuja, Nigeria: World Health Organization/Federal Ministry of Health. https://www.who.int/mental_health/evidence/nigeria_who_aims_report.pdf.

World Health Organization. Maternal Health in Nigeria: Generating Information for Action. https://www.who.int/reproductivehealth/maternal-health-nigeria/en/#:~:text=Spotlight%20on%20Nigeria&text=Nigeria%20is%20also%20the%20country,all%20global%20maternal%20deaths%20happen.&text=In%20fact%2C%20a%20Nigerian%20woman,risk%20is%201%20in%204900.

World Health Organization. NCDs and Development (Chapter 2). https://www.who.int/nmh/publications/ncd_report_chapter2.pdf.

World Health Organization. Noncommunicable Diseases. https://www.who.int/health-topics/noncommunicable-diseases#tab=tab_1.

World Poverty Clock. Kamla Foundation. https://kamlafoundation.org/wp-content/uploads/2019/01/World-Poverty-Clock.pdf.

Yu, Shu, and Franziska Ohnsorge. 2019. The Challenges of Informality. Let's Talk Development, January 18. https://blogs.worldbank.org/developmenttalk/challenges-informality#:~:text=While%20offering%20the%20advantage%20of,and%20poverty%20and%20income%20inequality.

Zimmerman, Mary Ko. 2020. Comparative Health-Care Systems. *Encyclopedia of Sociology*. Updated February 10. https://www.encyclopedia.com/social-sciences/encyclopedias-almanacs-transcripts-and-maps/comparative-health-care-systems.

Index[1]

---

[1] Note: Page numbers followed by 'n' refer to notes.

© The Author(s), under exclusive license to Springer Nature Singapore Pte Ltd. 2022
P. C. Aka, J. A. Balogun, *Healthcare and Economic Restructuring*,
https://doi.org/10.1007/978-981-16-9543-8

191

Printed in the United States
by Baker & Taylor Publisher Services